ISBN 978-1-331-29304-0
PIBN 10170046

1 MONTH OF
FREE
READING

at

www.ForgottenBooks.com

By purchasing this book you are
eligible for one month membership to
ForgottenBooks.com, giving you
unlimited access to our entire
collection of over 700,000 titles via
our web site and mobile apps.

To claim your free month visit:

www.forgottenbooks.com/free170046

Similar Books Are Available from
www.forgottenbooks.com

TOURS IN WALES,

BY

THOMAS PENNANT, ESQ,

𝔚𝔦𝔱𝔥 𝔑𝔬𝔱𝔢𝔰, 𝔓𝔯𝔢𝔣𝔞𝔠𝔢, 𝔞𝔫𝔡 𝔒𝔬𝔭𝔦𝔬𝔲𝔰 𝔍𝔫𝔡𝔢𝔵,

BY THE EDITOR,

JOHN RHYS, M.A.

PROFESSOR OF CELTIC IN THE UNIVERSITY OF OXFORD:

TO WHICH IS ADDED,

An Account of the Five Royal Tribes of Cambria, and of the Fifteen Tribes of North Wales and their Representatives, with their Arms, as given in Pennant's History of Whitford and Holywell.

VOL. II.

CAERNARVON:
PRINTED AND PUBLISHED BY H. HUMPHREYS.
1883.

TOUR IN NORTH WALES,

MDCCLXXIII.

———

AFTER a descent of no great length, enter

MEIRIONEDDSHIRE,

into that portion for ever to be distinguished in
the *Welsh* annals, on account of the hero it produced, who made such a figure in the beginning
of the fifteenth century. This tract was antiently
a comot in the kingdom of *Mathrafal*, or *Powys;*
and still retains its former title *Glyn-dwrdwy*, or
the valley of the *Dee*. It extends about seven GLYN-DWR-
miles in length; is narrow, fertile in grass, bound- DWY.
ed by lofty hills, often cloathed with trees; and
lies in the parishes of *Llangollen, Llandysilio,
Llansantffraid*, and *Corwen*.

THE tract once belonged to the lords of *Dinas
Brân*. After the murder of the two eldest sons of
Gryffydd ap Madoc the last lord, the earl *Warren*, who had usurped the property of the eldest,
appears to have been seized with remorse for his

crime; and, instead of removing the other object of his fear, as a *Machiavelian* politician would have done, procured from *Edward* I. a grant of this tract to *Gryffydd Vychan*, third brother to the unhappy youth, dated from *Rhuddlan* the 12th of *February* 1282[a]. *Owen Glyndwr* was fourth in descent from this nobleman[b].

I RETURNED from hence, by the same road; crossed the *Dee* at *Llangollen;* and, after a ride of about a mile, deviated, in a little fertile vale, to the abby of

ABBY OF VALLE CRUCIS.

LLAN-EGWEST, GLYN-EGWEST MONACHLOG, or DE VALLE CRUCIS, solemnly seated at the foot of the mountains, on a small meadowy flat, watered by a pretty stream, and shaded with hanging woods. The valley in which the abby stood was called, long prior to the foundation of the religious house, *Pant y Groes*, or the *Bottom of the Cross*, doubtlessly from the antient column erected in memory of *Eliseg*. This was a house of *Cistertians*, founded in the year 1200, by *Madoc ap Gryffydd Maelor*, lord of *Bromfield*, and grandson by the mother's side to *Owen Gwynedd* prince of *Wales*. I cannot discover any of the endowments, further than half the tithes of *Wrexham*, bestowed on it by *Reyner* bishop of St. *Asaph*,

---

[a] *Rotuli Walliæ*, 87.

[b] The historical account af *Owen Glyndwr* is inserted in the Appendix, Nº VII. ED.

who died in 1224; and the other half, by his successor bishop *Abraham*, in 1227. The following
bishop, *Howel ap Ednyfed*, presented it with the
church of *Llangollen*[b]. The monks obtained besides the patronage of several other livings; such
as *Wrexham, Rhiwabon, Chirk, Llansantfraid*, and
Llandegla; but their title to these, as well as to
Llangollen, was disputed by bishop *Anian*, com-
mouly known by the name of *Y Brawd du o Nannau*, or the black brother of *Nanney*, a *Dominican*,
consecrated in 1268[c]; who brought his cause
before the pope's delegates, the official of *Canterbury*, and the abbot of *Tallelechew*, and obtained
a decision in favor of him and his successors; but
as there was some doubt about the patronage of
the church of *Llandegla*, they allotted (in lieu of
it) to the abby a third of the tithes of *Bryn-
Eglwys*[d].

THE landed endowments were not inconsider- REVENUES.
able. In the year 1291, the abbot was found to
have near the monastery, a grange, with three
ploughlands, a mill, and other conveniencies, valued
at £3   0   0
The granges of *Bodhange, Tregam, Rud-
ryn*, and *Baketon*, set for 5 10   0
Also the dairy-farm of *Nante*, the grange
of *Nustroyz, Convenet*, and *Grennych-*

---

[b] Goodwin, 657.   [c] Idem, 658.   [d] Ibid.

amt, set for 3 19   8

Also the grange of *Wyrcessam*, consisting
of one ploughland and some pasture,
valued at 0 15   0

And thirty cows, at the expence of thirty shillings.

THE whole of his establishment was fourteen
pounds fourteen shillings and eight pence[e]. At
the dissolution, the revenue of the house was found
to be (according to *Dugdale*) 188*l.* *per Annum.*
Speed makes it 214*l.* 3*s.* 5*d.* The last abbot was
John Herne, who received an annuity of 23*l.* on
his surrender. This, and 10*l.* 13*s.* 4*d.* in annuities
to some surviving monks, were the only charges
remaining in 1553[f].

Two of the abbots, *Dafydd ap Jeven Jerworth*
and *Icôn* or *John,* were celebrated by the bard
Guttun Owain, who flourished about the year 1480.
He highly commends their hospitality: speaks of
their having four courses of meat, bright silver
dishes, claret, &c. *Guttun* does not forget the piety
of the house, and is particularly happy in being
blessed by abbot *John* with his three fingers
covered with rings[g].

THE freemen of *Llangollen* made a grant, in
part of the river near their town, of a fishery to

[e] *Willis's St. Asaph,* 178.   [f] *Willis's Abbies,* ii. 312.
[g] *Sebright, MSS.*

the monks of *Valle Crucis*. *F*or want of a seal of
their own, they affixed to their grant that of *Madoc*,
the founder of the abby. The monks erected new
works on the river for the purpose of taking the
fish: this caused a dispute between them and the
freemen. The last referred it to the abbot and
five monks of their own choice, who were to adjust
the matter on oath. *Madoc* and his secretary,
John Parvus, appointed a day for the purpose.
The assembly was held; the oath solemnly admi-
nistered; and the abbot and monks made the
decision in their own favor. They alleged, that
they had bought the right of erecting what works
they pleased, and of repairing of them, from the
heirs of *Llangollen*. The prince confirmed the
decree, and the donation of the fishery, by an
instrument dated in 1234.

THIS house was dissolved in 1235,([1]) and is said
to have been the first of the *Welsh* that underwent
that fate. It remained in the crown till the 9th of
James I. who granted it to *Edward Wotton*, afterwards created lord *Wotton*. In 1654, we find a
lady *Margaret Wotton*, a recusant, to have been
in possession; and that it was put under sequestration by orders of the commissioners from the ruling
powers.

THERE still remain the ruins of the church, and CHURCH.
part of the abby: the last inhabited by a farmer.

([1]) The date must be wrong. T.P.

The church was built in form of a cross, in diffe rent styles of architecture. The most antient is that of the east end, where the windows are in form of long and narrow slips, pointed at top. The window at the west end is large, divided by stone tracery; and above is a round window of elegant work. Above it is an inscription in memory of the person who repaired or re-built this part: an honor frequently paid to benefactors of this kind. It is in this form; AD. ADAM. DMS. *Fecit Hoc opus. Pace Beata quiescat.* Amen. And just beneath, are the letters M. D... probably part of the date; the rest being lost. We cannot ascertain the person intended in this line. He was probably one of the house of *Trevawr*, in which that name occurs more than once; as *Adam* or *Adda Fawr* of *Trevawr*; and *Adam* or *Adda ap Jorwerth Ddu* of *Pengwern*.

THE capitals of the pilasters within the church, are finished with elegant foliage. In the north transept, is a cloister of two arches; an arch that once contained a tomb; and near it a double *benctoire*, or holy water pot.

MUCH of the building is made of the coarse slaty stone of the country. The door and window frames of fine free-stone.

THE abbot's apartment was contiguous to the church. There opens from it a small space, where

PILLAR OF ELISEG.

he might stand to hear the holy offices performed below.

THE lower part of the abby is vaulted, and supported by rows of low pillars; now divided into different rooms. In front is a large window with curious stone tracery, which reaches to the ground. Within seems to have stood a small stair-case, which led to the fratry, a paved room above the arches.

IN one of the present bed-chambers is a stone (now part of a chimney-piece) carved with running foliage, with this imperfect inscription: *Hic jacet* .... ARVRVET. This is the only relique of any tomb; that of the founder, who was buried here[h], is no more: nor yet that of *Gryffydd ap Madoc Maelor*, lord of *Dinas Brân;* who, after siding with the enemies of his country, in 1270, was deposited within these walls[i].

ABOUT a quarter of a mile higher up the vale, I met with the remainder of a round column, perhaps one of the most antient of any *British* inscribed pillar now existing.

PILLAR OF ELISEG.

IT was entire till the civil wars of the seventeenth century, when it was thrown down and broken by some ignorant fanatics; who thought it had too much the appearance of a cross, to be suffered to stand. It probably bore the name of one;

[h] *Powel*, 255. 293.   [i] Idem, 321. 327.

for the field it lies in is still called *Llwyn-y-groes,*
or the Grove of the Cross, from the wood that surrounded it.   It was erected at so early a period, that
there is nothing marvellous, if we should perceive
a tincture of the old idolatry, or at lest of the
primeval customs of our country, in the mode of it
when perfect.

THE pillar had been sepulchral; and folly and
superstition paid it the usual honors.   It was a
memorial of the dead; an improvement on the rude
columns of *Druidical* times, and cut into form, and
surrounded with inscription.   It is among the first
lettered stones that succeeded the *Meini-hirion,*
Meini-Gwŷr, and *Llechau.*   It stood on a great
tumulus; perhaps environed with wood, according
to the custom of the most antient times, when
standing pillars were placed under *every green
tree*[k].

IT is said that the stone, when complete, was
twelve feet high.   It is now reduced to six feet
eight.   The remainder of the capital is eighteen
inches long.   It stood infixed in a square pedes-
tal, still lying in the mount: the breadth of which
is five feet three inches: the thickness eighteen
inches.

THE beginning of the inscription gives us nearly
the time of its erection; and informs us of the

---

[k] *Kings,* ii. 17. See the learned *Rowlands,* 52.

person to whose memory it was dedicated: ' *Con-* ' *cenn* filius *Catteli, Catteli* filius *Brochmail, Broch-* ' *mail* filius *Eliseg, Eliseg* filius *Cnoillaine, Concenn* ' itaque pronepos *Eliseg* edificavit hunc lapidem ' proavo suo *Eliseg.*' Within these few years the *tumulus* was opened, and the reliques of certain bones found there, placed as usual in those days, between some flat stones.

THIS *Concenn,* or *Congen,* was the grandson of *Brochmail Ysgithrog,* the same who was defeated in 607 at the battle of *Chester*[1] The letters on the stone were copied by Mr. *Edward Llwyd:* the inscription is now illegible; but, from the copy taken by that great antiquary, the alphabet near-ly resembles one of those in use in the sixth century[m].

ONE of the seats of *Concenn* and *Eliseg* was in this country. A township adjacent to the column bears, from the last, the name of *Eglwyseg;* and the picturesque tiers of rocks are called *Glisseg* for the same reason. The habitation of this prince of *Powys* in these parts was probably *Dinas Brân,* which lies at the head of the vale of *Glisseg.* Mr. *Llwyd* conjectures, that this place took its name from the interment of *Eliseg;* by a similar instance in the county of *Caermarthen;* where the place in which a monumental stone stands, is called *Pant y*

[1] BEDÆ *Hist.* lib. ii. c. 2. p. 80.
[m] Vide *Doctor* MORTON's *Table of Alphabets.*

Polion,([1]) corruptly for *Pant Pawlin,* from *Pauli-nus,* the person it was inscribed to:

> Servator fidei patriæque semper amator:
> Hic PAULINUS jacet cultor pientissimus æqui.

THERE are two ways from this pillar: the usual is along the vale, on an excellent turnpike-road leading to *Ruthin;* the other is adapted only for the travel of the horseman; but far preferable, on account of the romantic views. I returned by *Valle Crucis;* and, after winding along a steep midway to the old castle, descended, and crossing VALLEY OF the rill of the *Brân,* arrived in the valley of *Glis-*
GLISSEG. *seg;* long and narrow, bounded on the right by astonishing precipices, divided into numberless parallel strata of white limestone, often giving birth to vast yew-trees: and on the left, by smooth and verdant hills, bordered by pretty woods. One of the principal of the *Glisseg* rocks is honored with the name of *Craig-Arthur.* That at the end of the vale, called *Craig y Forwyn,* or the maiden's, is bold, precipitous, and terminates with a vast natural column.

THIS valley is chiefly inhabited (happily) by an independent race of warm and wealthy yeomanry, undevoured as yet by the great men of the country.

([1]) This cannot be, as *P*aulinus could only yield in Welsh *Peulin,* as in fact it has in South Wales in Capel Peulin, while the present pronunciation of *P*aul, as Pôl, is a mere attempt to imitate the English. J.R.

In order to reach the great road, I pursued a path up a steep ascent to the left; and about midway visited a house noted for being the residence of one *Edward Davies*, a low partizan and plunderer on the side of the usurper during the civil wars.   He was best known in his own country by the title of *Cneifiwr Glâs*, or the *Blue Fleecer*, from his rapacity, and the color of his cloaths; and was considered as a fit instrument of the tyranny of the times.   In 1654, he was appointed, by the commissioners for sequestration, steward of the court-leet within the manor of *Valle Crucis*, being recommended to the office by colonel *George Twisleton*.   The *Cneifiwr* seems to have not been over-true to his own party, when his interest stood in the way.   He was accustomed to take even the royalists under his protection, on receiving a proper reward.   He once concealed Sir *Evan Llwyd* of *Bodidris*, at the time that a considerable sum was ordered for his apprehension.   He lodged him in a cellar below the parlor; then summoning his people, ordered them, in a seeming rage, to sally out in quest of Sir *Evan*, stamping with his foot, and declaring, that if the knight was *above ground*, he would have him.

CNEIFIWR GLAS.

After continuing an ascent for a little space longer, reach the pass called *Bwlch y Rhiw Velen*, and fall again into the great road.   This place is distinguished by the deaths of two of the sons of

BWLCH Y RHIW VELEN.

Llowarch Hên, the *Cambrian* prince of the sixth century; who were slain in battle, and whose loss the princely bard, their father, deplores in an elegy, of which these lines are a fragment:

> Bedh GUELL yn y *Rhiw Velen,*
> Bedh SAWYL yn *Llan Gollen*[n]

> GUELL found a grave in *Rhiw Velen,*
> SAWYL, in *Llan Gollen.*

LLOWARCH HEN left his country to expel the *Saxons* and *Irish* out of this part of *Britain.* He leaves us ignorant of the event: all he acquaints us with is, that he lost twelve sons in the generous attempt.

FROM the height above *Rhiw Velen,* is a very extensive prospect of the hundred of *Yale;* hilly, fertile in grass, abundant in cattle; but in this part dreary, and destitute of hedges and woods: banks, for the most part, supply the place of the first; and brakes of the latter. Near this spot is *Plâs yn Yale,* the seat of the antient family of the *Yales,* descended from *Osborn Fitzgerald* earl of *Desmond,* who came over with *Gryffydd ap Cynan;* the chief of his descendants are the *Vaughans* of *Corsegedol.* After some descent, cross the *Alyn,* here a trifling rill (which, after running for some time, receives much increase) waters the rich vales of *Mold* and *Hope;* and passes between the pic

[n] *Llwyd's Archæol.* 259.

turesque banks from near *Caergwrle* to *Gresford*,
where it goes through an extensive flat, and falls
into the *Dee* midway between *Holt* and *Eaton*
Boat. Leave, a little to the left, a place called
Hafod yr Abad, the site of one of the country-
seats of the abbot of *Valle Crucis.* Close to the
road-side lies *Tommen y Rhodwydd*(¹), once a fortress known by the name of the castle of *Yale*°, built
by *Owen Gwynedd*, about the year 1148ᵖ. This
is the place *Leland*, mistakenly, calls a castle
belonging to *Owen Glyndwr*�q. It consists of a
vast artificial mount, with another still loftier near
one end, the keep of the place. These are surrounded with a great foss and rampart; and have
only a single entrance. At present, there are not
the lest reliques of the superstructure: which was
probably of wood; for we are told, that this short-
lived castelet was burnt nine years after its erection, by *Jorwerth Goch ap Meredydd*ʳ

Iᴛ is in this manner we must account for the
total disappearance of many *Welsh* castles, whose
names are preserved in history; and whose vestiges
we have sought for in vain. They were made of
wood, as was very customary with several antient

WOODEN CASTLES.

(¹) In that case the *rhod* would be the same as *rawd* in *beddrod*
or *bedd-rawd*, a sepulchre, from *bedd*, a grave, and as *rawd* in *gaeaf-
rawd*, a winter abode; the Irish word is *ráth*, and a curious com-
pound used by Adamnan in his *Vita S. Columbæ* is *ratabusta*, which
means much the same as the Welsh *bedd-rawd*. J.R.

° *Powel*, 201.   ᵖ Ibid.   q *Itin.* v. 35.   ʳ *Powel*, 208.

nations, and with others of later date. The *Per sians*, on the approach of the *Spartans*, secured themselves within their wooden walls: and *Cesar* found great resistance from a tower in the *Alpine* castle of *Larignum*, made of the timber of the *Larix*, or the *Larch*, which was found to be incombustible[s]. In later times, the castle of *Bamborough* was built originally by *Ida* with wood; the burgh of *Murray* was fortified by the *Danes* with the same material. The people of the same county, in 1228, had castles of wood[t]; and, a century after these more recent instances, *William de Melton*, archbishop of *York* in 1317, fortified the mount in that city, called the *Old Bale*, with planks eighteen inches thick.

WHENSOEVER we find an antient fortress totally vanished, and we cannot account for the disposal of the materials in the erection of any neighboring buildings, we must suppose that they had been constructed of wood; and that they had been destroyed by fire, either flung into them by means of torches, or by *veltæ*, or vast masses of combustibles rolled against them by the force of numbers, as was the practice of the antient *Scandinavians*, described by *Olaus Magnus*.

FROM *Tommen y Rhodwydd* I crossed the country for about two miles to the village of *Llandegla*,

LLANDEGLA.

---

[s] *Vitruvius*, lib. 2. c. 9. p. 35.
[t] *Annals of Scotland*, 149.

noted for its vast fairs for black cattle. The church
is dedicated to St. *Tecla,* virgin and martyr; who,
after her conversion by St. *Paul,* suffered under
Nero at *Iconium.*

About two hundred yards from the church, in
a quillet called *Gwern Degla,* rises a small spring,
with these letters cut on free-stone: A. G θ Ľ : G.
The water is under the tutelage of the saint; and
to this day is held to be extremely beneficial in the
Clwyf Tegla, St. *Tecla's* disease, or the falling-
sickness. The patient washes his limbs in the
well; makes an offering into it of four pence;
walks round it three times; and thrice repeats the
Lord's prayer. These ceremonies are never begun
till after sun-set, in order to inspire the votaries
with greater awe. If the afflicted be of the male-
sex, like *Socrates,* he makes an offering of a cock
to his *Esculapius,* or rather to *Tecla Hygeia;* if
of the fair-sex, a hen. The fowl is carried in a
basket, first round the well; after that into the
church-yard; when the same orisons, and the same
circum-ambulations are performed round the church.
The votary then enters the church; gets under the
communion-table; lies down with the Bible under
his or her head; is covered with the carpet or
cloth, and rests there till break of day; departing
after offering six pence, and leaving the fowl in
the church. If the bird dies, the cure is supposed

St. Tecla's
Well.

to have been effected, and the disease transferred to the devoted victim.

BODIDRIS. FROM hence I visited the house of *Bodidris*, a large and antient place, belonging to *Evan Lloyd Vaughan*, esq[u]. of *Corsygedol*, in right of his mother *Margaret*, daughter of Sir *Evan Lloyd* baronet, the last male of the family: descended from *Llewelyn ap Ynyr ap Howel ap Moriddig ap Sandde Hardd;* who, by his valor in battle, obtained from his prince *Gryffydd ap Madoc*, lord of *Dinas Brân*, the honorable distinction in his arms of four bloody strokes, or, in the heralds phrase, paly of eight, *or* and *gules.* For, while he was talking to his prince after the fight, with his left hand smeared with blood, he accidentally drew it across his sword, and left on it the marks of his four fingers. The prince observing this, ordered him to carry them on his shield; and at the same time bestowed on him the township of *Gelligynan* in this neighborhood, as a more substantial mark of his favor[x].

BODIDRIS takes its name from *Idris*, son of *Llewelyn* AURDORCHOG, *or of the golden torques*, the antient lord of *Yale*. It stands in two coun-

---

[u] Now to Sir *Thomas Mostyn* baronet, in right of his mother, niece to *Evan Vaughan*, esq. ED.

[x] By grant dated in *Yale* on the vigil of St. *Egidius* in 1256. *Salesbury Pedigree*, p. 51.

ties, *Flintshire* and *Denbighshire;* the long table in the hall having an end in each.

FROM hence I continued my journey to *Llanar-* *mon,* a village whose church is dedicated to St. *Germanus* bishop of *Auxerre;* who, with St. *Lupus,* contributed to gain the famous *Victoria Alleluiatica* over the *Picts* and *Saxons* near *Mold.* He was a most popular patron, and has numbers of other churches in *Wales* under his protection. An image of an ecclesiastic, still to be seen in the church-wall, is called his. In *Leland*'s days, there was a great resort of pilgrims, and large offerings at this place'; and, probably, to this imaginary resemblance of him.

IN the church is the tomb of a son of the bloody-fingered warrior above mentioned, carrying on his shield the arms won by his father, inscribed around, *Hic jacet Grufudd ap Lhewelyn ap Ynyr.* At his feet lies a dog gnawing a heap of intestines. The tradition of the country is, that he engaged in a *crusade,* in which he lost his life by a wound in the abdomen; that his bowels fell out, and were seized by a dog, as expressed by the sculptor. If he fell in the romantic cause of the holy sepulchre, the artist must have forgotten to place him cross-legged, the monumental distinction of all such knights-errant. The tomb is a chest cut out of one stone,

' *Leland Itin.* v. 35.

in which his body was put, and sent home. The lid is another stone, with his effigies carved out of it.

TUMULI.   SEPULCHRAL *tumuli* are very frequent in this parish. I was present at the opening of one, com posed of loose stone and earth, covered with a layer of soil about two feet thick, and over that with a coat of verdant turf. In the course of our search, were discovered towards the middle of the tumulus, several urns made of sun-burnt clay, of a reddish color on the outside, black within, being stained with the ashes they contained. Each was placed with the mouth downwards on a flat stone; above each was another stone, to preserve it from being broken by the weight above. Mixed with the loose stones, were numerous fragments of bones; such as parts of the thigh-bones, the arm- bones, and even a scull. These had escaped the effects of the fire of the funeral pile, and were de- posited about the urns; which contained the resi- duum of the corpse, that had been reduced to pure ashes.

I SHALL mention in the following pages the high antiquity of a custom which was in use among the most polished nations, among the *Greeks* and *Romans*, as well as among the most barbarous people. The antient *Germans* practised this rite, as appears from *Tacitus*[z]. The *Druids* observed

----

[z] *De moribus German.*

the same, with the wild addition of whatsoever was
of use in this life, under the notion that it would be
wanted by the deceased in the world below; and
in confirmation of this, arms, and many singular
things, of unknown use, are to this day discovered
beneath the places of antient sepulture[a].

THE remote *Sarmatæ*, and all the *Scandinavian*
nations, agreed in the burning of the dead; and the
Danes distinguished by this, and the different
funeral ceremonies, three several epochs[b].

THE first, which was the same with that in
question, was called *Roisold* and *Brende-tiide*, or
the age of burning.

THE second was styled *Hoigold*, and *Hoielse-
tiide*, or the age of *tumuli*, or hillocks. The corpse
at this period was placed entire, with all the ornaments which graced it during life. The bracelets,
or arms, and even the horse of the departed hero,
were placed beneath the heap. Money, and all
the rich property of the deceased, used to be buried
with him, from the persuasion that the soul was
immortal[c], and would stand in need of these
things in the other life. Such was the notion,
both of the *Gauls* and of the northern nations.
Among the last, when piracy was esteemed honorable, these illustrious robbers directed that all
their rich plunder should be deposited with their

---

[a] *Mela*, lib. iii. c. 2.   [b] *Wormii Mon. Danic.* 40.
[c] *Pomponius Mela*, lib. iii. c. 2.

remains[d], in order to stimulate their offspring to
support themselves, and the glory of their name,
by deeds of arms. Hence it is we hear of the
vast riches discovered in sepulchres, and of the
frequent violation of the remains of the dead, in
expectation of treasures, even for centuries after
this custom had ceased.

THE third age was called *Christendoms-old*, when
the introduction of Christianity put a stop to the
former customs: for 'Christians,' as the learned
physician of *Norwich* observes, 'abhorred this
' species of obsequies; and though they stickt not
' to give their bodies to be burnt in their lives,
' detested that mode after death; affecting rather
' depositure than absumption, and properly sub-
' mitted unto the sentence of GOD, to return not
' unto ashes, but to dust again.'

FROM the remarks of these able writers, we may
learn the time of the abolition of the custom of
burning among the several nations; for it ceased
with paganism. It therefore fell first into disuse
with the *Britons;* for it was for some time retained
by the *Saxons* after their conquest of this kingdom;
but was left off on their receiving the light of the
gospel. The *Danes* retained the custom of urn-
burial the last of any: for all the northern nations
who had any footing in these kingdoms, they were

---

[d] *Bartholini Antiq. Dan.* 438.

the latest who embraced the doctrines of Christianity.

I CANNOT establish any criterion by which a judgment may be made of the people to whom the different species of urns and tumuli belonged, whether they are *British, Roman, Saxon,* or *Danish.*

SOME of the tumuli consist of heaps of naked stones, such as those in the isle of *Arran;* in many parts of *Scotland;* and in some parts of *Cornwall.*

OTHERS are composed, like this of *Llanarmon,* of stones and earth, nicely covered with earth and sod. Of these the base is in certain places level with the ground, in others, surrounded with a trench: they were sometimes formed of earth only. *O*thers are of a conoid form, and some oblong; of which there is an example in the neighborhood of *Bryn y pys,* called the *Giant's Grave.* *F*inally, other places of antient sepulture consisted only of a flat area, encompassed, like the *Druidical* circles, with upright stones; and such were those of *Ubbo,* and of king *Harald,* in *Sweden*[e].

THE urns are also found placed in different ways; either with the mouth resting downwards upon a flat stone, secured by another above; or with the mouth upwards, similarly guarded.

[e] *Suecia Antiqua et Hodierna,* tab. 315.

VERY frequently the urns are discovered lodged
in a square cell composed of flags.   Sometimes
more than one of these cells are found beneath a
carn or *tumulus*.   I have even met with, near
Dupplin in *Perthshire*, not fewer than seventeen,
disposed in a circular form[t].   When many are
found together, the tumulus was either a family-
cemetery, or might have contained the reliques of
a number of heroes who perished with glory in the
same cause: for such honors were paid only to the
great and good.

THE urns found in these cells are usually surrounded with the fragments of bones that had resisted the fire; for the friends of the deceased were
particularly careful to collect every particle, which
they placed, with the remains of the charcoal,
about the urns, thinking the neglect the utmost
impiety.   We have no certainty of the ceremonies
used by the antient *Britons* on these mournful
occasions; but from many circumstances which we
continually discover in our tumuli, there appear
many, analogous to those used in antient *Greece*
and *Rome*.

THE *Greeks* first quenched the funeral pile with
wine, and the companions and relations of the
departed performed the rest.   Such was the ceremony at the funeral of *Patroclus*.

<hr>

[t] *Tour in Scotland*, :ii. 106.

Where yet the embers glow,
Wide o'er the pile the sable wine they throw,
And deep subsides the ashy heap below.
Next the white bones his sad companions place,
With tears collected in the golden vase.
The sacred reliques to the tent they bore;
The urn a veil of linen cover'd o'er.
That done, they bid the sepulchre aspire,
And cast the deep foundations round the pyre;
High in the midst they heap the swelling bed
Of rising earth, memorial of the dead[g].
POPE.

THE duty of collecting the bones and ashes fell
to the next of kin. Thus, *Tibullus* pathetically
entreats death to spare him in a foreign land, least
he should want the tender offices of his nearest
relations:

Me tenet ignotis ægrum *Phæacia* terris,
  Abstineas avidas, mors violenta, manus!
Abstineas, moras atra! precor, non hic mihi mater,
  Quæ legat in mæstos ossa perusta sinus.
Non soror, *Assyrios* cineri quae dedat odores,
  Et fleat effusis ante sepulcra comis.
DELIA non usquam[h]!

Here[i], languishing beneath a foreign sky,
An unknown victim to disease, I lie;
In pity, then, suspend thy lifted dart,
Thou tyrant, Death; nor pierce my throbbing heart:
No mother near me, her last debt to pay,
Collect my bones, my ashes bear away;
No sister o'er my funeral pile shall mourn,
Nor mix *Assyrian* incense in my urn:
Nor, *Delia*, thou, oh thou my soul's first care!
Shall with thy dear, dishevell'd locks, be there.
R. W.

[g] *Iliad*, lib. xxiii. lin. 310.
[h] *Elegia*, lib. i. el. 3.   [i] In *Phæacia*.

I BEG leave to add the account given by *Virgil* of the funeral rites of *Pallas*[k]. We find in it many ceremonies that were used by the northern nations. Animals of different species were burnt or deposited with the body. The spoils of war, and weapons of various kinds, were placed on the pile; the bones and ashes were collected together; and a heap of earth, or a *tumulus*, flung over them. Each of these circumstances are continually discovered in our barrows. Horns, and other reliques of quadrupeds, weapons of brass and of stone, all placed under the very same sort of tombs as are described by *Homer* and *Virgil*. Perhaps the other ceremonies were not omitted; but we have no record that will warrant us to assert that they were in all respects similar.

Jam pater *Æneas*, &c.

The *Tuscan* chief and *Trojan* prince command,
To raise the funeral structures on the strand,
Then to the piles, as antient rites ordain,
Their friends convey the relicks of the slain.
From the black flames the sullen vapours rise,
And smoke in curling volumes to the skies.
The foot thrice compass the high-blazing pyres;
Thrice move the horse, in circles, round the fires.
Their tears, as loud they howl at ev'ry round,
Dim their bright arms, and trickle to the ground.
A peal of groans succeeds; and heav'n rebounds
To the mixt cries, and trumpet's martial sounds.
Some, in the flames, the wheels and bridles throw,
The swords and helmets of the vanquish'd foe:

[k] Lib. xi. l. 184.

Some, the known shields their brethren bore in vain,
And unsuccessful jav'lins of the slain.
Now round the piles the bellowing oxen bled,
And bristley swine, in honour of the dead.
The fields they drove, the fleecy flocks they slew,
And on the greedy flames the victims threw.   PITT.

SINCE I am engaged in this funebrious subject, it will be fit to observe, that a discovery of an entire skeleton, placed between flags of a proportionable size, was made near this place. This, as well as others similar in different parts of our island, evinces that the antient inhabitants did not always commit their bodies to the fire: for, besides this instance, a skeleton thus inclosed was found in one of the *Orknies*[1], and others in the shire of *Murray;* and with one of the last an urn with ashes, and several pieces of charcoal[m]; which shews that each practice was in use in the same age.

UPON the bank of the river, near the village of *Llanarmon*, is a vast artificial mount, called *Tommen y Vardra*,[1] once the site of a castelet; the reliques of which appear in a small square foundation. The river bounds one side of the mount, a deep ditch the other. Not far from it is a great natural cavern of a considerable height, for some

TOMMEN Y VARDRA.

[1] Letter from the Rev. Mr. *Low* of *Birsa*.

[m] *Tour Scotl.* 1769, quarto ed.

[1] *Y Vardra* means *Y Fuerdref*, the town of the mayor or the steward, a place-name of frequent occurrence in Wales. J.R.

space: it then lowers and extends to an unknown length.

FROM *Llanarmon* I continued my journey along the bad roads of that parish. The country now grows more contracted, by the approximation of the hills. On one side are the rocky ledges of TRE'R YRYS. limestone, in the township of *Tre'r Yrys*,([1]) rich in lead-ore; and which is supposed to have taken its name from *Gyris*, who made the first collection of *Welsh* proverbs, known by the name of *Mad-waith hên Gyrys o Jal*, or the good work of old *Gyrys* of *Yale*.

ON the left are the *Clwydian* hills, which divide this country from the vale of *Clwyd*. These are cultivated pretty high; are free from rocks; and covered with heath.

THERE is a *Bwlch*, or pass through these hills, of a most remarkable name, lying between the summits called *Moel Eithinen*, and *Moel Fenlli*. BWLCH AGRICLA. This is called *Bwlch Agricla*,([2]) or the pass of *Ag*

([1]) This is now called *Eryrys*, the village so called being one of the highest in Wales: it would seem to be derived from *eryr*, eagle, in the same way as *Eryri*, as the neighbourhood of Snowdon is called in Welsh. J.R.

([2]) This is impossible, as Agricola must in Welsh become *Aircol* or *Aercol;* the former as a matter of fact occurs in the Nennian Genealogies, and the latter will be found in Skene's Four Anc. Books of Wales, ii. 173; see also i. 318. It would now be *Aergol* or *Aergwl*, but I should guess the name here meant to have been *Y greig-le, Y grug-le*, or the like. J.R.

ricola; and, since there is no other translation to
be given of the *Welsh* word, we may conjecture
this to have been his passage to *Mona.* That the
Romans were in after-times resident in these parts,
is evident from the number of coins found in the
neighborhood, particularly in the parish of *Llan
ferres,* where abundance of *Denarii* have been met
with.

MOEL FENLLI, or *Benlli's* hill, is remarkable for
having on it a strong *British* post, guarded as
usual by dikes and fosses. This probably was possessed by a chieftain of that name; for *Nennius*[n]
speaks of such a *regulus* of the country of *Yale;*
but, as is too usual with our antient historians,
blends so ridiculous a legend with the mention of
him, as would destroy the belief of his existence,
did not the hill remain a possible evidence. St.
Germanus, says the abbot, designed to make this
Benlli a visit; but meeting with a most inhospitable reception, was kindly entertained by a servant of the king in his humble cottage; who killed
his only calf, dressed, and placed it before the saint
and his companions. This goodness met with its
reward; for lo! the next morning the identical
calf was found alive and well with its mother.

A LITTLE beyond this pass, entered the parish
of *Llanferres,* rich in mineral. Pass through the

MOEL
FENLLI.

LLANFERRES.

[n] C. xxx. xxxi.

village, and by the church.   The last is dedicated
to St. *Berres (Britius)* disciple of St. *Martin* the
Hungarian, and his successor in the bishoprick of
Tours, the latter end of the fourth century.   The
church at this time was rebuilding, chiefly by the
bounty of Mrs. *Catherine Jones* of *Clomendy*(¹).

THE east end of the old church was repaired in
1650, by Dr. *John Davies*, the author of the
Welsh-Latin dictionary, a most skilful antiquary;
native of this parish.

In the course of my ride, cross the turnpike-
road between *Mold* and *Ruthin;* which, after a
long ascent, passes *Bwlch Pen-y-Barras*, a spot
extremely worthy of the traveller's attention, on
account of the beautiful view over the vale of
Clwyd.

MY route this time led me eastward, along the
great road, into the county of

FLINT.

THIS spot being confirmed to it by the event of
a most expensive law-suit, in the court of exchequer, in 1763, between the *Grosvenor* family and

---

(¹) *Clomendy* is in the parish of *Llanferres*.   *Richard Wilson*, the
great landscape painter, was a relative of Mrs. *Catherine Jones*, and
the last years of his life were passed there, and at *Mold*.   He is said
to have painted the sign of the roadside inn called the *Loggerheads*,
which is near *Clomendy*.   T.P.

the lords of the manor of *Mold:* the first claming
it as part of the mineral grant of the hundred of
Yale; the others affirming it to be part of the
county of *Flint,* and within the parish of *Mold.*
The decision, which was in favor of the lords of
Mold, is recorded on an arch over a noted stone,
called *Carreg Carn March Arthur;* which was
then adjudged to be the boundary of the parish of
Mold in the county of *Flint,* and of *Llanferres* in
that of *Denbigh.*

I CONTINUED along the great road; and, within
two miles of *Mold,* hung long over the charming
vale which opens with exquisite beauty from *Fron,*
the seat of the ingenious the Reverend *Richard
Williams. Cambria* here lays aside her majestic
air, and condescends to assume a gentler form, in
order to render less violent her approaching union
with her *English* neighbor. It were to be wished
she had acted with more moderation, and not out-
shone it at the rate, the most partial *Saxon* must
allow it to have done.

THIS was antiently called *Ystrad-Alyn,* or the
Strath of the *Alyn;* a comot in the cantref *Y
Rhiw:* inhabited by a hardy race, at perpetual
feud with the men of *Cheshire* on one side, and the
men of *Yale* on the other: for my countrymen
never suffered their active swords to rust; in default of *Saxon,* they would take up with the blood
of their *Cambrian* neighbors.

On the first regulation of the *Welsh* counties by *Henry* VIII. this vale ,then called *Molesdale*, with the continuation of it which went under the name of *Hopesdale*, were annexed to the county of *Denbigh;* but, in the 33d year of the same monarch, were given to *Flintshire*.

Almost the whole is seen from this spot; a delicious composition of rich land finely bounded by gentle risings, watered by the *Alyn*, and varied with a pretty town and fine church in the middle; with numerous seats, groves and well cultivated farms. Among the former appears conspicuous, Leeswood. *Leeswood*, the seat of the late Sir *George Wynne*, rising palace-like along a fine slope on the south side of the vale, surrounded with woods and lawns. The distant view is not less beautiful. The three fine estuaries of the *Dee, Weever*, and *Mersey*, the hills of *Cheshire*, and the more remote range of those of *Shropshire, Staffordshire, Derbyshire, Yorkshire, Lancashire, Westmoreland*, and *Cumberland*, complete this beautiful scene.

Nerquis. Nerquis chapel, not far from hence, is a neat building with a pretty spire steeple. Within is a large gothic niche, elegantly carved, which once held the image of the Virgin, and is called (as all similar niches in *Wales* are) *Cader Fair*, or *the seat of Mary*. Not far from the chapel is *Nerquis* house, a good old seat, built in 1638 by *John*

Wynne, esq. of the line of *Edwyn,* lord of *Tegengl.*
Thomas Pindar esq. son to the famous merchant
Sir *Paul,* had for a short time possession of it, by
his marriage with Miss *Wynne,* the heiress of the
place.   Their son *Paul* was created a baronet in
1662, and dying single the estate devolved by ma-
ternal right to *Paul Williams* esq. of *Pont y*
Gwyddel.   On the death of *Edmund Williams*
esq. in 1737, it fell to his sister°; now relict of
Robert Hyde esq. who enjoys it with great hospitality.

FROM hence to the town of *Mold* is a pleasant   MOLD.
ride.   *Mold* consists principally of one broad and
handsome street on a gentle rising, in the midst of
a small but rich plain.   The church placed on an
eminence, is of the time of *Henry* VII. and is
adorned with a very handsome steeple built of late
years.   Before the Reformation, it belonged to the
abby of *Bustlesham,* or *Bysham,* in *Berkshire.*
The living is a vicarage, and has dependent on it
the chapelries of *Nerquis* and *Treyddyn.*   Near
the last is a vast *maen-hir,* or monumental stone,
called *Carreg y Llech,* five feet high, seven broad,
and eighteen inches thick, set erect on a tumulus
coarsely paved.

THE architecture of the church of *Mold* is of   CHURCH OF MOLD.
the gothic of the beginning of the sixteenth cen-

° Her grand-daughter Miss *Gifford* is the present possessor. Ed.

tury; the windows large, and their arches obtuse.
Within and without, is a row of animals carved, as
usual at that period.   The same may be observed
on the old building over St. *Winefrede's* well.
The inside is extremely elegant; consisting of a
nave and two ailes, supported by seven arches,
whose pillars are much to be admired for their
lightness.   They are composed of four round pilasters, with the intermediate space hollowed, and
the capitals elegantly carved.   Between the
springs of every arch is an angel holding a shield,
on which are either the arms of benefactors, or the
instruments of the Passion.   The arms of the
Stanlies, who long possessed this manor, are very
frequent.   Among the other sculptures, is the
Veronica, or face of our Saviour impressed on a
handkerchief given to him by a woman on his way
to the place of crucifixion.   He took it, wiped his
face, and returned it with the miraculous impres-
sion.   This precious relique is preserved in St.
Peter's at *Rome,* and the woman worshipped as a
saint, under the name of the *Handkerchief;* which
at first was called the *Vera Icon,* or true image;
but becoming thus personified, received the title
of St. *Veronica.*   Beneath two windows above the
chancel, are carved in a rude manner, the nails,
pincers, and other symbols of the crucifixion.

MONUMENTS.   AT the eastern ends of the two ailes are three
gothic niches elegantly carved.   They formerly

were filled with images, now destroyed. The two
in the south aile are almost hid with monuments.
Among them is a very superb one in memory of
Robert Davies esq. of *Llanerch*, with his figure in
a standing attitude, and dressed in a *Roman* habit.
He died *May* 22d 1728, aged 44.

NEAR it is a mural monument of his grandfather, another *Robert Davies*[p], of *Gwysaney*[q], the
paternal seat and the residence of the family, before
the acquisition of *Llanerch* in the vale of *Clwyd*,
by the marriage of this gentleman with *Anne*,
daughter and heiress to Sir *Peter Mutton* knight.

NEAR this is an antient mural monument, in
memory of *Robert Warton*, alias *Parfew*. He was
first abbot of *Bermondsey*, and elected to the
bishopric of St. *Asaph* in 1536. He lived much at
Denbigh and *Wrexham* during his continuance in
this see[r]; and was removed to that of *Hereford* in
1554, where he died in 1557. He was unjustly
accused of impairing the revenues of this diocese:
on the contrary, it appears, that he had been a
considerable benefactor to the churches of *Gres-*

[p] This gentleman died in 1666.

[q] *Gwysaney* stands not far from *Mold;* a most respectable old
house, beautifully situated: it was of strength sufficient to be garrisoned, in the time of the civil wars; and was taken, on the 12th of
April 1645, by Sir *William Brereton**.

[r] *Willis's Bangor*, 341. *Cathedrals*, i. 521. *Athenæ Oxon.* i. 682.

* *Whitelock*, 142.

ford, Wrexham, and *Mold;* which, probably, he
found in an unfinished state.   He was interred at
Hereford, under a handsome tomb with his effigies;
but this grateful memorial of his benevolence to
the church of *Mold* was erected, as an inscription
beneath once stated, by one *John ap Rys.   Hoc
opus factum fuerit, per John ap Rys.*   Above are
his arms in a shield, quartered with those of the
see of St. *Asaph;* and over them a label, inscribed
Robtus pmissione Divina Epus ASSAV.   An angel
supports one end; a bishop the other.

THE epitaph on the reverend Doctor *Wynne,*([1])
composed by himself, several years before his decease, merits publication.

WILLIAM WYNNE of *Tower,* D. D.
Some time fellow of *All-Souls* College in *Oxford,*
and rector of *Llanvechan* in this diocese,
departed this life
aged [s]
In conformity to an antient usage,
from a proper regard to decency,
and a concern for the health of his
fellow-creatures, he was moved to give
particular directions for being buried
in the adjoining church-yard,
and not in the church[t].

([1]) A few years ago the Church was enlarged, and Doctor *Wynne's*
grave is now inside the building. T.P.

[s] He died *March* 3d 1776, aged 77. And this, now, fills the blanks.

[t] Doctor *Verheyen,* professor of physic at *Louvain,* was actuated
by the same humane principle. He died in 1710, and left the following epitaph, expressing, '*P*artem sui materialem hic in cœmeterio
condi voluit, ne templum dehonestaret, aut nocivis halitibus inficeret.'
Keysler's Travels, i. Letter xxx. p. 279. Quarto edit.

And, as he scorned flattering of others
while living, he has taken care to prevent
being flattered himself when dead,
by causing this small memorial to be
set up in his life-time.
GOD, be merciful to me a sinner!
Heb DDUW, *Heb ddim.*

LATELY was dug up in the church-yard a stone
with the following inscription.

Fundamentum
Ecclesiæ CHRISTUS
1597.

W As . Cps

THE bishop was *William Hughes,* who died in
1600. The inscription must have been on a stone
used in some repairs, for the church was certainly
founded about the time I mention.

AT the north end of the town stands the mount, BAILEY-
to which it owes the *British* and *Latin* names, HILL.
YR WYDDGRUG, and MONS ALTUS, *the lofty* or
conspicuous mount. This is partly natural, partly
artificial. Our *British* ancestors, and afterwards
the *Saxons* and *Normans,* taking advantage of so
defencible an eminence, cut it into form, and placed
on it a castle. It is possible, that the *Romans*
might also have had some concern in it; for a
beautiful gold coin of *Vespasian* was found here;
but this being the only proof of its having been pos-

sessed by them, I shall not insist on it any farther than to urge the probability; *Mold* being in the neighborhood of many of their mines, and of places where much of their money has been found.

THE mount is now called the *Bailey*-hill, from the word *Ballium*, or castle-yard. It appears to have been strongly fortified by great ditches, notwithstanding its arduous ascent. It is divided into three parts: the lower *Ballium* or yard; the upper; and the keep, or *Donjon*. The tops of the two first are levelled by art; and are all separated by deep fosses. The keep was on a part greatly and artificially elevated; and round its edges are a few stones, the only reliques of the fortress. On one side of the upper yard are found vast quantities of bones, some human; others of animals, mostly domestic, such as of oxen, sheep, horses and hogs, and a few remnants of horns of stags and roe-bucks.

THE summit of this hill commands a limited but most exquisite view of the circumjacent vale; and to the west, *Moel famma*([1]) rises with awful pre-eminence among the *Clwydian* hills.

THE first certain account which I find of this place is in the reign of *William Rufus*, when it

---

([1]) The proper spelling is no doubt *Moel Fammau*, the Mothers' Mountain, the ladies in question being of the class of the divine *Matres* once worshipped by the Celts, especially in Gaul: see Elton's Origins of English History (London, 1882) p. 264. J.R.

was in possession of *Eustace Cruer*[u], who then did homage for *Mold* and *Hopedale;* he, probably, having been the person who had wrested them from the antient owners.

In the end of the reign of *Henry* I. or the beginning of that of *Stephen, Robert,* called, from his residence at this place, *de Montalto,* high steward of *Chester,* and one of the barons of the *Norman* earls, became owner of it. We are informed, that the castle was at this time very strong; and that it had been often besieged; but never taken, till the *Welsh,* no longer able to bear the ravages of the garrison, attempted, in 1144, the reduction of it, under the conduct of their gallant prince *Owen Gwynedd.* The garrison, for a considerable time, defended the place with great courage; but at length it was taken by storm; part of the defendants slain, the others taken prisoners, and the fortress razed to the ground[x]. 1144.

After this it was again restored; for we find in the *æræ Cambro-Britannicæ*[y], that it was taken in the winter of 1198, by *Llewelyn ap Jorwerth;* and about the year 1267 it was a third time besieged, taken, and demolished, by *Gryffydd ap Gwenwynwyn,* lord of *Powys.* 1198.

The gentry of *Ystrad alun* or *Molesdale* were

---

[u] *Powel,* 151.   [x] *Powel,* 199.
[y] At the end of *Llwyd's* Commentariolum, 157.

among the principal complainants of wrongs done
to them by *Roger de Clifford*, justiciary of *Chester*,
and his deputy *Roger Scrochil*, a little before our
subjection by *Edward* I. They alleged, that their
lands were taken from them; that they were grie-
vously and unjustly fined on trivial occasions; and
that, after paying a sum for exemption from the
English laws, they were obliged to submit to a
trial by jury, or by twelve men, contrary to the
usage of their country[z].

MUCH of the country was, in this reign, so
covered with woods, that *Edward*, before his conquest of *Wales*, was obliged to cut a passage
through them, in the tract between *Mold* and a
place then called *Swerdewood;* and to direct, that
nothing should be required for the damage done
to the owners[a]. I find he called in a number of
cutters for this purpose; and that in the next year,
not fewer than two hundred cutters and colliers
(carbonarii) were summoned out of the forest of
Dean, and the county of *Hereford,* under the conduct of *Gilbert de Clare* earl of *Gloster.*

IN the year 1322, Sir *Gryffydd Llwyd,* a valiant
gentleman, who was knighted by *Edward* I. on
bringing the news of the birth of his son *Edward*

---

[z] *Powel,* 356.

[a] *Rotuli Walliæ,* 75. Anno 9 *Edward* I. We find a similar order
in *Rymer.*

of *Caernarvon;* and, who, after our conquest, adhered to the *English,* till he thought their yoke intolerable; rose in arms, over-run all *North Wales,* and the *Marches,* and, among others, seized on this castle; but his attempt was unsuccessful, he being defeated, and taken prisoner[b].

FROM this time we hear no more of it as a place of defence. *Matthew Paris* and *Dugdale*[c] confound it with *Hawarden,* and assert it to have been attacked or taken by *Dafydd,* brother to the last *Llewelyn.* *Mold* continued in possession of the posterity of *Robert,* who did homage for it in 1302, at *Chester,* to *Edward* prince of *Wales;* but in 1327, the last baron, in default of male issue, conveyed it to *Isabel,* queen of *Edward* II. for life; and afterwards to *John* of *Eltham,* younger brother to *Edward* III.; who died without issue, and his possessions reverted to the crown.

1302.

1327.

I AM uncertain how long the crown reserved this lordship. I find it was granted to the *Stanley* family, perhaps to Sir *John Stanley,* by *Henry* IV. at the same time that he bestowed on him *Hope* and *Hopedale.* The earls of *Derby* possessed it till the execution of earl *James;* after which, both the manors of *Hope* and *Mold*(1) were purchased

---

[b] *Powel,* 383. *Wynn,* 313.

[c] *M. Paris,* 885. *Dugdale Baron.* i. 527.

(1) *Mold* was granted, together with *Hawarden,* to Sir *Thomas Stanley* by *Henry* VI. in 1443. Sir *Thomas* was summoned to Parlia-

by certain persons, who enjoyed them till the Res
toration: subsequent to that event, a reference was
made by his majesty, in 1662, to the lords, respecting the re-purchase of those manors by the
earl of *Derby;* in which it had been agreed by his
lordship to pay the parties, on the 26th of *March*
1664, the sum of eleven thousand pounds, and to
be put into full possession.   The lords imagined
that every thing had been adjusted; but the earl
of *Derby* refusing to perform his part, the referees
layed the affair before the king; who, on the 14th
of *June* 1664, ordered that the former purchasers
should remain in quiet possession.   The *Derby*
family, by some means, regained the lordship of
Hope; but that of *Mold* is at[d] present the property
of lady *Vincent.*   The mineral profits of the manor, which have, at times, been very considerable,
are equally divided between her ladyship, the
Trevors, and *John Lloyd* esq. of *Havodunos.*

ment, as *Baron Stanley,* in 1456, and died in 1459, when he was
succeeded by his more celebrated son Sir *Thomas Stanley,* afterwards earl of *Derby.*   In 1484, *Richard* III. granted "the castle,
manor, and lordship of *Hope,*" along with a number of other manors,
and various lands situate in different counties, to this nobleman.   It
was in consequence of the peculiar character of the language used in
the grant of *Richard* III. that the manor of *Hope* was recovered in
1680, by the then Earl of *Derby,* after a long lawsuit with Mr. *John*
Trevor.   The whole case is fully reported by Sir T. Raymond under
the name of *Murrey* v. *Eyton.* T.P.

   [d] This Lordship was recently purchased by Sir *Thomas Mostyn*
from his brother-in-law *Thomas Champneys* esq. ED.

FROM *Mold*,([1]) I tok the west side of the vale;
a tract filled with numerous seats of gentlemen of
independent fortunes, as yet not caught and ab-
sorbed in the gulphy vortex of our *Leviathans*.
These are the remnants of the custom of gavel-
kind, so prevalent formerly in *North Wales*, and
which have remained unimproved by those accidents which, by time and chance, happen to many.
I digressed a little to the right, to see the magnificent gates of *Leeswood*, the seat of the late Sir
George Wynne([2]) baronet; and a little higher up to
Tower, to enjoy the witty, the lively, and agreeable
conversation of the reverend Doctor *William
Wynne* (now departed). This gentleman was one
of those who kept the patrimony derived from a
long train of ancestors, without increase, yet with-

TOWER.

([1]) An account of a remarkable gold corslet found close to *Mold*,
is given in the Arch. Camb. for 1848, p. 98. T.P.

([2]) Sir *George Wynne*, who was created a baronet in 1731, "acquired a fortune by a lead mine, which in 20 years yielded £360,000.
This he spent in every kind of extravagance, electioneering, draining
a bog and building his house on it, which stands pleasantly under a
hill, with good gardens, and a pair of wrought iron gates made by
the same hand as those at Chirk." (Gough's *Camden*.) *Richard
Wilson*, the painter, was related to this family of *Wynne*, of *Leeswood*, and Sir *George Wynne* took him when very young to *London*,
and assisted him to learn his profession. *Wilson* first practised
portrait painting, but during a long visit which he paid to *Italy*, he
discovered the real bent of his genius, and became a landscape
painter. His great merits were not sufficiently appreciated by his
contemporaries, and he retired into *Wales*, and spent the latter part
of his life there. *Wilson* was buried in *Mold* churchyard, May 15th,
1782. T P.

out impair. The house is small; but part of it is a
true specimen of the border-houses on the confines
of *England* and *Scotland:* a square tower of three
stories. In the lower, still remains a staple in the
cieling; a memorial of the rudeness of the times.
During the wars between the houses of *York* and
Lancaster, this place was inhabited by *Reinallt
ap Gryffydd ap Bleyddyn*, one of the six gallant
captains who defended *Harlech* castle on the part
of *Henry* VI. He and his people were in continual feud with the citizens of *Chester*. In 1465,
a considerable number of the latter came to *Mold*
fair; a fray ensued between the two parties; a
dreadful slaughter was made on both sides; but
Reinallt got the victory; took prisoner *Robert
Bryne* linen-draper, and mayor of *Chester*, in 1461,
whom he led to his tower, and hung on the staple
in his great hall. An attempt was made afterwards to seize *Reinallt;* and two hundred tall men
sallied from *Chester* for that purpose. He retired
from his house to a neighboring wood, permitted
part of his enemies to enter the building; then
rushing from his cover, fastened the door; and
setting fire to the place, burnt them without mercy:
he then attacked the rest, pursued them to the sea-
side, where those who escaped the sword, perished
in the channel. *Reinallt* received his pardon from
Thomas lord *Stanley*, lord of the council of *Wales*,
which was afterwards confirmed under the great

seal by *Edward* IV. His actions were celebrated
at the time, in poems still extant; particularly by
Lewis Glyn Cothi, in an *Awdl*°, in praise of *Reinallt*. It seems *Lewis* had married a widow of
Chester, against the consent of the inhabitants;
who spoiled him of all his effects. This whetted
the poet's satire: 'Who summons the ministry of
' angels and of devils to his assistance; and pours
' a profusion of curses on *Caer Lleon* and its
' people. He wishes water to drown, fire to burn,
' and air to infect the hated place; and that grass
' might grow in every part, except the sacred
' edifices, of this habitation of the seven deadly
' sins.'

THE TOWER, in old times, was called after the
name of this hero. It was also named *Bryn-coed*,
from the wood that might have surrounded it. In
the time of *Leland* it was inhabited by *John Wynn
ap Robert*.

I DESCENDED into my former road; went by
Pentrehobin, a good old house built in 1540, the
property of *Trevor Lloyd* esq[f]. This gentleman,
and the *Lloyds* of *Farn* (now extinct) a house
about three miles farther up this vale, were des-

° A *Cywydd* and an *Awdl* differ in these respects: the first consists of couplets generally of seven syllables; the last of stanzas of
different lengths of metre; somewhat like a *Pindaric* ode.

[f] Now of *Rice Thomas* esq. of *Coed Helen* in right of his wife, sister to *Tr. Lloyd* esq. ED.

cended fron *Edwyn* lord of *Tegengl,* who had a numerous progeny seated in this and other parts of
Flintshire.   Passed along the course of the *Terrig,*
or the *violent;* at this time a trifling brook; but
often of a tremendous swell and fury.   On quitting its channel, go by *Leeswood,* or *Coed-Llai,* the
antient seat of my worthy relation *Thomas Eyton*
esquire[g].   The *Davieses* of *Gwysaney,* the *Wynnes*
of *Tower,* and this family, sprung from *Cynric
Evell,* or *the Twin,* son of *Madoc ap Meredydd*
prince of lower *Powys*[h].   He was styled lord of
Eglwyseg; and had beside, for his portion, *Molesdale,* and *Treyddyn* in the parish of *Mold;* which,
by the custom of gavel-kind, became divided among
his posterity; part of which, these families, his
descendants, still enjoy.

FARTHER on is *Hartsheath,* the house of *Guillim Lloyd Wardle* esquire, descended, by the female
line, from the *Lloyds* of the same place, of the stock
of *Edwyn.   Catherine Lloyd,* daughter and heiress
of([1]) ——— *Lloyd* of *Hartsheath* esq. married,
before the year 1681, a person who styled himself

---

[g] At present the residence of his nephew, the Rev. *Hope Wynne
Eyton.* ED.

[h] *Madoc* died in 1160.

([1]) The name of the father of the lady who married Sir St. *John
Gwillym,* according to Reynolds, was *Edward Lloyd.*   In 1697 *Lady
Gwillym* married *Richard Lloyd,* Esq.   Reynolds says that she was
alive, and about 120 years old in 1738.   See his *Heraldry,* printed at
Chester, 1739. T.P.

Sir St. *John Gwillym;* the country people call him a son of *Oliver Cromwell.* He gave the *Guillim* arms exactly as they are in *Guillim's* heraldry, retaining those of *Hatheway* and adding those of *Lloyd,* and improperly assumes the bloody hand, as there never was a baronet of his name. I have his seal affixed to a letter of his, written in a fair hand, dated *June* 6th, 1681; his motto, *Spes potentior viribus.* He was buried *Jan.* 17, 1689, she, *Feb.* 5, 1739, both in the family vault of the *Lloyds* in *Mold* church. There is an excellent half-length portrait of him at *Hartsheath.* The house is most beautifully seated on a long rising, insulated by the vale, and finely wooded and cultivated. It stands on the southern extremity, and commands a most elegant view of the valley, divided by the insulated rock of *Caergwrle,* soaring out of it, and capped with a ruined castle.

A LITTLE further up the vale stands *Plâs-Têg;* PLAS-TEG. a singular house, belonging to the *Trevors;* but, for many years, occupied by farmers[i]. The *Trevors* acquired it by the marriage of *Robert Trevor* of *Brynkinallt,* with *Katherine* daughter of *Llewelyn ap Ithel* of *Mold* and *Plâs-têg.* It is built with great regularity and simple grandeur. In the centre is a hall forty-three feet long by twenty-

[i] Its late owners Lord and Lady *Dacres* added some offices to the antient mansion, and resided there occasionally. It is now in possession of ——— *Roper* esq. ED.

three; there is a spacious stair-case; and above is a dining-room of the same dimensions with the hall, and twelve feet nine inches high. At each corner of the house is a square wing or tower, consisting (as does the centre) of five floors. In each is a room twenty-two feet six, by nineteen six; and within each of these rooms a closet thirteen feet seven inches square.

THIS house was built in 1610 by Sir *John Trevor*[k], a second son of the branch of *Trevalyn*. The design is attributed to *Inigo Jones;* but I doubt the tradition. It wants both the *Grecian-gothic* ornaments of his worse days, and the pure *Grecian* of his best.

CAERGWRLE. FROM hence I pursued my journey to *Caergwrle*, a village on the banks of the *Alyn*, in the parish of *Hope* or *Estyn*, whose form speaks it to have been a *Roman* station, which appears very evident to the antiquarian eye, from the summit of the adjacent rock, the site of the castle. The precints shew themselves to have been rectangular, with one side formed by the slope along the banks of the river. Here is yet preserved the antient disposition, in three broad streets, running parallel, and three narrower intersecting them at right angles. It had been only a small place, an outpost to *Deva;* but possessed the usual concomi

---

[k] Epitaph in *Hope* church.

tants of *Roman* luxury. In *Camden's* time (1606) a *hypocaust* was discovered near the place five ells long, four broad, and half an ell high, cut out of the live rock. The floor was of brick set in mortar: the roof supported by brick pillars; and consisting of polished tiles, perforated; on these were laid certain brick tubes which conveyed the heat to the room above. On some of those tiles were inscribed LEGIO XX[1], which point out the founders. I have also been credibly informed, that *Roman* bricks were found in the ruins of the old house of *Hope*, the seat of the family of the same name. I have also heard, that large beds of iron cinders have been discovered near *Caer Estyn* in this parish, the supposed works of the *Roman*.

BESIDES these proofs, here is the trace of a *Roman* road, pointing from the village towards *Mold*, and which is visible in two or three places; especially in the fields to the south of *Plâs-têg*. I think that part of the present road was a portion of the *Roman*. An artificial mount stands close on its course. Another road points towards *Ha-* *warden;* which increases my suspicion of that having been also a *Roman* out-post. As the word *street* is generally a sign of a *Roman* road, there might have been a third on the *Wrexham* side of *Caergwrle*; for we find on that road, *Croes y street*

---

[1] *Camden*, ii. 828.

passing over a place called *Cefn y Bêdd*, or the
hill of the grave, and leading to the castle. These
roads formed the approach to some of the mineral
parts of *Wales*, where *Roman* money has been
found.

MR. EDWARDS makes a happy conjecture respecting the etymology of the name of this place.
Caer Gawr Lle([1]), or the camp of the *Giant Legion*,
Lleon Gawr; for the *Britons* bestowed that title
on the twentieth legion, to imply its power; a term
analogous to *Victrix*, giving it the strength of a
giant[m].

THIS place, in the division of *Wales* by *Roderic*
the great, formed part of the *Cantref y Rhiw.*
When the *Saxons* made a conquest of our borders,
they comprehended it in their hundred called *Exe-
stan*, and added it to the county of *Chester*. We
find in the Doomsday book, that *Hope* (which
gives name to the parish) was held at that period
by one *Gislebert;* before by *Edwevin* a freeman.
In after times, this tract was known by the name

([1]) This is utterly impossible, as *Caer Lleon Gawr* is only Chester,
and means literally, the Castra of Lleon the Giant. *Lleon*, which is
really the Latin *legionis*—is taken to have been the name of a man,
who is then further called a giant: so thoroughly has *Lleon* got his
personal character established, that he appears in his place in a
Dictionary of Eminent Welshmen! In no case could it be the Welsh
for *Victrix.* J.R.

[m] This gave rise to the fable of *Chester* having been built by *Lleon
Gawr*, a mighty giant. See p. 139. CAMDEN, by mistake, calls the
legion *Leon Vawr.*

of *Hopedale.* On the division of *Wales* into counties by *Edward* I. it was annexed to *Flintshire;*
but was severed from it, and added to *Denbighshire* by *Henry* VIII.; and in the same reign, restored to the former county. It is a common notion in the country, that the last was effected by
the interest of the earl of *Derby,* in order to have
his *Welsh* estates in the same county; for at that
time the family was possessed of *Hawarden, Molesdale,* and this manor; which had been granted, on
January 1st 1401, by *Henry* IV. to Sir *John
Stanley*(1). The family had, at the same time, the
lordship of *Maelor Saesneg,* which was a portion of
Flintshire since its first being formed into a county.
This manor of *Hope* is the only one possessed at
present in *Wales* by the earl of *Derby.* I find
that in 1388, *Richard* II. made a grant of the
territory of *Hope* and *Hopedale* to *John de Holland* earl of *Huntingdon*[n], a most potent lord; who,
after the deposition of his master, was beheaded
by the populace at *Plessy* in *Essex.*

THE castle of *Caergwrle* stood on the summit of   CASTLE.
a great rock, precipitous on one side, and of steep
ascent on the others. Some of the walls, and part

---

(1) *Hawarden* and *Molesdale* were granted to Sir *Thomas Stanley,*
afterwards the 1st lord *Stanley,* by Henry VI. on October 14th,
1443. *Hope* was granted by *Richard* III. to the 2nd lord *Stanley*
on Sept. 17th, 1484. T.P.

[n] *Dugdale's Baron.* ii. 78.

of a round tower, still remain, sufficient to shew that its size was never great. Close, on the accessible parts, it was protected by very deep fosses cut through the rock. On the north-east side, there is a pretty extensive area; and round its verge, the vestiges of a rampart of earth and stones, and a foss, such as is usual in the *British* posts; it may be therefore supposed, that it had been possessed by the *Britons* in early times; and that

CAER ESTYN. it served to defend, in conjunction with *Caer Estyn*, a *British* post of one rampart and ditch, on the opposite side of the dale above the village, the entrance through this pass into *Wales*. Here the vale almost closes, leaving only room enough for the *Alyn* to flow through its picturesque dingles, till it gains the open country near the church of *Gresford*.

FOUNDER.   I CANNOT trace the founder of this castle. It probably was one of the few *Welsh* fortresses that we have to boast of. Its oblong form, its comparative deficiency of towers, and its general agreement in structure with others whose origin I am acquainted with, making me willing to suppose it the work of our countrymen, after they had recovered possession of this tract. In the reign of *Owen Gwynedd*, I find it part of the estates of *Gryffydd Maelor*[o]

[o] *Powel,* 211.

DAFYDD, brother to *Llewelyn*, last prince of *Wales*, held it from *Edward* I. *Dafydd* made great complaints of the injurious treatment he met with from *Roger de Clifford*, the justiciary of *Chester*, who cut down his woods about *Hope*, and endeavored to dispossess him of his rights[p]. When *Dafydd* took up arms in defence of his brother, he left a garrison in this castle; but in *June* 1282, it surrendered to the *English* monarch. As soon as it came into his possession, he bestowed it, with all its appertenances, on his beloved consort *Eleonor*[q]; from which it acquired the name of *Queen Hope*. The queen lodged here in her way to *Caernarvon*, where her husband sent her to give the *Welsh* a ruler born among them. Either at this time, or soon after, the castle was burnt by a casual fire.

IN 1307, the first of *Edward* II. this castle and manor were granted to *John de Cromwell*, on condition that he should repair the castle, then in a ruinous state: and in 1317, he was directed to raise fifty foot-soldiers for the wars in *Scotland*, out of his lands in this country[r]. *F*rom his death I find a gap in the succession, till the time they were given to Sir *John Stanley*.

CAERGWRLE, with *Hope*, is a prescriptive bo-

JOHN DE CROMWELL.

---

[p] *Powel*, 350.   [q] AYLOFFE's *Rot. Walliæ*, 87.
[r] *Dugdale Baron.* i. 44, 45; *Rotuli Scotiæ*, 136.

rough, and, in conjunction with *Flint*, &c. sends a member to parlement.

BRYN YOR-KYN. WEST of the castle, on a lofty hill, is *Bryn Yorkyn*, the paternal seat of *Ellis Yonge*, esq*. a descendant of the fertile stock of the often-men- tioned *Tudor Trevor. Jorwerth*, the twelfth in descent, marrying the daughter of *William le Yonge* of *Croxton*[t], called his children after their mother's name, which was continued by the family

HOPE. LLEWELYN AP DAFYDD AP MEREDYDD, a des- cendant of *Ynyr* of *Yale*, had estates in this parish, which were forfeited in the reign of *Henry* IV. for his adherence to *Owen Glyndwr*, and be- stowed on *Jenkin Hope*, great grandson of *Hugh Hope* of *Hawarden*[u].

THE parish is divided by the *Alyn:* the village and church of *Hope* lye about a mile from the **CHURCH.** castle, on the north side of the stream. The church is dedicated to St. *Cynfar*. The monuments of note are, two to the *Trevors* of *Plâs-têg;* one, which is mural, to Sir *John Trevor* knight, founder of that house, and secretary to the earl of *Notting- ham*, victor over the invincible *armada*, and comp- troller of the navy in the reigns of *Elizabeth* and *James* I. He died at his neighboring seat, in 1629, aged 67.

* Deceased. ED.   *Salusbury Pedigree*, 36. b.
[u] The same, p. 52. b. 67.

THE other is also mural; with two kneeling figures: the man in a gown and ruff; the lady with a kerchief over her .neck. This wants an inscription; but by the arms appears to have belonged to a *Trevor*.

THE first charter given to *Hope*, was by *Edward* the black prince, dated from *Chester*, in the twenty-fifth year of the reign of his father, or 1351. He orders that the constable of the castle for the time being should be the mayor, who was, after taking the sacrament, to swear on the holy evangelists, that he would preserve the privileges of the burgesses, granted in the said charter; and that he should chuse out of them annually, on *Michael mas*-day, two bailiffs. He adds also most of the other advantages granted in the charters of those times; all which were afterwards confirmed by *Richard* II[x].

ABUNDANCE of limestone is burnt into lime on *Caergwrle* hill, a lofty mountain composed of that species of stone; from which a vast quantity is carried into *Cheshire*. Near the top are found, in loose earth, numbers of the bodies called *entrochi*, ENTROCHI. of a curious and uncommon sort, with round protuberant joints. Fossilists suppose them to have been parts of some species of arborescent sea-star, whose branches bear a resemblance to these substances.

[x] *Sebright MSS.*

In former times, mill-stones were cut out of the rock on which the castle stands, which is composed of small pebbles lodged in grit.

On *Rhyddyn* demesne, belonging to Sir *Stephen* SALT SPRINGS. *Glynne*[y], adjoining to the *Alyn*, are two springs, strongly impregnated with salt; which, in dry weather, used to be the great resort of pigeons to pick up the hardened particles. These were formerly used as a remedy in scorbutic cases. The patients drank a quart or two in a day; and some boiled the water till half was wasted, before they took it. The effect was, purging, griping, and sickness at the stomach, which went off in a few days, and then produced a good appetite. Dr. *Short* gives an instance of a woman in a deplorable situation from a scurvy, who was perfectly restored by the use of these springs.

From the village of *Hope*, I returned on the north side of the valley; re-passed *Mold*; and, MAES-GARMON. about a mile west of the town, visited *Maes-Garmon*; a spot that still retains the name of the saintly commander in the celebrated battle, the *Victoria Alleluiatica*, fought in 420, between the

---

[y] Unfortunately there has been a very quick succession in this house. Sir *John*, and his very worthy son Sir *Stephen*, have died since the publication of the first edition of this book; and now the fortunes rest in the infant[*] Sir *Stephen*.

[*] The marriage of the latter with the amiable daughter of Lord *Braybroke*, and the birth of another *Stephen*, affords the gratifying prospect of the continuance of this worthy family. ED.

Britons, headed by the bishops *Germanus* and *Lupus,* and a crowd of pagan *Picts* and *Saxons* who were carrying desolation through the country. This event happened in *Easter* week, when the Christian army, wet with their recent baptism in the river *Alyn,* were led by their holy commanders against the pagan host. *Germanus* instructed them to attend to the word he gave, and repeat it. Accordingly, he pronounced that of ALLELUIA. His soldiers caught the sacred sound, and repeated it with such ecstatic force, that the hills re-echoing with the cry, struck terror into the enemy, who fled on all sides; numbers perished by the sword and numbers in the adjacent river[z]

SUCH is the relation given by *Constantius* of *Lyons,* who wrote the life of St. *Germanus,* within thirty-two years after the death of the saint. It has heen objected by cavillers, that the *Saxons* were not at that time possessed of *Britain.* That may be admitted; but the learned USHER overthrows the objection, by rightly observing, that those people had, long before, made temporary invasions of our island, and committed great ravages in several parts; and calls to witness *Ammianus Marcellinus*[a]: and to his authority I may add, that the *Romans* found it necessary to have, in the

---

[z] *Brit. Eccles. Antiquitates,* 335.　*Paulus Diaconus,* lib. xv. c. 12, and BEDÆ, lib. i. c. 20, describe the action.

[a] Lib. xxvi. c. 4.

later times, a new officer to watch their motions, and repel their invasions, a *comes littoris* SAXONICI *per* BRITANNIAS.

MAES-GARMON, the scene of this celebrated victory, lies near *Rhual*, the pleasant seat of *Thomas Griffith* esq. whose uncle, *Nehemiah Griffith,*([1]) erected a column, with the following inscription, to perpetuate the memory of the spot.

Ad Annum
CCCCXX.
Saxones Pictiq. bellum adversus
Britones junctis viribus susceperunt
In hac regione, hodieq. MAESGARMON
Appellata: cum in prælium descenditur
Apostolicis *Britonum* ducibus GERMANO
Et LUPO, CHRISTUS militabat in castris:
ALLELUIA tertiò repetitum exclamabant;
Hostile agmen terrore prosternitur;
Triumphant
Hostibus fusis sine sanguine;
Palmâ Fide non Viribus obtentâ.
M. *P.*
In VICTORIÆ ALLELUIATICÆ memoriam
N. G.
MDCCXXXVI.

RHUAL. RHUAL was built in 1634 by *Evan Edwards* esq[b]. secretary to *Richard* earl of *Dorset,* and

---

([1]) *Nehemiah Griffith* was a man of letters, and the author of a forgotten poem called the *Leek*. T.P.

[b] At *Rhual* is preserved a portrait of *Evan Edwards,* said to have been painted by *Vandyck;* here are also two curious heads, on wood, of *Richard* earl of *Dorset,* and of his countess, the celebrated *Anne Clifford.* Among the collection are several family pictures by *Ed-*

member, in the parlement of 1628, for *Camelford*. *Mary* his grand-daughter married *Walter Gryffith* esq. of *Llanfyllyn*, and conveyed the estate into the family of the present possessor. Almost all the houses built in *Wales*, from the beginning of the seventeenth century to about the time in which this was founded, are in the form of a *Roman* H. The mode of architecture had been practised long before, as is evident from the good house of *Pentrehobin*, and here and there the example was followed in the same century, but most generally in the period just mentioned.

*F*ROM hence I proceeded towards *Kilken;* and saw in my way *Hesp-alun*[c], the place where the river *Alyn*, like the sullen *Mole* or mourning *Guadiana*, sinks under ground, continues a subterraneous course for half a mile, and then emerges to the day. About two miles distant from this place lies the church of *Kilken*, beneath *Moel Famma*, the highest division of the *Clwydian* hills. These run in a chain from above *Prestatyn* on the estuary of the *Dee*, from north to south as far as *Moel Yr Accre* in *Llanarmon* parish; when they join the mountain *Cefn du*, extending to the parish of *Gwyddelwern*. These admit no passage the whole

ward Bellins and *Gilbert Jackson*, names unknown in the list of artists, but whose merits entitle them to a place among the more celebrated painters. They flourished about the year 1632. ED.

[c] *i. e.* the dry *Alun.*

way, excepting that of *Bodfari*, without climbing
the steep sides, and going through the *bwlchs*
formed high up between the round heathy heads,
that rise from the mass more than two-thirds of
the way to the summits; and which form, from the
west side of the vale of *Clwyd*, a most beautiful
view, especially in the season when it glows with
the purple flowers of the heath. A few birds,
lovers of exalted situations, are still to be found
here; a few black and red grous[d] have escaped the
rage of shooters; and I have seen the *ring-ouzel*
about the lower parts. These hills are composed
of a mixed soil, clay, and gravel. The stone[e] is of a
shattery laminated nature, and bad for most œco-
nomic uses. The sides abound in springs, which
descend in small rills, to the great benefit of the
inhabitants of the rich slopes.

KILKEN CHURCH. THE church of *Kilken* is remarkable for its
carved roof; which is said to have been brought
from the church at *Basingwerk* abby on the disso-

[d] The first species is totally, and the latter nearly extinct on this chain of hills. ED.

[e] The strata which principally form this elevated range, consist of a coarse argillaceous schistus. ED.

The editor seizes this opportunity of pointing out an error which appears in Mr. *Aikin's* generally correct Tour of *North Wales*. He says, p. 182, 'The vale of *Clwyd* is bounded by *Moel-vamma* and other lime-stone hills;' whereas, that mountain and nearly the whole of the chain is composed of an argillaceous schistus, on whose basis calcareous strata are only found occasionally. ED.

lution: and thus to have fulfilled a prophecy of our *Robin Ddu*, who, when he saw it put up by the monks, observed, it would do very well for a church beneath *Moel Famma*.

IN this parish, on the side of the turnpike-road, not far from *Kilken hall*, is the noted *Ffynnon Leinw*, or the *flowing well*; a large oblong well with a double wall round it. This is taken notice of by *Camden* for its flux and re-flux; but the singularity has ceased since his time, according to the best information I can receive.

FFYNNON LEINW.

NEAR this well, is *Kilken hall*, a seat of a branch of the *Mostyns*, now the property of the reverend Mr. *Edwards*[f] of *Pentre*, in *Montgomery-shire*, in right of his first wife, *Charlotte Mostyn*, heiress of the place.

THIS fountain lies in the vale of *Nannerch·* which extends one way to *Mold;* and at the other joins with that of *Bodfari*, the inlet into the vale of *Clwyd*. The *Wheeler*, a pretty stream, rises on the east side; and after a short course, falls into the *Clwyd*. The house of *Penbedw*, the seat of *Watkin Williams* esq[g]. is a great ornament to this little valley. In this gentleman's library are some remains of the collection of Sir *Kenelm Digby*, some curious illuminated books; and the

VALE OF NANNERCH.

PENBEDW.

[f] At present of his son *Thomas Mostyn Edwards* esq. ED.

[g] Watkin Williams esq. died towards the close of the year 1808. ED.

superb pedigree[h] of the *Digby* family, and its alli-
auces, with all the arms and tombs that were extant, painted in a most exquisite manner, at the
expence of above a thousand pounds; a vast sum
at the time of the compilation, in the year 1634.

PENBEDW is seated in a manor of the same
name, granted, *July* 17th 1544, by *Henry* VIII.
and witnessed by queen *Catherine Parr*, to *Peter
(Pyers) ap Howel*, alias *Peter Mostyn*, of *Wespre*,
in consideration of the payment of seventy-three
pounds in hand. The grant recites, that it had
been parcel of the possessions of the earl of *Kent*,
in the commot of *Dogbylyn*, in the county of
Denbigh.

IN the meadows below the house, is a part of a
druidical circle, and a small *tumulus*. On one of
the summits of the mountain, at a great height
BRITISH POSTS. above the house, is a very strong *British* post,
with two ditches of prodigious depth, with suitable
dikes on the accessible sides: and on that which is
inaccessible, is a smooth terrace, levelled along the
hill, probably a place for exercising the possessors.
MOEL ARTHUR. This post is called *Moel* ARTHUR, perhaps in
honor of our celebrated prince. This is one of the
chain of posts that defended the country of the

h Mention is made of it in *Wood's Athenæ Oxon.* ii. 354, and the
Brit. Biog. iii. 1313. By permission of Mr. *Williams*, I caused several of the tombs to be copied; and that of Lady *Venetia Digby* to be
engraven in the *Antiquary's Repertory*.

Ordovices, and their successors, against the inroads
of invaders. They are far from being peculiar to
that nation; but were the common mode of defence
throughout the whole island. I conjecture that
their origin was very early; but that they were occasionally made use of in after-times, even as low
as those of *Owen Glyndwr.* Almost all are rendered defensible in the same manner, by deep
ditches and high banks, formed either of earth or
loose stones, with one, but generally two entrances. In the description of that of *Caractacus*
by *Tacitus,* their formation is exactly shewn:
*Tunc montibus arduis, et si qua clementer ac-
cedi poterant, in modum valli saxa præstruit*[1]
They are of no certain shape; but the precinct
conforms to that of the hill. They are gene- THEIR USES.
rally destitute of water, which evinces, that they
were not intended as places of long abode,
but merely temporary retreats for their families,
herds, and flocks, on a sudden invasion. The
fighting men kept the field, while all that was dear
or valuable was committed to these *asyla,* under a
proper garrison.

THEY are always placed within sight of one
another; so that by fire, or other signals, notice
might be given of the approach of an enemy. The
first that forms this chain is *Moel Hiraddug,* MOEL HIRADDUG.
about two or three miles from the sea, on a rocky

[1] *Taciti Annales,* lib. xii. c. 33.

hill, in the parish of *Cwm*.   Possibly, prior to the
castle of *Diserth*, another post might have been on
that rock; and in such case, should be esteemed
the first post, the guard of the shore; and the great
artificial mount above *Newmarket*, called *Cop yr
Goleuni*, or *Mount of Light*, which may be seen
from most of the others, might be the spot from
whence the signal was given of the approach of the
enemy by sea, whether they were *Saxons* or plundering *Scoti*.

MOEL
Y GAER.

THE next to *Moel Hiraddug*, is a *Moel y Gaer*,
in the parish of *Bodfari*, above the entrance of the
inlet into the vale of *Clwyd*.

BRYN Y
CLODDIAU.

THE third are the vast entrenchments on *Bryn
y Cloddiau*, or the hill of ditches.   This is the
largest we have; being a mile and a half in circuit,
and defended by single, double, triple, and even
quadruple ditches, according to the exigencies of
the sides.   In the foss next to the area, are numbers of hollows, as if designed for lodgments of
men, on a particular guard.

MOEL
Y CRIO.

SECOND
MOEL
Y GAER.

MOEL Arthur is the next.   Almost opposite to
it, on *Halkin* mountain, on the highest part, is
Moel y Crio; a vast artificial mount, that seems to
be a middle post between this and the *Moel y
Gaer* in *Northop* parish; but our ignorance in the
art military of those days, prevents us from pointing out the immediate use.

· NEXT succeeds *Moel Fenlli.* Beneath that is another post, on a lesser hill, which juts into the vale of *Clwyd,* and is called by the common name of *Moel y Gaer.* These are all that seem destined for the defence of this part of the country.

CAER ESTYN, and the post opposite on *Caer-gwrle* rock, defended that front. *F*arther on was *Hawarden;* and still farther, where the vale of *Cheshire* gains upon our country, was that of the *Rofts,* in the parish of *Gresford.* I could give a long list of these posts, perhaps as far as the *Severn* sea, in the country of the *Silures,* and the *Trans-sabrine* parts of the *Cornavii;* but these suffice for the present purpose.

SOON after passing *Penbedw,* I reached *Nan-nerch,* a hamlet with a small church, noted for little but a monument in memory of *Charlotte Theophila Mostyn,* wife to *Richard Mostyn* esq. former owner of *Penbedw,* and daughter and co-heiress (with her sister *Margaretta Maria,* who married Sir *John Conway* of *Bodrhyddan*) to *John Digby,* son of the famous Sir *Kenelm;* by which means, several choice morsels of his collection came into our country.

In the chancel window were once these words: *Orate pro bono statu Howell ap John ap Dda ap Ithel,* who is thought to have been founder of the church.

MOEL FENLLI.

AND THIRD MOEL Y GAER.

CAER ESTYN.

NANNERCH.

THIS valley forms one boundary of the mineral
tract of our county.   I shall now take a kind of a
bird's eye view of the whole, which I have surrounded, in the course of my tour, beginning with
the northern extremity.   The highland part may
be divided into two.   The first is insulated by
valley, plain, and sea.   The farther point is *Dalar*
Goch, or the rock of *Diserth,* bounded by the rich,
arable flats of *Rhuddland;* the course is continued
southward through the parishes of *Cwm,* *Tre-*
meirchion, and *Caerwys,* bounded by the vale of
Clwyd, and that of *Bodvari.*   The parishes of
Skeifiog, and *Nannerch* succeed, and after them a
portion of *Kilken,* when this mineral tract takes a
turn above the parish of *Mold* at *Rhos Esmor* in
that of *Northop;* and then faces the east in the
parishes of *Halkin* and *Holywell,* in those of *White-*
ford, Llanasa, Gwaenyskor, and *Meliden,* and
makes a point towards the west, where it unites
with the rock of *Diserth.*

THE second division is separated from the first
by a deep depression of the country between *Rhos*
Esmor, and the parish of *Mold.*   There is even in
the lower parts, on the west side, a chain of mines.
But the land rises again at *Mold* mountain, and
the mineral tract is continued through the parishes
of *Llanferres,* the eastern sides of *Llanarmon,*
Llandegla, the *Glisseg* rocks, and *Minera* above
Wrexham.

THE middle of the first division is entirely lime- LIMESTONE.
stone, as is the western side, from *Dalar Goch* to
Rhos Esmor: from thence, or on the eastern side,
the strata alter. Towards the skirts of the hills,
they change to that flinty substance called *chert*, CHERT.
more or less pure. Lower down they degenerate
into a black shale stone, soon decomposed by the SHALE.
air. So far lead-ore is found. Soon after these
strata, free-stone commences, and coals are found, FREE-STONE.
which continue to the shore, and under the sea,
till they appear on the opposite side in the penin-
sula of *Wiral*, and again beyond the estuary of
the *Mersey*.

THE same observations might be made on the
strata in the second division. Limestone beds are
continued on the western side beyond the *Glisseg*
rocks, and in their neighborhood on both sides of
the *Dee*. The veins in *Minera* lie in an impure
gritty chert. The sudden change of strata is very,
observable. The transition may be immediately
seen on each side of the narrow vale of *Nannerch*,
limestone forming the one, and the shattery slaty
stone composing the other.

WERE I to continue my aërial speculation, I
should see a discontinuance of the limestone strata
till they rose on the opposite side of the vale of
Clwyd. My eye would catch the most remote
part on the northern side of *Red Wharf-bay* in
Anglesey, insulated far from any other. The great
VOL. II. F

promontories of *Llandudno* and *Rhiwledin,* or the
greater and lesser *Ormshead* (the first at times rich
in copper) would next appear. *Penmaen Rhos,*
and the continued precipices along the coast of
Denbighshire, succeed in the nearer view, many of
them productive of lead-ore. And, finally, the
detached rocks of *Henllan* beyond *Denbigh,* and
Coed Marchon beyond *Ruthin,* which yield to the
industrious farmer, by their excellent lime, a manure more certainly productive of wealth, than the
precarious search after the deep-hid minerals.

THE limestone and the chert of our mineral
tracts are of unknown depth; neither their bottom,
nor that of the fissures or veins which cross them,
have ever been discovered. The ore of lead has
DEPTH OF been followed to the depth of a hundred and thirty,
VEINS. or a hundred and forty yards, and then has ceased;
but the unprofitable vein appears below unclosed.
Our mines, as I have shewn before, have been
worked from very early times[k], but not without
long interruptions. But as several of our veins
have been pursued for a hundred years past, the
point may be affirmed of the depth to which they
bear ore in our country.

THEIR   THE veins run either north and south, or east
COURSE. and west. But it is remarkable, that the lead ore
got in the first, scarcely ever produces a quantity

[k] *P.* 69, vol. i.

of silver worth the refiner's labor. The ores of *Mold* mountain, and of *Minera*, yield scarcely any silver.

THE minerals of the tracts in question, are ore of lead, calamine, or *Lapis calaminaris;* and the mineral, that answers the same purpose, called by the miners *black jack.*

Our ores of lead differ in quality. The lamel- ORES OF LEAD; THEIR lated, or common kind, usually named *potters ore*, PRODUCE yields from fourteen to sixteen hundred and a OF LEAD. quarter of lead, from twenty hundred of the ore: but the last produce is rare.

THE quantity of silver produced from our lead OF SILVER. is also variable. The upper part of the vein of lead ore is always richest in silver; the bottom, in lead. Our refiners will assay any lead that will yield ten ounces in the ton of lead and upwards. The usual produce is fourteen ounces: sixteen have been gotten; but acquisitions of that kind within this circuit are extremely uncommon.

SOME years ago, a green lead ore was discovered GREEN LEAD ORE. in the *silver rake* on *Halkin* mountain. Only a small quantity was found, which yielded about thirteen hundred and a quarter from a ton of the ore. It was of a very stubborn quality, and re- sisted the greatest powers of the blast furnace before it would yield any metal.

BROWN, OR
CAULK.

THE brown or whitish stoney species of ore,
called *Caulk*[1], produces from five hundred and a
quarter to eleven hundred of lead from the ton.
The smelters likewise get from what is called *waste*,
or the hillocks, which are the refuse of good ores,
so mixed with clay, gravel, stones, or calamine, as
not to be separated but by fire, from ten to thirteen hundred of lead per ton.

RICH MINES.

WE have had at different periods mines productive of vast wealth in several parts of this tract.
The richest vein was discovered about fifty years
ago at *Rowley's* rake, or *Pant y Pwll dwr* on
Halkin mountain, continued with some interrup-
tion into a small inclosure, the property of Sir
George Wynne of *Leeswood*, and the freehold of
Mr. *David Hughes;* which, in less than thirty
years, yielded to different proprietors, adventurers,
and smelters, above a million of money.   The
reader will naturally expect to find in these parts a
nation of *Cræsus's;* but *citò parta citò dilabuntur.*([1])
It is at this time an undetermined question, whether more wealth has been gotten out of the earth,
or more lost in the search after the prizes in this
subterraneous lottery.

MUCH of the ore obtained in our country is

---

[1] Not to be confounded with *Sulfate* of *Barytes*, the *Caulk* of *Derbyshire*. ED.

([1]) Sir *George Wynne* is probably the person who is here alluded to. T.P.

smelted in the several furnaces belonging to different companies: much also is exported in the form of ore. I wished to be acquainted with the annual quantity smelted from those of the country; but found, by reason of the ores imported from *Scotland* and other parts, that the computation would be of insuperable difficulty. All the lead and ore is exported from the port of *Chester*, a small quantity excepted, consumed by the plumbers and for other purposes in the adjacent parts. I therefore refer the reader to the Appendix[m], for the number of tons sent from that port in the years 1771, 1776. By the favor of Mr. *Jken*, collector, I am permitted to say, that, from the year 1758 to *Christmas* 1777, the following quantities have been entered in the custom house, foreign and coast ways.

Lead.				*Lead ore.*		*Litharge.*	
Tons.	*c.*	*qrs.*	*lb.*	*T.*	*c.*	*T.*	*c.*
79533	11	2	16	12840	6	2767	7

I CANNOT ascertain the quantity of ounces of silver produced from our ores, for the reasons just assigned. I can only say, that the company of a single smelting house, did obtain in the

		O~			*Oz.*
Year	1754	12160.	In 1774		5693.
	1755	1276.	1775	–	6704.
	1756	7341.	1776	–	4347.

[m] Nᵒ II.

THE reader need not to be told, that the former were the years of mineral plenty; and such, as I must say, are seldom known.   There are five other smelting-houses; but I believe none equalled this in quantity of silver.   This precious metal is chiefly bought by the artificers at *Sheffield* and *Birmingham.*

CALAMINE.   CALAMINE is found in great abundance in the veins of limestone and chert, in the same manner as the ores of lead.   Where there is plenty of the former, there is little or none of the latter.   The calamine is also entirely confined to the eastern side of the county.   About a thousand tons of this mineral is annually exported.   I have mentioned, in p. 84, vol. i. how little it was known in *Flintshire* till within these sixty years; and may here add, that we were indebted to *John Barrow,* a native of *Somersetshire,* who being well acquainted with that mineral in his own country, pointed out to us its uses.

CALAMINE assumes various shapes and colors; green, yellow, red, and black; it often has a stony appearance, and is often like the lattice-work of bones.   The richest looks like bees-wax; but that species is not common any more than the curious crystallized specimens.

ANOTHER ore of *Zink,* called here *black jack,* is met with in our mines.   We have it mineralized with sulphur and iron of a bluish grey and yellowish.

brown color, and of the color of the dark semipellucid ambers. *Cronstedt* calls the first ZINCUM *ferro sulphurato mineralisatum;* the other ZINCUM *calciforme cum ferro sulphuratum,* N° 1. *a.*

THESE were engrossed by patent by a *Bristol* company, and carried there to aid the making of brass.

SPARS of different kinds are found in the limestone veins; particularly the variety called *Iceland* crystal, *spatum islandicum,* the refracting spar, which represent objects seen through it double[m]

ICELAND CRYSTAL.

PETROLEUM, or rock-oil, is found sometimes in crevices of the mines; it has an agreeable smell, and is esteemed serviceable in rheumatic cases, if rubbed on the parts affected. The miners call it *Ymenyn tylwyth têg,* or the *fairies butter,* belonging to the benign species; perhaps the same with those (in superstitious days called *knockers*) which, by repeated strokes, were believed to direct the miners to a rich vein. But, in fact, the noises often heard in mines are discovered to proceed from the dropping of water. These *dæmones montani,* as *Agricola*[n] calls them, never infest our mines, except in form of damps of both species,

FAIRIES BUTTER.

KNOCKERS.

[m] The rarer mineral the *Carbonate of Barytes,* is found on the side of *Rhialt* hill, between *Holywell* and *St. Asaph.* ED.

[n] This very able writer, in one instance credulous, says, that twelve men were killed at once by one of these *Dæmones truculenti,* in the mine of ANNEBERG. *De anim. subter.* 491.

the *suffocating* and the *fire.* The last is very frequent in the coalpits, but rare in the mines of lead,
unless in those parts where the shale begins, or
stone attendant on coal. The first° kills instanta
neously, by its *mephitic* vapour, and is a disaster
common to neglected vaults, and draw-wells.
FIRE-DAMP, The other^p is inflammable, and burns and destroys
in a dreadful manner, as the colliers, through negligence, in not setting fire to the vapor before it
gets to a head, do often experience. The most
tremendous instance was on *February* 3d, 1675,
in a coalwork, at *Mostyn*, which I shall relate from
the *Philosophical Transactions*^q; and so conclude
the account of our mineral concerns.

IN MOSTYN   ' THE damp had been perceived for some time
COLLIERY.
' before, resembling fiery blades darting and cross-
' ing each other from both sides of the pit. The
' usual methods were taken to free the pit from
   this evil. After a cessation of work for three
' days, the steward thinking to fetch a compass
' about from the eye of the pit that came from the
' day, and to bring wind by a secure way along
' with him, that, if it burst again, it might be done
' without danger of men's lives, went down, and
' took two men along with him, which served his

° Carbonic Acid Gas. ED.

p Hydrogen Gas. ED.

q N° 136, or Vol. ii. 378, *Lowthorp's* Abridgement. The account
was drawn up by Mr. *Roger Mostyn.*

' turn for this purpose. He was no sooner down,
' but the rest of the workmen that had wrought
' there, disdaining to be left behind in such a time
' of danger, hastened down after them; and one of
them more indiscreet than the rest, went head-
' long with his candle over the eye of the damp-
' pit, at which the damp immediately catched, and
' flew to and fro over all the hollows of the work,
with a great wind, and a continual fire; and, as
' it went, keeping a mighty great roaring noise on
all sides

' THE men, at first appearance of it, had most
' of them fallen upon their faces, and hid them-
' selves as well as they could, in the loose slack, or
' small coal, and under the shelter of posts; yet,
' nevertheless, the damp returning out of the hol-
' lows, and drawing towards the eye of the pit, it
' came up with incredible force; the wind and fire
' tore most of their clothes off their backs, and
' singed what was left, burning their hair, faces,
' and hands; the blasts falling so sharp on their
' skin, as if they had been whipt with cords. Some
' that had least shelter, were carried fifteen or six-
' teen yards from their first station, and beaten
' against the roof of the coal, and sides of the post,
' and lay afterwards a good while senseless; so that
' it was long before they could hear or find one
' another. As it drew up to the day-pit, it caught
' one of the men along with it, that was next to

' the eye; and up it comes, with such a terrible
' crack, not unlike, but more shrill, than a cannon,
' that was heard fifteen miles off, with the wind;
' and such a pillar of smoak, as darkened all the
' sky over-head for a good while. The brow of the
' hill above the pit was eighteen yards high, and
' on it grew trees of fourteen or fifteen yards long;
' yet the man's body, and other things from the
' pit, were seen above the tops of the highest trees,
' at least 100 yards. On this pit stood a horse-
' engine of substantial timber, and strong iron
' work; on which lay a trunk, or barrel, for wind-
' ing the rope up and down, of above 1000 pounds
' weight; it was then in motion, one bucket going
' down, and the other coming up full of water.
' This trunk was fastened to that frame with locks
' and bolts of iron; yet it was thrown up, and carried a good way from the pit; and pieces of it,
' though bound with iron hoops and strong nails,
' blown into the woods about: so likewise were the
' two buckets; and the ends of the rope, after the
' buckets were blown from them, stood a while up-
' right in the air like pikes, and then came leisurely
' drilling down. The whole frame of the engine
' was stirred, and moved out of its place; and those
' men's clothes, caps, and hats, that escaped, were
' afterwards found shattered to pieces, and thrown
' amongst the woods a great way from the pit[r].'

[r] On the 6th of *April*, 1807, there was a dreadful recurrence of

FROM *Nannerch*, I continued my journey along the narrow vale, picturesquely ornamented with hanging woods. Leave the church of *Skeifiog* on the right. In this parish was shot, a few years ago, that singular bird, the *Hoopoe*, vol. i. N° 90. of the *British Zoology*. This species is of the size of a *stare;* easily distinguishable by its large crest; long, slender, incurvated bill; and by having only ten feathers in the tail. I can add to my former account, that the *Arabs* call it the *messenger bird;* not only from the resemblance which the crest bears to the plumes that decorate the caps of *Chaous* or *Turkish* messengers; but also because the *Mahometans* believe it to have been the bird

the same calamity in *Mostyn* colliery, by which *twenty-eight* persons were either instantaneously destroyed, or died in consequence of the effects of the inflamed gas. A warning, it might have been thought, sufficient to rouse the attention of the over-lookers, and render the workmen more cautious! but, alas! on the 10th of *March*, 1809, notwithstanding the accumulation of the fatal damp had been evident for several days, an explosion again took place, and occasioned the death of *twenty-two* others. Thus, in the short period of two years, by the culpable negligence of some, the rashness and blind belief in predestination of others, *fifty* industrious colliers have been deprived of their existence, *twenty-six* women rendered widows, and *sixty-six* young children fatherless.

The effects of the fiery vapor on the human body were precisely similar to those described by Mr. *Mostyn;* but it did not appear in other respects to have acted with equal violence, nor was the report of the explosion, though considerable, heard at any distance. It may be remarked, that the pits in which the *hydrogen* gas accumulates so frequently, are in the immediate vicinity of the sea, and not remote from the "Burnt Rock," described in the preceding volume of this work, p. 26. Some of the adjacent strata contain *pyrites*. ED.

which (when birds could speak) held a conversation with *Solomon,* and to have been the courier which carried on the epistolary correspondence between that wise monarch and the *Sabœan* queen[s].

CAERWYS.

AT the junction of the vales of *Nannerch* and *Bodfari,* I ascended to *Caerwys;* a town mouldering away with age. It consists of four streets, crossing each other at right angles, answering to the four points of the compass. The name, as *Camden* has long since observed, savors of great antiquity. *Caer,* the fortress, and *Gwŷs,*([1]) a summons, which shews it had been, in early times, the place of judicature. I will not assert that it had been a *Roman* station, notwithstanding I am credibly informed, that in the present century[t], a number of copper coins were found in a bottom below the town; and there still remains in the parish, a Latin inscription, cut in rude letters, on an unhewn upright stone[u] to this effect: *Hic jacit mulier bo . . . . obiit.* The stone is four feet six inches high, and three in breadth. Multitudes of

[s] *Bochart Hieroz.* pars ii. p. 347. Also, *Universal 'Antient Hist.* iv. 107. notes.

([1]) The *gwŷs* was not issued from a *caer,* but from a *llŷs* or court. It is not improbable that the Welsh word *caer* is the Latin castra planed down: in that case Caerwys would be *castrensis,* or] *castrense* with *oppidum* or some such a word understood. J.R.

[t] The eighteenth. ED.

[u] This curious relic of antiquity, which was applied to the purpose of a gate post, has been removed to the garden at *Downing.* ED.

tumuli are scattered over the neighborhood, and one very near to it. This plain, probably, had been a field of battle. Whether this inscription referred to any heroine that fell on this place, I will not dare to affirm.

CAERWYS[x], with a neighboring town now lost, called *Tref Edwyn*, and *Rhuddlan*, had been, from very early time, the seats of the judicature for these parts of *Wales*. In 1281, the noblemen of *Tegengl* layed before the archbishop of *Canterbury* (who came down on the Christian design of reconciling the differences between *Edward* I. and *Llewelyn*) the infringement of their liberties in this particular; asserting, that it was the tenor of their privilege to be judged according to the laws of *Wales*, at those three places; and that the best men of the country were taken because they desired to be judged at *Tref Edwyn*, by the laws of *Wales*[y]. How far their complaints were remedied does not appear: but when justiciary courts were in after-times appointed, *Caerwys* recovered its antient honors. In this town were held the great sessions. It had its town-hall, and its jail; and was the place of execution. It remained the place of judicature till sometime past the middle of the seventeenth century, when the courts were removed to *Flint*.

[x] *Powel*, 360.   [y] Ibid.

IN the year 1241, or the 26th of *Henry* III.
that prince granted to the inhabitants of *Tegengl*,
a charter[z], exempting them from the *amobr;* but
at the same time imposing on them an obligation
to find twenty-four people, who were to keep the
peace of the country: and obliging this town,
Picton, Axton and other hamlets, to find three
men each, to work three days in the harvest, as
they were wont in the days of the two preceding
Welsh princes. This seems to have been issued
during some temporary advantage which *Henry*
had over the *Welsh.*

CAERWYS has the most considerable fairs for
cattle, sheep, and horses, in all the county. They
are of great antiquity. The first *John Trevor,*
bishop of St. *Asaph,* appears among the subscrib-
ers to a charter for a market in 1356; but the
markets have now failed entirely, since the increase
of *Holywell.*

THE earl of *Plymouth* is lord of this manor;
and possesses, by purchase of an ancestor, the
estate of the *Griffiths* of *Caerwys-hall,* descended
from *Ednowen-Bendew,* one of the fifteen tribes.
Over the door of *Caerwys-hall* is "*Piers,* and
M. Griffith, 1589." It had been a tolerable good
house, with a gate-way.

[z] *Mostyn MSS.*

THE other manors([1]) in *Flintshire* are[a]

Mostyn,	Sir *Roger Mostyn*[1].
Picton and *Axton,*	Sir *Pyers Mostyn.*
Hawarden,	Sir *Stephen Glynne.*
Mold,	Lady *Vincent*[2].
Maylor,	Sir *Thos. Hanmer* and *Philip Lloyd Fletcher* esq.
Ewloe,	John *Davies*[3] esq.
Holywell,	Sir *Tho. Egerton*[4].
Prestatyn,	Rev. *Richard Williams*[5]
Coleshill,	*Paul Panton* esq.
Hope,	Earl of *Derby.*

But what gave a particular glory to the town of *Caerwys*, was the honor it had of being the place of the *Eisteddfod,* or the sessions of the bards and minstrels for many centuries. It was the resort of those of a certain district; as *Aberffraw* in *Anglesey* was of those of that island, and the neighboring county; and *Mathrafal* of those of the land of *Powys.* The reason that these places were thus distinguished, was, because the two last were the residence of princes; and *Caerwys,* on account of the royal palace that stood below the town, the residence of *Llewelyn ap Gryffydd.*

([1]) The two united townships of *Merford* and *Hoseley* are another manor in *Flintshire.* T.P.

[a] In 1809.

[1] Sir *Thomas Mostyn.*
[2] Sir *Thomas Mostyn.*
[3] *Bryan Cooke* esq.
[4] Created Earl *Grey de Wilton.*
[5] *Richard Wilding* esq.

THESE *Eisteddfods* were the *British Olympics.*
Fired at first with generous emulation, our poets
crowded into the list, and carried off the prize,
contented with the mere honor of victory.   At
length, when the competitors became numerous,
and the country oppressed with the multitude,
new regulations of course took place.   The disappointed candidates were no longer suffered to
torture the ears of the principality with their
wretched compositions.   None but bards of merit
were suffered to rehearse their pieces; and minstrels of skill, to perform.   These went through a
long probation: judges were appointed to decide
on their respective abilities; and degrees suitable
were conferred, and permissions granted for exercising their talents, in the manner that will be related in the following pages.   The judges were
appointed by commission from our princes; and
after the conquest of *Wales,* by the kings of *England,* notwithstanding *Edward* I. exercised a
political cruelty over the bards of his time, yet
future princes thought fit to revive an institution
so likely to soften the manners of a fierce people.
The crown had the power of nominating the
judges, who decided not only on the merit, but the
subject of the poems; and, like our modern lord
chamberlains, were sure to licence those only which
were agreeable to the *English* court.

BEFORE I enter on the account of the succession

of *British Eisteddfods,* I shall just mention the
high antiquity of the character that made, in after- ANTIENT
BARDS.
times, the principal figure in these meetings. The
Bardi (the *Beirdds* of the *Britons*) were of great
authority among the *Celtic* nations: the *Germans*
were animated in battle by verses delivered in a
deep and solemn tone[b]; among the *Gauls*[c], they
sung the actions of great men; and particularly
celebrated in their hymns, the heroes who fell in
fight:

> Vos quoque qui fortes animas belloque peremtas
> Laudibus in longum vates dimittitis ævum
> Plurima securi fudistis carmina BARDI.
> LUCAN 1.

> You too, ye bards, whom sacred raptures fire
> To chaunt your heroes to your country's lyre,
> Who consecrate in your immortal strain,
> Brave patriot souls in righteous battle slain;
> Securely now the tuneful task renew,
> And noblest themes in deathless songs pursue.
> ROWE.

IT is highly probable, that the bards and minstrels were under certain regulations during the
time of *Druidism;* but we find no proofs of them
till long after; till the days of *Cadwaladr,* last IN TIME OF
CADWALADR.
king of *Britain,* who died at *Rome* about the year
688. *Of* him, it is said, that being at an assembly
of this nature, with his nobles, there came a minstrel, and played in a key so displeasing, that he

---

[b] *Tacitus de mor. German.*
[c] *Strabo,* lib. iv. 302. *Athenæus,* lib. vi. 246.

and all his brethren were prohibited, under a severe
penalty, from ever playing in it any more; but
were ordered to adopt that of *Mwynen Gwynedd,*
or the sweet key of *Gwynedd*[d].

OF ARTHUR.   I imagine, that previous to this, there had been
musical regulations in *Britain;* for I find that a
tune, called *Gosteg yr Halen,* or the *Prelude of
the Salt,* was always played whenever the salt-seller
was placed before king *Arthur's* knights, at his
round table[e].

AFTER *Cadwaladr,* the next princes who undertook the reform of our minstrelsie, were *Bleyddyn*
OF GRYFFYDD *ap Cynfyn* and *Gryffydd ap Cynan.*   The first
AP CYNAN.
was cotemporary with the Conqueror; the last
with king *Stephen.*   These enacted, that no person
should follow the *profession* of bard or minstrel,
but such only who were admitted by the *Eisteddfod,* which was held once in three years.   They
were prohibited from invading one another's province: nor were they permitted to degrade themselves by following any other occupation.   Neither
of these were to demand above ten shillings in any
article, under pain of losing the whole, besides
being suspended from their profession for three
years[f].

AFTER the times of the princes, the great men,

---

[d] *North Wales.*   [e] Mr. *Morris's MSS.* of *British* music.
[f] *Leges Wallicæ,* 35.

their descendants, took these people under their care and protection, allowing them the liberty of circuiting their respective territories thrice a year, viz. at *Christmas*, *Easter* and *Whitsuntide;* and the whole principality once in three years.

THE bards were in the highest repute. I cannot give a stronger idea of the esteem they were in, than by citing from the *Welsh* laws, the account of their rank in the prince's court, and the various rewards and fees they were entitled to, and the severe penalties that were enacted to preserve their persons from insult. They were supposed to be endowed with powers equal to inspiration. They were the oral historians of all past transactions, public and private. They related the great events of the state; and like the *Scalds* of the northern nations, retained the memory of numberless transactions, which otherwise would have perished in oblivion. They were likewise thoroughly acquainted with the works of the three primary bards, *viz.*, MYRDDYN AP MORFRYN, MYRDDYN EMRYS, and TALIESIN BEN BEIRDD. But they had another talent, which probably endeared them more than all the rest to the *Welsh* nobility; that of being most accomplished genealogists, and flattering their vanity, in singing the deeds of an ancestry derived from the most distant period.

THE BARDD TEULU, or COURT BARD, held the eighth place in the prince's court. He possessed

his land free. The prince supplied him with a
horse and woollen robe, and the princess with
linen[g]. He sat next to the governor of the palace at the three great festivals; for, at those seasons, the governor was to deliver him his harp.[h]
On the same festivals, he was also to have the
Disdain's, or steward of the houshold's garment
for his fee.

WHEN a song is called for, the *Cadeir-fardd*, or
the bard who has got the *badge of the chair*, is first
to sing a hymn in glory of GOD; after that, another
in honor of the prince. When those are over, the
Teuluwr, or bard of the hall, is to sing some other
subject.

IF the princess calls for a song after she has
retired from table to her apartment, the *Teuluwr*
must sing to her highness in a low voice, lest he
should disturb the performers in the hall. *John
Dafydd Rhys* says, that the subject was to be on
death; but I rather follow *Wotton*, who, instead of
angau, which signifies *death*, prefers the word
amgen, or a *separate subject* from what was sung
in the hall.

WHEN the bard goes with the prince's servants
on a plundering expedition, and performs before
them his animating compositions, he is to have the
finest heifer of the booty; and in case the detach

---

[g] *Leges Wallicæ*, 35.   [h] The same, 35, and 16.

ment was drawn up in order of battle, he was to sing at their head, the *praises of the* British *monarchy*. This was to remind them of their antient right to the whole kingdom; for their inroads being almost always on the *English* territories, they thought they did no more than seize on their own.

THE prince bestowed on him an ivory chess-board; others say a harp; and the princess a golden ring. His lodging was to be with the governor of the palace.

WHEN he is required to sing with other bards, by way of distinction, he is to have a double portion.

IF the bard asks any favor of the prince, he must sing one of his compositions: if of a nobleman, three: if of a common person, he must sing till he is so weary as to rest on his elbow, or to fall asleep. This, I fear, shews our bards were a very importuning race, and required a check; yet still they were in high estimation. Their *Gwerth*, or compensation for their life, was rated at cxxvi cows[i], and any injury done them, at vi cows and cxx pence.

THE *Merch-Gobr* of his daughter, or marriage fine of his daughter, was cxx pence. Her *cowyll*, *argyffreu*, or nuptial presents, was thirty shillings; and her portion three pounds[k]. It is remarkable,

MERCH-GOBR.

---

[i] *Leges Wallicæ*, 37. [k] Ibid. 37.

that the PENCERDD GWLAD, or chief of the
faculty, was entitled to the *merch-gobr*, or *amobr*
for the daughters of all the inferiors of the faculty
within the district, who payed xxiv pence on their
marriage; which not only shews the antiquity, but
the great authority of these people.

THE PENCERDD was not among the officers[1] of
the court: but occasionally sat in the tenth place.
He also had his land free; was to perform much in
the same manner as the court bard, whom he seems
to have taken place of, whenever he attended; for,
when the *Pencerdd* was present, the former sat
only in the twelfth seat.   No other was to play
without license from him.   His death was valued
at cxxvi cows; and any injury done him at vi cows,
and cxx pence.   Each of the chief musicians was
to receive from their lord, the first, a harp; the
second, a *crwth;* the third, a pipe; which, on their
deaths, were to revert to the lord[m].

THE prince's harp was valued at cxx pence, and
that of *Pencerdd* at the same; the key at xxiv
pence: a gentleman's harp was estimated at lx
pence.

POWELL[n] says, that *Gryffydd ap Cynan* brought
over with him out of *Ireland*, divers cunning mu
sicians, who devised in a manner, all the instrumental music now used.   With all respect to our

---

[1] *Leges Wallicæ*, 68.   [m] Ibid. 68.   [n] 191.

sister kingdom, I must imagine, that if our instruments were not originally *British*, we were copyists from the *Romans*, who, again, took their instruments from the *Greeks*. Methinks I see the model of a harp in fig. 7. tab. lxxvi. of the supplement of *Montfaucon*, volume iii.; of the *crwth* in Doctor Burney's Psalter, tab. v. fig. 4. or his *Etruscan* lyre, fig 10.; and of the pipe, in several simple pipes, before it received from us the addition of the horns, from whence it got the title of *pib-gorn*, and the *English* name of *cornet*[o].

A commission for holding an *Eisteddfod* at *Caerwys*, in 1568, is still in possession of Sir *Roger Mostyn*, together with the Silver harp; which had from time immemorial been in the gift of his ancestors, to bestow on the *chief of the faculty*. This badge of honor is about five or six inches long, and furnished with strings equal to the number of the muses. The commission is the last of the kind which was granted; and is in form following:

By the Quene.

ELIZABETH, by the grace of God, of *England*, *Fraunce*, and *Ireland* Quene, defendor of the fayth, &c. to our trustie and ryght wel beloved Sr *Richard Bulkley* knight, Sir *Rees Gruffith*

---

[o] See figures of the *crwth* and *pib-gorn* in *Archæologia*, iii. tab. vii.

knight, *Ellice Price* esquio^r, Doctor in cyvill lawe, and one of our counsail in our marches of *Wales,* *William Mostyn, Jevan Lloyd* of *Yale, Jhn Salusbury* of *Ruge, Rees Thomos, Maurice Wynne, Will*^{m} *Lewis, Peres Mostyn, Owen Jhn ap Ho*^{ll} *Vaughan, John Will*^{m} *ap John, John Lewis Owen, Moris Gruffydd, Symound Thelvall, Ellice ap W*^{m} *Lloyd, Rob*^{t} *Puleston, Harry Aparry, William Glynne,* and *Rees Hughes,* esquio^{rs}, and to every of them, greating. Wheras it is come to the knowledge of the lorde president and other o^r said counsail in o^r marches of *Wales,* that vagraunt and idle psons, naming themselfs mynstrells, rithmors, and barthes, are lately growen into such an intollerable multitude wthin the principalitee of *Northwales,* that not only gentlemen and others, by theire shameles disorders, are oftentimes disquieted in theire habitacons; but also thexpert mynstrells and mucisions in toune and contry therby much discouraged to travail in thexercise and practize of theire knowledge; and also not a litle hyndred in theire lyvings and pferm^{ts}. The reformacon wherof, and the putting of these people in ord^r, the said lorde president and counsail have thought verey necessarye, and knowing you to be men both of wysdome and upright dealing, and also of experience and good knowledge in the scyence, have apointed and authorized you to be commissioners for that purpose. And forasmuch as o^r said coun-

sail of late, travayling in some pte of the said principalitee, had pfect understanding or credible report, that thaccustomed place for thexecucon of
the like comssyon, hath bene heretofore at *Caroyes*
in our countie of *Fflynt;* and that *William Mostyn*
esquio[r], and his ancest[rs] have had the gyfte and
bestowing of the sylver harpe apptayning to the
cheff of that facultie, and that a yeares warning at
the least hath bene accustomed to be geaven of
thassembly and execucon of the like comissyon.
Our said counsail have, therfore, apoynted thexecucon of this commissyon to be at the said towne
of *Caroyes,* the *Monday* next aft[r] the feast of the
blessed Trynitee, w[ch] shall be in the yeare of o[r]
Lorde God 1568[p].

AND therfore we require and comand you, by
the aucthoritee of these psents, not only to cause
open pclamacons to be made in all ffayo[rs], m[r]ketts,
townes, and other places of assembly w[th]in our
counties of *Anglize, Carn[r]von, Meyryonneth, Denbigh,* and *Fflynt,* that all and ev[ry] pson and psons
that entend to maynteigne theire lyvings by name
or color of mynstrells, rithmrs, or barthes, wthin
the *Talaith* of *Aberfiowe,* comphending the said
fyve shires, shal be and appeare before you the
said daye and place, to shewe their learnings ac-

---

[p] This was the last *Eisteddfod* held at *Caerwis.* The prize was
adjudged by *Sion ap William ap Sion. Sebright MSS.*

cordingly: but also that you, xx^{tie}, xix^{en}, xviii^{en}, xvii^{en}, xvi^{en}, xv^{en}, xiiii^{en}, xiii^{en}, xii^e, xi^n, x^{en}, ix, viii, vii, or vi of you whereof youe, Sr *Richard Bulkley,* Sr *Rees Gruffith, Ellice Price,* and Wm *Mostyn,* Esquio^{rs} or iii^{ee}, or ii of you, to be of the nomb^r to repayre to the said place the daye aforesaid, and calling to you such expert men in the said facultie of the *Welshe* musick, as to you shall be thought convenient to pceade to thexecucon of the pmiss^s, and to admytt such and so many as by your wis-domes and knowledges you shall fynde worthy into and und^r the degrees heretofore in semblable sort, to use exercise and folowe the scyences and facultes of theire pfessyons in such decent ord^r as shall apptaigne to eche of theire degrees, and as yor discrecons and wisdomes shall pscribe unto them, geaving straight monycons and comaundm^t in o^r name and on o^r behalf to the rest not worthy that they returne to some honest labo^r and due exercise, such as they be most apte unto for mayn-tenaunce of their lyvings, upon paine to be taken as sturdy and idle vacaboundes, and to be used according to the lawes aud statutes pvided in that behalf, letting you wyth o^r said counsaill look for advertisem^t by due certificatt at your handes of yor doings in thexecucon of the said pmis^s. For seeing in any wise that upon the said assembly the peas and good order be observed and kept accord-ingly, assertayning you that the said *Willm Mostyn* hath pmised to see furnyture and things necessary pvided for that assembly at the place aforsaid. Geven under o^{r} signet at o^{r} citie of *Chester* the xxiiith of *October*, the nynth yeare of o^{r} raigne.

Signed her Hignes counsaill, in the m^{r}ches of WALES[q].

IN consequence, an *Eisteddfod* was held on the 26th of *May* following: and on this occasion the following persons received their degrees:

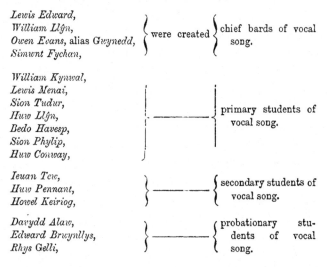

Lewis Edward, *William Llŷn*, *Owen Evans*, alias *Gwynedd*, *Simwnt Fychan*,	were created	chief bards of vocal song.
William Kynwal, *Lewis Menai*, *Sion Tudur*, *Huw Llŷn*, *Bedo Havesp*, *Sion Phylip*, *Huw Conway*,	———	primary students of vocal song.
Ieuan Tew, *Huw Pennant*, *Howel Keiriog*,	———	secondary students of vocal song.
Davydd Alaw, *Edward Brwynllys*, *Rhys Gelli*,	———	probationary students of vocal song.

[q] Another *Eisteddfod* was held here in the fifteenth of *Henry* VIII. *July* the 2d, in which the old laws are confirmed respecting bards, in the manner I recite. *Richard ap Howel ap Jevan Vychan*, of *Mostyn*, and Sir *William Gryffydd*, and Sir *Roger Salusbury*, presided, assisted by *Gryffydd ap Evan ap Llewelyn Vychan*, and *Tyder Aled*, a famous bard.

INSTRUMENTAL MUSIC.

HARP.   *Sion ap Rhys Bencerdd,* *William Penllyn,* *Hwlkin Llwyd,* } were created { chief bards and teachers of instrumental song.

HARP.   *Thomas Anwyl,* *Dᵈ Llwyd ap Sion ap Rhys,* *Edward ap Evan,* *Robt. ap Howel Llanvor,* *Humphrey Gôch,* — chief bards (but not teachers) of instrumental song.

HARP.   *Richard Glyn,* *Robert Llwyd,* *Evan Penllyn,* *Lewis Llanvor,* — primary students of instrumental song.

HARP.   *Huw Dai,* *Huw ap Morus.* *Siamas Morlas,* *Sion Niwbwrch,* *Ellis Gruffydd,* — secondary ditto.

HARP.   *Lewis Berain,* *Ieuan ap Meredydd,* *Gwalchmai ap Davydd,* — probationary students of instrumental song.

CRWTH.   *Siamas Eutyn,* *Evan Penmon,* — chief bards and teachers of instrumental song.

CRWTH.   *Robert ap Rhys Gyttyn,* *Thomas Môn,* *Sion Ednyved,* *Thomas Grythor,* — chief bards (but not teachers) of instrumental song.

CRWTH.   *Sion Ddu Grythor,* — primary student of instrumental song.

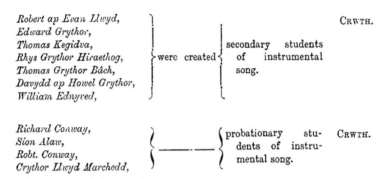

It must be observed, that players on crwths with three strings, taborers, and pipers, were reckoned among the ignoble performers: they were not allowed to sit down, and had only a penny for their pains.

The different degrees were comprehended in this list. There were four in the poetical, and five in the musical faculty. The lowest, or more properly what should be called a candidate or probationer, was *Y. Dyscybl Yspâs*, or the *lowest disciple*, who was obliged (if a candidate for poetry) to understand the construction of five species of *Englyns*, and to compose them before a *Pencerdd*, who was to declare upon his conscience, that he was endowed with a true poetical genius. After this he commenced

Dyscybl Dyscyblaidd, *Discipulus disciplinabilis:* here he becomes a graduate; but must understand twelve of our different metres, and produce specimens of each of his own composition; and if in three years time he does not, by his merit, acquire the next degree, he is degraded from this. If he succeeds, he then proceeds to the degree of

DYSCYBL PENCEIRDDIAIDD, or candidate for the degree of *Pencerdd*, when he must understand the propriety of expressions, and the different metres, and compose in twenty-one species; and if in three years he does not attain by his own merit to the next degree, he falls back into that of *Dyscybl dyscyblaidd*; otherwise he becomes a

PENBARDD or PENCERDD, chief of the faculty he was candidate in; when it was necessary he should be accomplished in every branch of his art. He then received the badge of the silver-harp; or that of a golden or silver chair, which he wore upon his shoulder. He also was placed with much ceremony on a magnificent chair, part of the *furnyture* mentioned in the patent; was there invested with his degree; and then acquired the honorable name of *Cadeirfardd* or *Bardd cadeiriawg*. A *Pencerdd* might challenge any other to rehearse or sing for the prize, after giving a year and a day's notice. If he succeeded, he carried it off; if not, he lost his degree; and the victor kept the prize for life, but was obliged to produce it annually on the *Eisteddfod*.

In instrumental music there were five degrees; which differ nothing from those in the other faculty, except in the two lowest: 1. The *Dyscybl yspas heb râdd*, or without a degree; 2. *Dyscybl yspas graddawl*, or graduated; 3. *Dyscybl dyscyblaidd*; 4. *Dyscybl penceirddiaidd*; 5. *Pencerdd.* These, like the others, were to be attained by their respective merits in the science; but as their qualifications are expressed in technical terms of *British* music, it is past my skill to give an explanation. None but a *Pencerdd* should presume to become an instructor. The chief of our days, was that uncommon genius, the blind Mr. John Parry, late of Rhiwabon, who had the kingdom for his *Cylch clera*, or musical circuit, and remained unrivalled.

Our Pencerdds thus qualified, were licensed to sing, or to perform under certain restrictions. By the law of our princes, particular regard was paid to their morals: ' They were to be no make- ' bates, no vagabonds, no ale-house haunters, no ' drunkards, no brawllers, no whore-hunters, no theeves, nor companions of such; in which things, ' if they offend, everie man, by the statute, is made ' an officer, and authorized to arrest and punish ' them; yea, and to take from them all that they ' have about them[r].'

They were prohibited from uttering any scan-

[r] *Powel*, 192

dalous words in speech or whispers; detraction,
mocking, scoffing, inventing lies, or repeating them
after others, under pain of fine and imprisonment:
nor were they to make a song of any person
without his consent; nor to enter any man's house
without formal leave first obtained.

EVERY *Penbardd* and *Pencerdd* was allowed to
take in disciples for a certain space of time, but
not above one at a time. A disciple was not qualified to make another. Each was to be with his
teacher during *Lent*, unless prevented by sickness
or imprisonment, under pain of losing his degree.
He was obliged to shew every composition to his
teacher before it was publicly sung. They were
not to follow the practice of *cler y dom*, i.e. dung-
hill bards and musicians, or any other species of
vagabond minstrels. They were enjoined a month
before each festival, to settle their routes with
their respective teachers, lest too many of them
should crowd to the same places; only one being
allowed to go to a person who paid ten pounds a
year rent; and two to such who payed twenty
pounds, and so on in proportion to those of higher
rank: and every teacher was obliged to keep a
copy of these rules, to shew and inculcate to his
pupils in time of *Lent*, when they came for their
instructions.

No person was to mimic, mock, or scoff at the
awenyddion on account of their mental absence,

or when they had on them the AWEN or *poeticus furor;* from an opinion that no bard, duly authorized, could ever meditate on improper subjects.

To whatsoever house they came in the time of wakes, they must remain there while the feasting lasted; unless they had leave from the master of the house, or were invited by another. If they wandered from house to house, they were to be apprehended as strollers and vagabonds, and to be deprived of their *clera*[s], which was forfeited to the use of the church. If they got intoxicated, they forfeited their reward; but if they violated the chastity of wife or maid, they were fined and imprisoned, and lost their *clera* for seven years.

THEIR fees or rewards were regulated. *A dyscybl dyscyblaidd* was entitled to 3s. 4d. for his *cowydd.*

A DYSCYBL PENCEIRDDIAIDD received for the same species of composition 6s. 9d.

HIS teacher, or the *Pencerdd*, had no more; only the master of the house usually presented him with a garment, or some other mark of favor.

The minstrels received these rewards; a *dyscybl yspas graddawl* had only 1s. upon each of the great festivals.

---

[s] Or their pay. Sometimes it signifies the act of their perambulation.

A DYSCYBL DYSCYBLAIDD, at the same seasons
2s· and a *dyscybl penceirddiaidd* 3s. 4d.

A PENCERDD the same, besides a voluntary
gratuity. He was also entitled to fees at royal
and other weddings; and upon their *cylch clera*,
which was permitted only once in three years.
But besides these fees, in order to encourage the
clerwyr to keep up the language and the memory
of the exploits and pedigrees of the *Britons*, they
were allowed a penny out of every ploughland,
and a halfpenny out of every half ploughland of
their district.

THE *Penbardd* and *Pencerdd*, in his circuits,
frequented only the houses of the gentry; but if
he degraded himself by visiting the commonalty,
he was only to expect the fee of a common *clerwr*,
whose province it was to visit the *plebeian* houses.

THE following were the persons who were allotted to entertain the vulgar ears. A person la-
boring under any infirmity; such as blindness,
lameness, &c. a *dyscybl yspas*, a *dyscybl dyscyblaidd*, and *dyscybl penceirddiaidd*. The first regulation was founded on humanity.

No public festivity, great feast, or wedding
could be duly solemnized without the presence of
the bards and minstrels. A glorious emulation
arose among them; and prizes were bestowed on
the most worthy. In 1176, the lord *Rhys* prince

of *South Wales*, made a great feast[t] at *Christmas*,
on account of the finishing his new castle at
Aberteifi; of which he proclaimed notice through
all *Britain* a year and a day before; great was
the resort of strangers, who were nobly entertained; so that none departed unsatisfied. Among
deeds of arms, and variety of *spectacles*, RHYS
invited all the bards of *Wales*, and provided *chairs*
for them, which were placed in his hall, where
they sat and disputed, and sang, to shew their
skill in their respective faculties: after which, he
bestowed great rewards, and rich gifts on the
victors. The bards of *North Wales* won the
prizes; but the minstrels of *Rhys's* houshold ex-
celled m their faculty. On this occasion the
Brawdwr Llys, or *judge of the court*, an officer
fifth in rank, declared aloud the victor, and received from the bard, for his fee, a mighty drink-
ing-horn, made of the horn of an ox; a golden
ring, and the cushion on which he sat in his chair
of dignity[u]

THE bards of those times often accompanied
their voices with the harp, as they were wont of
old, in the manner described by *Ammianus Marcellinus*[x]. There was also another species of musician, of an inferior kind, called *Datceiniad*, who

[t] *Powel*, 237.

[u] *Leges Wallicæ*, 28.   [x] Lib. xv. 9.

accompanied the musical instruments of others
with his song. He was inferior to both bard and
minstrel; yet it was requisite he should be possessed of a considerable degree of knowledge in
both sciences; he ought to be able to tune the harp
and *crwth:* to shew his skill in playing several
notes and keys, and to be perfectly conversant in
what are called the twenty-four measures of instrumental song; and to be able to sing with judgment and melody. He was likewise to be master
of reading justly, and writing correctly. He was
not only to understand the twenty-four modes of
metrical compositions; but to exhibit specimens
of his own, at lest in three of them; and if he met
with any old song faultily transcribed, he was to
rectify it. He was also to carry with him a harp
or a *crwth* in a white case. He was further required, not only to be a ready waiter at table,
but to be an expert carver of every species of fowl.
At the weddings of any of the royal family, his
office was to wait on the bride.

On those occasions, I am reminded of another
custom in which the bards were concerned. After
their nuptial feast, a *Pencerdd* was constituted
CYFF CLER, or *pillar of the clêr*, and seated in a
chair surrounded by the other bards standing, who
made him the subject of their merry and ludicrous
compositions, to raise mirth in the company. He
was that day to make no reply; but on the next,

he was to divert the hall at the expence of the inferior bards; and was also to compose a poem upon a subject given him suitable to his dignity.

THE lowest of the musical tribe was sometimes DATCEINIAD. admitted. This was the *Datceiniad pen pastwn*, or he that sung to the sound of his club; being ignorant of every other kind of instrument. When he was permitted to be introduced, he was obliged to stand in the middle of the hall, and sing his *cowydd* or *awdl*, beating time, and playing the symphony with his *pastwn* or club; but if there was a professor of music present, his leave must be first obtained before he presumed to entertain the company with this species of melody. Where-ever he came he must act as a menial servant to the bard or musician[y].

I SHALL conclude this account of the *Eisteddfods* and my Tour, with the description of the poetical genius of the *Welsh* by *Michael Drayton*[z],

[y] Several parts of this account are translated from *Cambrobrytannicæ Cymraecæce Linguæ Institutiones;* a very rare book, written by Doctor *John Davydd Rhys*, of *Llanfaethlu* in *Anglesey*, printed in 1592. He took his doctor's degree at *Sienna;* but was educated at *Oxford.* He returned to his own country, where he practised with great success. At the request of Sir *Edward Stradling*, of St. *Donats,* he composed this book. He tells us, he wrote the first part at Mr. *Morgan Meredydd*'s in *Radnorshire;* the rest at a place of his own in *Brecknockshire,* as he says, at the age of seventy, and under the shade of a hawthorn grove. *Vide* his preface.

[z] POLY OLBION, song iv.

who elegantly and faithfully records the various
personages concerned in the entertainments.

   '————— some there were bards, that in their sacred rage
   ' Recorded the descents and acts of every age:
   ' Some with their nimble joints that struck the warbling string,
   ' In fingering some unskill'd, but us'd to sing
   ' To others harp; of which you both might find
   ' Great plenty, and of both excelling in their kind,
   ' That at the *Stethva* oft obtain'd a victor's praise:
   ' Had won the silver harp, and worn *Apollo*'s bays:
   ' Whose verses they deduc'd from those first golden times
   ' Of sundry sorts of feet, and sundry suits of rhimes.
   ' In *Englins* some there were, that in their subject strain;
   ' Some makers that again affect a loftier vein,
   ' Rehearse their high conceits in *cowyths;* other some
   ' In *owdells* theirs express, as matter haps to come.
   ' So varying still their moods, observing yet in all
   ' Their quantities, their rests, their ceasures metrical;
   ' For, to that sacred art they most themselves apply;
   ' Addicted from their birth to so much poesy,
   ' That in the mountains, those who scarce have seen a book
   ' Most skilfully will make, as though from art they took.'

END OF THE FIRST PART.

PART II.

DOWNING

ST. ASAPH, DENBIGH, RUTHIN, CORWEN, BALA,

DINAS-MOWDDWY, DOLGELLEU,

BARMOUTH, HARLECH, YS*PYTTY*, LLANRWST,

SNOWDONIA,

*P*ENMORFA, LLYN, CAERNARVON, ANGLESEY,

BANGOR, CONWY.

TOUR IN NORTH WALES,

PART II.

———

IN this, the sequel of my former tour, I directed my course westward from *Downing*, passed by *Whiteford*, our parish-church, and ascended the hill of *Garreg*ᵃ, or the *Rock*, a high and most conspicuous part of the country. The *Romans* took advantage of it, and placed on its summit a *Pharos*, to conduct the navigators to and from *Deva*, along the difficult channel of the *Seteia*(1) *Portus*. The building still remains. I hope my friends will not deem me an antiquarian *Quixote*, and imagine that I mistake, in this my second sally, a building, hitherto supposed to have been a windmill, for a *Roman* light-house. It is tolerably entire ; its form is circular ; the height considerable ; the inner diameter twelve feet and a half ; the thickness of the walls four feet four inches. The doors, or entrances, are opposite to each other ; over each is a square funnel, like a

PHAROS.

Hist. of *Whiteford*, iii. ED.

(1) The *Seteia* is not now supposed to be the *Dee*, but some more northern river, probably the *Mersey*. J.R.

chimney, which opens on the outside, about half
way up the building. On each side is a window.
About four feet from the ground are three circular
holes, lined with mortar, as is frequent in *Roman*
buildings; and penetrate the whole wall, for purposes now unknown.

WITHINSIDE are the vestiges of a stair-case,
which led to the floors, of which there appear to
have been two. Along such part of the upper,
which was conspicuous from the channel, are eight
small square openings, cased with free stone (the
rest of the building being of rude lime-stone, bedded in hard mortar) and each of these were separated by wooden pannels, placed in deep grooves,
the last still in a perfect state. In each of these
partitions were placed the light, which the *Romans* thought necessary to keep distinct, or to prevent from running into one, lest they should be
mistaken by seamen for a star. *Periculum in cor-
rivatione ignium ne sidus existimetur*[b].

To the building is very evidently a broad and
raised road, pointing from the east; and near its
upper end are the marks of a trench, which surrounded and gave protection to this useful edifice.
Descend, and near the foot of the hill leave on the
left *Maen Achwynfan*, the cross described in my

[b] *Plinii Hist. Nat.* lib. xxxvi. c. 12.

former tour. *Glol,* an inclosed mountain a little farther on, has among the bushes various circular foundations of stone unmortared building. About a mile from hence, visit the small town of *New-* NEWMARKLT. *market,* almost the entire creation of its then owner, *John Wynne,* esq. of *Gop,* who died in the present century. The antient name of the parish is *Trelawnyd,* for which I can find no satisfactory reason. In the churchyard is a handsome old cross. Here is fixed one of the charity-schools, founded and opened in 1726, by doctor *Daniel Williams*(1), a dissenting minister, with an endowment of eight pounds a year; a charity which he extended to every county in *North Wales,* distinguishing that at *Wrexham,* the place of his birth, by an annual salary of fifteen pounds. He also established a fund, I believe, to each, from which the children are apprenticed, at five pounds apiece.

*F*ROM the town I ascended the hill, called *Cop-* Cop. *a'r'leni,* on whose summit is a most enormous carnedd, or tumulus, formed of lime-stones. It was probably the site of a *specula,* or exploratory tower, and memorial of some chieftain. If *Roman,* perhaps *Paulinus* gave name to it, *Cop-Paulini.* There is great uncertainty in these derivations: I may possibly as well abide by my former etymology of *Cop yr Goleuni*c, or the Mount

(1) *Dr. Daniel Williams* is best known as the founder of a public Library in *London.* T.P. c See p. 62 of this volume.

of Lights; for it might have been a place of signals by fire of the approach of an enemy by sea,
or a *station* of the *holy fires,* the *Coel Ceithie* of
the *Druids,* similar to the *Karn Gollewa,* the
carn of lights, and *Karn Leskyz,* or carn of burn-
ings, of the *Cornish,* supposed by the learned
BORLASE[d] to have been used for similar purposes.
The tract from hence to *Caerwys* was certainly a
field of battle: no place in *North Wales* exhibits
an equal quantity of *tumuli;* but all sepulchral,
as is proved by the urns discovered in them: they
are of a far inferior size to the first, and covered
with turf. It will not be too hazardous a conjecture to suppose, that in this place was the slaughter of the *Ordovices* by *Agricola,* when our gallant nation was nearly extirpated. Part of the
brow of the hill is called *Bryn y Saethau,* or *the
Hill of Arrows,* from being the station of the
archers in the engagement.

RETURN along the ridge of the hill, marked in
its whole length with verdant tumuli, the tombs
of antient heroes. See beneath me the little
church of *Gwaen-yskor,* remarkable for its antient
register.

GWAEN-
YSKOR.

LLANASAPH. DESCEND to the church and villages of *Llanasaph,* the former dedicated to *St. Asaph,* whose
festival is kept on the first of *May. Laurence*

[d] *Antiq. Cornwall,* 131.

Child, Bishop of *St. Asaph,* in 1385, procured
the impropriation of this church to supply his cathedral with lights[e], and repair the ruins occasioned by the wars. In my approach from these
high lands towards the shore, observe the ruins of
a small chapel at the little hamlet of *Gwespyr,*
near *Talacre,* one of the seats of Sir *Pyers Mostyn,*
Baronet, a branch of the house of *Mostyn.* His
adjacent quarry is noted for the excellence of the
free-stone; and his vast and profitable warren beneath, for the delicacy of the rabbets, by reason of
their feeding on the maritime plants.

Pass over *Gronant-Moor.* There is a tradi-   GRONANT.
tion, that its extent was so great, that the people
on this side could hold conversation over the channel with those of *Cheshire.* This may be exag-
gerated; but from authentic records, it appears,
that this flat was formerly very extensive, and that
it had been reduced to its present scanty limits by
the fury of the sea, which still possesses its antient
place. Previous to that catastrophe, it was possessed by the see of *St. Asaph,* by virtue of a
grant made by *Edward the Black Prince,* son of
Edward III. to *Llewelyn ap Madoc,* elected Bishop
of *St. Asaph* in 1357. The inundation happened
before the reign of *Henry* V. Previous to that
time, the Bishop paid annually into the exchequer

---

[e] *Willis's St. Asaph, App. No. xxi.*

at *Chester*, as an acknowledgement, the sum of
twenty marks: but *Henry* V. in 1414 and *Henry*
VI. in 1445 and 1451, in consideration of the
misfortune, released the see from that rent[t].   If
this record did not remain an incontestable proof
of the ravages of the ocean on this part of the
country, there exist other natural ones, that would
have given reasonable grounds for suspicion.   The
Hyle sands, which run for twelve or fourteen
miles parallel to the hundred of *Wiral*, in
Cheshire, and are divided from *Wales* by a narrow
channel, were once, in all probability, part of the
firm land of *England*.   A few miles to the west of
Gronant-Moor, under the parish of *Abergeleu*, in
Denbighshire, are to been seen at low water, very
remote from the shore, bedded in the sand, immense numbers of oak-trees, a forest before this
event.   Lastly, in the church-yard wall of *Abergeleu* is a dateless epitaph, in *Welsh*, signifying
that the person who was interred there lived three
miles to the north of that spot, a tract now entirely possessed by the sea.

A LITTLE beyond *Gronant* is the old seat of
Nant, formerly possessed by the *Conways*, a
branch of the *Conways* of *Bryn euryn*, near
Llandrillo Rhos, descended from *Gryffydd goch*
Lord of *Rhos*, and *Rhyfoniog*.

---

[t] *Will's St. Asaph*, 65. *App.* No. xxxi. xxxii.

ON approaching *Prestatyn*, about two miles from *Trelacre*, the flat becomes extremely fertile in corn, especially wheat, which is of distinguished excellence; and continues equally noted through all the flat tract, as far as *Rhuddlan*, where it is interrupted by the marsh, and is again continued along the coast far beyond *Abergeleu*. A little below *Prestatyn*-mill, in a meadow, is the site of its Castle: nothing more than an elevated space, with foundations consisting of stone and mortar and a foss at some distance from it, now remain. This little fortress was probably built by the *Welsh*, but wrested from them by the *English*, who were possessed of it in 1167, the only time I find any mention of it, when it was destroyed by *Owen Gwynedd*, *Cadwaladr* his brother, and *Rhŷs* Prince of *South Wales;* and all *Tegengle* reduced to the power of its lawful sovereign.

PRESTATYN-CASTLE.

THE lordship and village of *Prestatyn* lie in the parish of *Meliden*. This place was granted by *Richard* I. to *Robert Banaster*, who enjoyed it for three years and a half, and built the town, which was destroyed by *Owen Gwynedd*. *Robert de Crevecœur*, in the seventh year of *Edward* I. laid claim to it in right of his ancestor, *Banaster*. An inquisition was made, before a jury of twenty-four men[g]: their determination was in favour of *Robert;* since I find, by another record, that he

[g] *Sebright's MSS.*

died possessed of lands in *Maelor Saesneg*, and *Prestatyn*, which he held by the service of one knight's fee.

THE lordship of *Prestatyn* fell to the *Conways* of *Bod-rhyddan*, by the marriage of *Angharad*, daughter and heiress of Sir *Hugh de Crevecœur*. On the division of the estate, after the death of Sir *John Conway*, this lordship fell to the reverend *Richard Williams* of *Fron*, in right of his mother, youngest daughter of Sir *Thomas Longueville*, who possessed it in right of his first wife, one of the daughters of Sir *John Conway*.   Of late years Mr. *Williams* disposed of it to his brother-in-law *Richard Wilding* esq.

THE road from hence to *Diserth* is extremely pleasant, at the foot of high hills, rich in lead ore, with a fine and fertile flat to the right.   The white rock makes a conspicuous figure on the left, and its sides appeared deeply trenched by the miners in search of ore.   Near this place is the beginning of the vale of *Clwyd*, and the termination of the range of mountains, which bound it on the east. DISERTH CHURCH. At a small distance from hence lies the church of *Diserth*, in a picturesque and romantic bottom, beneath some rude rocks: the church overshaded with great yews, and the singular figure of some of the tombs form a most striking appearance. A water-fall in the deep and rounded hollow of a rock, finely darkened with ivy, once gave addi-

tional beauty to this spot; but of late the divert-
ing of the waters to a mill, has robbed the place
of this elegant variation. The stream, which is
little inferior to that of *Holywell*, flows principally
from a single well, called *Ffynnon Asaph*, or *St.
Asaph's Well*, in a dingle in the parish of *Cwm*,
about a mile distant. The fountain is inclosed
with stone, in a polygonal form, and had formerly its votaries, like that of St. *Wenefrede*.

ABOVE *Diserth* church, on a high rock, stand CASTLE.
the remains of its Castle. We cannot trace the
foundation of this fortress, which went by the
names of *Din-colyn, Castell y Ffailon,* and *Castell
Gerri*[g]. It probably was *Welsh*, and the last of
the chain of *British* posts on the *Clwydian* hills.
Henry III. in 1241, fortified it[h]; but its date was
but short, for in 1261 *Llewelyn ap Gryffydd* rased
both this castle, and that of *Diganwy*[i]. It was at
a siege of this place that *Eineon*, the son of *Ririd
Flaidd*, was slain[k]. A cross was erected on the
spot, called *Croes Eineon*, the shaft of which, ornamented with strange sculpture, now is supposed
to form the stile into the churchyard of *Diserth;*
in which is another cross, of very curious work-
manship.

THE castle occupied the summit of the rock,
whose sides are *escarpés*, or cut steep, to render

[g] *Llwyd's Itin.*   [h] *Powel*, 307.   [i] Same, 326.   [k] *Hengwrt, MS.*

the access more difficult.   On one part, beneath
the top, is a square out-work, with fosses cut in
part through the solid lime-stone.   The fragments
of the castle shew, that its ruin was not effected
by time; they lie in vast masses, overthrown by
mining, which was a common method of besieging,
very long before the use of powder.

IN a field a little to the south of the castle, is a
SIR ROBERT ruinous building, called *Siamber Wen.*   This is
POUNDER-
LING. said to have been the seat of Sir *Robert Pounderling*[1], once constable of the adjacent castle, a
knight valiant and prudent, who had one of his
eyes knocked out by a gentleman of *Wales,* in the
rough sport of tournament; but being requested
to challenge him again to *feates of armes,* on meeting our countryman at the *English* court, declined
the combat, declaring that he did not intend that
the *Welshman* should beat out his other eye[m]

MOEL   *Moel Hiraddug,* a *British* post, on a very steep
HIRADDUG.
and rocky hill, with an immense agger of loose
stones on the accessible part, stands to the south
of the castle, and forms the next to it in the chain
of fortresses[n].   On the east side, and on a place
called *Marian,* are long deep trenches, out of
which minerals have been dug, probably in the
times of the *Saxons;* the ore appears, by the fragments, and color of the rubbish, to have been

[1] *Llwyd's Itin. MS.*   [m] *Leland's Itin.* vi. 23.
[n] See p. 61 of this volume.

iron: and on the summit of the hill (which is in the parish of *Cwm*) is a great bed of beautiful red spar, which seems to take its tinge from the ore.

In the village of *Diserth* are two or three antient and large houses. One[n] belonged to the archdeacon of *St. Asaph*, till that office was annexed to the bishopric by *William Hughes*, prelate of this see, who in 1573 procured a faculty from Archbishop *Parker* to hold this dignity in commendam with his bishoprick. The last who held it was *Thomas Powel*, rector of *Hirnans* and *Llanfechan*, who died in 1589. It was at times the residence of the bishops, after they had made the acquisition. Bishop *Parry* died in it in 1623.

Cwm church, as the word signifies, is embosomed in hills, and fronts the vale of *Clwyd*. On a very antient stone in the church-yard is this inscription, *Hic jacet* TANGWISTE, *uxor* LLEWELIN *ap* INIR; but whether of *Inir* of *Yale* is uncertain.

Cwm Church.

From *Diserth* I rode to *Bod-rhyddan*, long the residence of the *Conways*, a family derived from Sir *Hugh Conway*, son of old *John Coniers*, of *Richmond*, *Yorkshire*, brother to *Jevan* Lord *Coniers*[o]: his son Sir *Henry*, by marriage with *Angharad*, heiress to Sir *Hugh Crevecœur* of *Prestatyn*[p],

Bod-rhyddan.

---

[n] This antient building has been taken down, and a new house erected for the use of the resident clergyman. Ed.

[o] Mr. *W. Mytton's Coll. Pedigrees.*   [p] *Salusbury Pedigree,* p. 68. b.

probably acquired the settlement in this country. *Prestatyn* continued possessed by the *Conways* till the death of Sir *John Conway* baronet, in 1721, the last of the male line, when the estate was divided.

ABOUT a mile and a half farther stands the small borough of *Rhuddlan*, seated high on the red, clayey banks of the *Clwyd*, and above *Morfa-Rhuddlan*, a marsh celebrated for the battle in 795, between the *Saxons* and *Welsh:* our monarch *Caradoc* fell in the conflict[q], and, I fear, victory declared against us. We do indeed say, that *Offa*, the famous king of *Mercia*, was slain here; but the *Saxon* chronicle places his death[r] the year before that battle. The fine plaintive *Welsh* tune, so well known by the name of *Morfa-Rhuddlan*, is supposed to have been composed on this occasion: for victories are not the only subjects for the harp. How beautifully does *David* lament the blood of the slain on the mountains of *Gilboa:* HOW ARE THE MIGHTY FALLEN, AND THE WEAPONS OF WAR PERISHED[t]

CASTLE.   THE castle has been a handsome building, in a square with two extremes placed at opposite corners, with a double round tower at each; and a single one at the two other corners. The court forms an irregular octagon. The ditch is large,

---

[q] *Powel*, 20.   [r] *Sax.* ch. 65.

faced on both sides with stone. The steep slope
to the river was defended by high walls, and square
towers: one is entire, and there are vestiges of
two others: the first is called *Twr-y-Silod;* another,
in the castle, was named *Twr-y-Brenhin,* or the
King's Tower.

To the south of the castle, at about a furlong
distance, is a large artificial mount, the site of another fortress, of very early date; the whole surrounded by a very deep foss (including also the
abby) which crosses from the margin of the bank,
near the ascent of the present road to *St. Asaph,*
to another parallel road; near which it is continued, then turns and falls nearly into the southern
part of the walled ditch of the castle: the whole
forming a square area of very great extent. These
different works were made at three several times.
The mount, now called *Tut-Hill,* and its superstructure (whatever it was) is thoroughly *British,*
and is said to have been built by *Llewelyn ap Sit-
sylt,* who reigned from the year 1015 to 1020[s].
It was a residence of our princes from that time:
but *Gryffydd ap Llewelyn,* in 1063, having given
offence to *Edward the Confessor,* by receiving
Algar, one of his rebellious subjects, was attacked by *Harold,* who in revenge burned the palace at *Rhuddlan*[t]. It was soon restored, and
as soon lost. *Robert,* afterwards surnamed of

[s] *Camden,* ii.   [t] *Powel,* 100.

Rhuddlan, a valiant *Norman*, nephew to *Hugh Lupus*, earl of *Chester*, conquered it from the *Welsh*, and by the command of *William* the Conqueror, fortified it with new works[u], and made it his place of residence; from whence he greatly annoyed our countrymen. The square towers are evidently of *Norman* architecture, and naturally adopted by the new owner. *Robert* received here a visit from our prince *Gryffydd ap Cynan*, who came to solicit aid against his enemies, from the *Norman* warrior, which he obtained; but on some quarrel attacked him in his castle, took and burnt the bailey, or yard, and killed such a number of his men, that very few escaped into the towers[x].

Henry II. in 1157, added new strength to the castle, and left a considerable garrison in it before he quitted the country. Notwithstanding this, *Owen Gwynedd*, in 1167, took and dismantled it; but it was afterwards re-fortified by the *English;* for it appears that this fortress had, with two others, been bestowed by *Henry*, with *Emma* his natural sister, on *Dafydd ap Owen*, son and successor to *Owen Gwynedd.* Here, in 1187, he entertained, very nobly, *Baldwin* archbishop of *Canterbury*, in his progress through *Wales*[y]. Possibly

---

[u] *Order. Vital.* 670.

[x] Life of *Gr. ap Cynan.* SEBRIGHT MSS.

[y] *Giraldi Cambr. Itin.* 872.   Sir *Richard Hoare's* Ed. xi. 134.

he resigned it again to the *English;* for I find that in 1214 it was besieged and taken by *Llewelyn ap Jorwerth,* his successor in the principality[z].

I MUST not omit relating, notwithstanding I am unable to give the year of the event, that *Randle Blundeville,* earl of *Chester,* was in this castle surprized by a body of *Welsh,* and lay in the utmost distress, until he was relieved by his lieutenant, *Roger Lacy,* alias *Hell;* who collecting suddenly a rabble of fiddlers and idle people, put the besiegers to flight. In reward, he received from the earl, *Magisterium omnium peccatorum et meretricum* TOTIUS CESTRESHIRE[a].

I FIND it in possession of *Edward* I. in 1277; who was so well convinced of its importance in the conquest of *Wales,* that he made it the rendezvous of all the forces destined for that purpose. It was the *place d'armes,* and the great magazine of provisions for the support of his army, in its advance into the country. The reigning prince, *Llewelyn ap Gryffydd,* knew the danger of leaving so consequential a place in the hands of his enemy: but it resisted all the most vigorous attacks made on it in 1281, by *Llewelyn* and his brother *Dafydd,* just reconciled to him by the sense

---

[z] *Powel,* 270.　　[a] *Leycester,* 142. This Earl of *Chester* held his earldom from 1182 to 1232.

of their common danger. Soon after, it proved
the place of confinement to the latter, not long
before his ignominious end at *Shrewsbury.*

In order to secure this fortress from any future
attempts of the *Welsh, Edward* turned all his
thoughts towards rendering it impregnable. He
accordingly began with an act of justice, that of
making recompence to *Master Richard Bernard,*
parson of *Rhuddlan,* for certain lands taken from
him for the purpose of enlarging the castle[b]; and
again, in 1282, made an exchange with the same
church, of six acres and a half, for the same uses[c]:
and on which he built the castle, whose ruins we
now survey. The finishing of it took a considerable time; for I find an order in 1291, for overlooking the works at the castles of *Rhuddlan,
Flint,* and *Chester*[d]. I cannot but remark here
the strong necessity of curbing the new-conquer'd
country with powerful garrisons; for notwithstanding all the ravages of long and barbarous wars, it
remained so exceedingly populous, that *Edward*
politically drafted out of it not less than fifteen
thousand men, in aid of his *Scottish* expedition[e].
The consequence proved almost fatal to him: for
while he lay encamped near *Linlithgow,* a national
quarrel ensued between the *English* and *Welsh*

---

[b] *Ayloffe's Rot. Walliæ,* 75.   [c] *Sebright MS.*
[d] *Rot. Walliæ,* 98.   [e] *Carte,* II. 264.

troops; and after great bloodshed, the latter separated themselves from his army[f].

DURING the civil wars of the seventeenth century, it was garrisoned on the part of the king; was taken by general *Mytton* in *July* 1646; and in the same year ordered by the parlement (in the phrase of the times) to be *slighted, i. e.* dismantled, with many other *Welsh* castles[g].

TAKEN BY
GENERAL
MYTTON.

IN respect to the civil history of *Rhuddlan*, I find that in the reign of *Edward the Confessor*, it made part of the great territories of earl *Edwin*, the last earl of *Mercia*, who at the time of the Conquest enjoyed this hundred, and part of *North Wales*[h]. *Edwyn ap Gronw*, one of the fifteen tribes of *North Wales*, seems to have been, under him, lord of these parts. It was then, by reason of the inroads of *Harold*, a waste; and continued so when it was possessed by *Hugh Lupus*. It then became the capital of the district: and *Hugh* enjoyed a moiety of the church, the mint, and mines of the iron[i] ore found in the manor, and a moiety of the water of *Clwyd, i. e.* of the mill and fishery on such part which belonged to earl *Edwin;* a moiety of the forests on the manor, and

---

[f] *Dalrymple's Annals,* II. 257.

[g] *Whitelock,* 231.   [h] *Dugdale's Baronage,* I. 11.

[i] Probably those which we have mentioned in the parish of *Cwm,* to which this manor might have extended; for *Dissarch,* or *Diserth,* adjoining to *Cwm,* is cited in *Doomsday-Book* as belonging to it.

of the toll, and of the village called *Bren:* and
there were at this time in *Rhuddlan* eight burgesses. All this *Hugh Lupus* granted to *Robert*
of *Rhuddlan*, with an addition of certain hamlets
dependent on the place; and a new borough was
erected with eighteen burgesses, who enjoyed the
same privileges with those of *Hereford* and *Bre-
tril:* and were exempted from all fines exceeding
twelve-pence, except in case of manslaughter,
theft, and *heinfare, i. e.* the depriving a person of
his servant[k].

A BOROUGH.   EDWARD I. made this town a free borough, appointed the constable of the castle for the time
being to be mayor, and the bailiffs to be chosen
annually by the burgesses on *Michaelmas*-day, who
were to be presented to the constable to be sworn.
The town was to have power of imprisoning, except in such cases as affected the life, or loss of
limb: when criminals of this nature were to be
committed to the castle, burgesses only were permitted to bail.   No *Jews* were to inhabit the
town.   The burgesses had a forest and free warren; a *gild cum hansa et loth et shoth, sok sak et
theam et infangenthest et lib. per totam terram de
Theoloniis, lestagio, Muragio, Danegeld, Gay-
wite, &c.*

THIS charter was given by the King at *Flint,*

---

[k] *Doomsday-Book.*

September 8th, in the twelfth year of his reign; *Testibus Rob. Bath & Wells,* &c. and confirmed by *Richard* II. at *Leicester,* and again at *Westminster.*

No constable has been appointed since the days of *Oliver Cromwell.*

THE burgesses contribute towards electing a member for the borough of *Flint.* Those who are qualified inhabit the place, and that part of the parish called *Rhuddland Franchise,* which extends above a mile from the town.

THE parlement said to have been held here in 1288, by *Edward* I. was probably no more than a council assembled by the conqueror, to divide his new conquests into counties, and to give salutary laws to the *Welsh;* to abolish any antient customs which the wise prince thought detrimental, and to introduce such of the *English* as would prove of use. This was not done hastily; for in the year preceding, a commission had been appointed, with *Thomas Beke,* bishop of *St. David,* president; who were to consider and report upon oath the different laws of both countries. From their resolutions was framed the famous STATUTE OF RHUDDLAN; in which, among many excellent institutions, were introduced sheriffs and coroners, their powers defined, and the principal crimes of the times pointed out: most of which

ITS PARLE-
MENT.

were acts of violence, rapine, and theft; such as might be expected to exist among a rude people, and which resulted more from the turbulence of the times than the want of wholesome laws[l].

A PIECE of antient building, called the Parlement House, is still to be seen in *Rhuddlan;* probably the place where the king sat in council. From hence he actually practised the well-known deceit of giving them a prince born among them, who never spoke a word of *English,* and whose life and conversation no man was able to stain[m]: all which our discontented nobility eagerly accepted, little thinking the person intended, to be the infant *Edward,* just born at *Caernarvon.*

BRIDGE.   THE bridge consists of two arches. It appears to have been rebuilt or repaired in 1595: that date with the arms of *St. Asaph,* and the initials of *William Hughes,* the bishop of that time, being cut in the battlements. The tides flow very little higher than this place, and bring up to the bridge flats or vessels of about seventy tons. The port of these parts is about three miles further, at the *vorryd,*([1]) or great *ford,* where the river discharges itself into the sea; and from whence much corn and timber are exported.

---

[1] See the *Statuta Walliæ* passim.   [m] *Powel,* 376.

([1]) *Vorryd,* that is to say, *Y Vorryd,* is more likely to have meant the Sea-ford. J.R.

IN the south end of the town is *Hendre,* an old
house, the property of *John Egerton* esq. of *Oul-*
ton, which, with a good estate[n] in this parish, with
some lands in *Tremeirchion* and *St. Asaph* parishes, descended to the *Oulton* family, by the
marriage of *Philip Egerton* esq. fourth son and
heir of Sir *Roland Egerton* with *Catherine,* sole
heiress and daughter of *Pyers Conway* of *Hendre.*
This *Philip* was living in 1655[o].

THE house called the *Gwindy,* or Wine House,
must not be forgotten. There are few towns in
Wales, which have not one of that name: but the
use has long been lost. In old times, most gentlemen's houses had one in their neighborhood, where
they met their friends and retainers, to *ymgampio,*
or to exert feats of activity. Here the gentleman
kept a cellar for wine, which he retailed for his
own profit. Here they passed the day in archery,
wrestling, throwing the sledge, and other manly
exercises. At first, the drinking was moderate:
but at length the purpose was abused; and these
places were made the sanctuary for all sorts of
crimes, committed by the dependents or friends of
the owner of the *Gwindy,* who were recommended
to his care: and there *Llawruddion, i.e.* persons
who came *red-handed* from a murder, were

[n] This property has been sold to the Rev. *Edward Hughes* of
Kinmael. ED.

[o] Pedigree of the *Egertons* of *Oulton.*

protected till composition could be made for their crimes.

CHURCH.   THE church is dedicated to *St. Mary.* It has nothing remarkable about it, except an antient gravestone, with a flowery cross and sword; the last the mark of the gentility of the person interred. The patronage of this church was granted in 1284 to the see of *St. Asaph,* in recompence for the loss of that of *Eglwysfach,* which had been taken from it, and bestowed on the abby of *Conwy*[p].

THE priory of black-friers stood about half a mile south of the castle. There is a fragment which bears marks of antiquity, the rest is disguised in the form of a farm-house and barn. We do not know the time of its foundation: but it was certainly before the conquest by *Edward* I. as *Anian,* or *Eineon de Schonan,* a friar of this house, was made bishop of *St. Asaph* in 1268. It suffered much in the wars between *Edward* and *Llewelyn,* but soon recovered its losses, towards which were allowed 17*l.* 10*s.*[q] besides a grant of a fishery on the *Clwyd* with one net, free from any obstruction[r]. On the dissolution, the house was granted to *Harry ap Harry,* and now belongs to *John Davies* esq; of *Llanerch.*

[p] *Willis's St. Asaph,* 159.   *Rot. Walliæ,* 92.
[q] *Rymer,* ii. 292.   [r] *Rot. Walliæ,* 90.

NEAR this place were certain lands called *Nun-neland* and *St. Marieland*[s]: but whether they had reference to any house of female religious, I cannot say.

THE hospital, which existed in 1281, stood between the town and *Bodrhyddan.*

As soon as *Edward* I. had finished the fortifications of *Rhuddlan*, and filled his new town with inhabitants, he and bishop *Anian* II. made different petitions to the pope, to remove the see of *St. Asaph* to this place[t]. They urged the solitude and insecurity of the former; its hazard from banditti, and the danger to which the body of the most glorious confessor *St. Asaph* was continually exposed: the king in particular adds, the great safety of this place, by reason of the vast works he had completed. But these petitions never took effect; frustrated either by the death of the pope, or the exhortation of the archbishop of *Canterbury*, to rebuild the cathedral on its antient site.

A LITTLE beyond the priory I descended the bank, and fording the *Clwyd*, soon came in sight of *St. Asaph.* The handsome extensive bridge, ST. ASAPH. the little town, and the cathedral mixed with trees, form a most agreeable view. The place is seated on the slope of a pleasant eminence: the cathedral

[s] *Sebright MSS.*
[t] *Rymer*, ii. 245. *Willis's St. Asaph*, 45. 149. 155.

on its summit. The *Clwyd* runs on the eastern
side: the *Elwy*, a most turbulent stream, on the
western: and from the last is taken the *British*
name of *Llan-Elwy*. The township in which it
stands, is also called *Bryn-Paulin*([1]); and one part
of it, *Bron y Wylfa*, or the þrow *of the watch:*
from which circumstances, as well as the great
fitness of the situation, between two rivers, I cannot but think that it was a place of encampment
of *Paulinus*, in his way to or from *Mona*.

Its ecclesiastical history may be spoken of with
more certainty. When *Kentigern*, bishop of *Glas-
gow*, was driven from his see in 543, he retired into
Wales, and established here a monastery for nine
hundred and sixty-five monks, instituted on the
same plan with that of *Bangor;* part for labor,
part for prayer. Here he built a church; and
having won over the *British* prince *Maglocunus*,
once his violent opponent, established here a see,
and was himself the first bishop. Being recalled
to *Scotland*, he nominated for successor, *Asaph*, or
Hassaph, a *Briton* of great piety and good family
(being grandson of *Pabo post Prydain*). He died
in 596, was buried in his cathedral, and gave name
to the place.

The church was first built of wood; but soon

after of stone. In 1247, during the wars of *Henry* III. the diocese was destroyed by fire and sword[u], and the bishop, who sided with the *English*, obliged to live on alms. In 1282, the cathedral was burnt CATHEDRAL. down; but ample amends were made to the see, by the grant of *Edward* I. of lands in *Newmarket, Nannerch, Dincolyn, Coed y Mynydd*, and a rich mineral tract in *Diserth:* four hundred and nine acres were given, each of which appears at that time to be valued at only six-pence[x]. In 1402, the church underwent new misfortunes; being burnt by *Owen Glyndwr*, together with the palace, and canons houses; who, strange to say! soon after brought over to his party, *John Trevor*, the injured bishop of the see, who was deprived on account of his revolt. After this the church remained in ruins for eighty years, when it was rebuilt by that worthy prelate, *Richard Redman*. The same building still remains, handsome, plain and neat. The present dean and chapter are now re-building (out of a fund vested in them for that purpose) the choir, after the inevitable dilapidations of time in the space of near four hundred years. The good imitation of the gothic, and the happy copy in the east window, of the noble remains in *Tintern* abby, will add no small beauty to the church[y].

[u] *Matthew Paris*, 642.   [x] *Sebright MSS.*
[y] This east window is now filled with handsome painted glass, executed partly at the expence of Bishop *Bagot*, and partly of several

ST. ASAPH.

THE tombs are very few. Here is one in an episcopal habit, supposed to commemorate that munificent bishop, *Dafydd ap Owen,* who died in 1512; and in the church-yard, near the west door, is a plain altar monument of bishop *Isaac Barrow,* who departed in 1680: and whose pious address I can read without any offence, howsoever papistical, zealots may think it.

Exuviæ ISAACI ASAPHENSIS Episcopi
In manum Domini depositæ
In spem letæ resurrectionis
Per sola CHRISTI merita.
Obiit dictus Reverendus Pater festi D. JOHANNIS BAPTISTÆ,
An. Dom. 1680. Ætatis 67.
Et translationis suæ undecimo.
O vos transeuntes in Domum Domini
In Domum orationis
Orate pro conservo vestro,
Ut inveniat misericordiam in die Domini.

FEW prelates were more distinguished for their piety and good works. He was first bishop of the *Isle of Man,* where he bought up all the impropriations, and settled them upon the church. He spent large sums in maintaining at school the youth of the island, and founded for them, at *Dublin,* three scholarships. In *St. Asaph* he repaired the cathedral, and mills; founded the almshouse for eight poor widows; and did numberless other

noblemen and gentlemen of the principality, whose arms are emblazoned on it. ED.

works of munificence and charity. Among his other merits was the education of his nephew, Doctor *Isaac Barrow*, the greatest of mathematicians, and geometricians, his pupil Sir ISAAC NEWTON excepted; and the soundest of divines, whose works will be read with admiration as long as the sense of religion remains.

IN the churchyard of the parish-church, is another tomb, singular enough, with foliage, a shield with a lion rampant, inscribed around, *Hic jacet Ranulfus de Smalwode;* and beneath the shield passes a sword, held by a hand. It is said to have been brought from *Rhuddlan;* but we are left unacquainted with the person whose memory it perpetuates[z].

PARISH-CHURCH.

THIS church stands at the lower part of the town, and serves for the use of the inhabitants of town and country, the cathedral not being used for that purpose.

THE members of the chapter are the dean, archdeacon (who is the bishop), six prebendaries, and seven canons. Besides these, belong to the church, four vicars choral, four singing men, four choristers, and an organist.

---

[z] An old drawing of this, and some other antient *Welsh* monuments, were most obligingly presented to me, by that excellent antiquary, the Rev. *William Cole*, of *Milton*, near *Cambridge;* a gentleman to whom I have been frequently indebted for variety of useful information.

THE present palace[a] is not very magnificent. It
was rebuilt by bishop *Dafydd ap Owen*, in 1503,
after it had lain in ruins an hundred years. Since
which time it has received very little real improvement.

THE diocese comprehends all *Flintshire*, excepting *Hawarden*[b] and the hundred of *Maelor* in
the same county; all *Denbighshire*, except the
deanery of *Dyffryn Clwyd*; all *Montgomery-
shire*, excepting seven parishes; the hundreds of
Mowddwy, Penllyn, and *Edeirnion,* in *Meirioneddshire;* and trespasses a little even on *Shropshire.* The number of livings are a hundred and
thirty; of which all, except seven[c], are in the
patronage of the bishop; as is the valuable
deanery.

THE road from *St. Asaph* along the common
called the *Row*([1]) is extremely beautiful: the vale is
watered by the *Elwy*, which runs beneath lofty

PONT YR
ALLT GOCH. banks, finely wooded: at its extremity is *Pont yr*

[a] The worthy and liberal prelate, the late *Lewis Bagot*, rebuilt the
greatest part of the palace, and by considerable additions rendered it
a residence adapted to the opulence of the see. ED.

[b] Vol. i. p. 131, of this Tour.

[c] Viz. Holywell, *Flintshire;* Kegidoc, alias St. George, *Denbighshire;* Kinnersley, Oswestry, Knocking, Whittington, Selattin, *Salop.*

([1]) This in spite of its English spelling is simply the Welsh, *Y Ro,*
the gravel, or the gravel shore, from *gro*, gravel; similarly, a place
in the Conwy Valley is called *Y Ro Wen,* but the natives take a delight in writing it *Roe Wen,* I believe. J.R.

allt Gôch, a noble bridge of one lofty arch, eighty-five feet in diameter. The *Elwy* here takes another direction, running west, and then north, along most romantic dingles, varied with meadows, woods, and cavernous rocks: neither is it destitute of antiquities. *Y ffynnon fair*, or our lady's well, a fine spring, inclosed in an angular wall, formerly roofed; and the ruins of a cross-shaped chapel, finely over-grown with ivy, exhibit a venerable view, in a deep-wooded bottom, not remote from the bridge; and, in days of pilgrimage, the frequent haunt of devotees. On an eminence above stands *Wyg-fair*, the seat of *John Lloyd* esq; in full enjoyment of this beautiful scenery. He is derived paternally from *Ednowain Bendew*, one of the fifteen tribes, and from *Hedd Molwynog*, by a female ancestor, in whose right he enjoys his antient seat of *Hafodynos*.

THE most capital view of these picturesque PENCRAIG. glens, is from *Pencraig*, on the grounds of Mrs. *Jones* of *Galt-vaenan;* from whence is a sight of three at once, together with an unspeakable variety of other objects, extremely worthy of a visit from every traveller.

At *Llanerch*, the chief seat of my kinsman, the LLANERCH. late *John Davies* esq ; formerly called *Lleweni Fechan*, about half a mile to the east of the bridge, I stopped a while to admire the charming view of the vale of *Clwyd*, with the magnificent boundary

between it and *Flintshire.* The intervening plain
is of matchless fertility: inclosures creep high up
the hills; the remaining part is divided into various
summits, in the season, glowing to the setting sun
with the purple flowers of the heath.   Churches
and neat mansions enliven the scene.   From *Tre-
meirchion-Green,* placed high above *Llanerch,* is a
very fine view of the whole vale, of the western
boundary, and of the lofty tract of *Snowdon.*   The
middle, from end to end, is enriched with towns
and castles; among which rises supreme, the rock
of *Denbigh,* topped with its great fortress.

TREMEIRCH-
ION.
In *Tremeirchion* church is the mutilated tomb
of Sir *Robert Pounderling,* before-mentioned.   By
his cross-legs it seems he had attained the merit
of pilgrimage to the holy sepulchre.

DAFYDD
DDU.
Under a handsome gothic arch lies, in priestly
vestments, well executed, the image of *Dafydd
Ddu,* or the black, of *Hiraddug.*   Underneath is
inscribed, *Hic jacet* David ap Roderic ap Madog.
He was vicar of this place, and dignitary of *St.
Asaph:* prophet and poet: and had a great concern
in regulating our prosody.   The *Daroganeu,* or
prophecies of *Robin Ddu,* so celebrated in *North
Wales,* I believe properly belong to *Dafydd,* who
flourished in 1340, above a hundred years before
the time of *Robin.*

In this church stood a cross, celebrated for its

miracles, which are celebrated in an *awdl*, or poem, about the year 1500, by *Gryffydd ap Ifan ap Llen Fychan*. The cross is now demolished, but the carved capital is still to be seen, in a building adjoining to the church-yard.

I~ the bottom, not far from *Tremeirchion*, lies, half-buried in the wood, the singular house of *Bachegraig;* now the property of Seignior *Piozzi*[d], in right of his wife *Hester Lynch*, widow of *Henry Thrale* esq; and daughter and heiress of the late *John Salusbury* esq. It consists of a mansion, and three sides, inclosing a square court. The first consists of a vast hall, and parlour: the rest of it rises into six wonderful stories, including the cupola, and forms from the second floor the figure of a pyramid: the rooms are small, and inconvenient. In the windows of the parlour are several pieces of painted glass, of the arms of the knight of the *holy sepulchre;* as his own with a heart at the bottom, including the letters R. C. his and his 1567. S. wife's initials, and beneath them, *cor unum, via una;* the arms of *Elystan Glodrydd;* those of his great partner Sir *Thomas Gresham,* and of several kingdoms with which these munificent merchants traded. There are besides some broken wheels, with a sword, the usual emblems of *St. Catharine:*

BACHEGRAIG.

[d] Mr. *Piozzi* died in 1809. ED.

by his order of knighthood he probably was a
Roman Catholic, and might pay particular respect
to that saint.   The bricks are admirable, and appear to have been made either in *Holland*, or by
Dutchmen upon the spot, for in certain pits near
the house are still to be seen specimens of a similar
sort: the model of the house was probably brought
from *Flanders*, where this species of building is
not unfrequent.   The country people say, that it
was built by the devil, in one night, and that the architect still preserves an apartment in it : but Sir
Richard Clough, an eminent merchant in the reign
of queen *Elizabeth*, seems to have a better title to
the honor.   The initials of his name are in iron on
the front, with the date 1567; and on the gate-
way that of 1569.

SIR *Richard* was a man of distinguished character, who raised himself, by his merit, from a
poor boy at *Denbigh*, to be one of the greatest
merchants of his time.   He was first a chorister at
Chester[e]*:* then had the good fortune to become
apprentice to the famous Sir *Thomas Gresham;*
and afterwards his partner; with whom he may
be considered as joint founder of the *Royal
Exchange*, having contributed several thousand
pounds towards that noble design.   His residence
was chiefly at *Antwerp*, where his body was in-

---

[e] *Fuller's* Br. Worthies, *Flintshire*, p. 40.

terred: his heart in *Whitchurch*, a neighboring
church. He is said to have made a pilgrimage to
Jerusalem, and to have been made knight of the
holy sepulchre: this is confirmed; for he assumed
the five crosses, the badge of that order, for his
arms[f]. His wealth was so great, that *Efe a aeth
yn Clough,* or *He is become* a CLOUGH, grew into a
proverb, on the attainment of riches by any person. He left two daughters: one he bestowed,
with this house, and certain tythes in *Llŷn,* on
Roger Salusbury, a younger son of *Lleweni;* the
other on a *Wynne,* of *Melay,* with whom he gave
the abby of *Maenan.* He also left the tythes of
Kilken to the school at *Denbigh.* They are now lost
to the school, being annexed as a sinecure to the
bishoprick of *St. Asaph.* His heirs probably enjoyed but an inconsiderable part of his wealth,
which is said to have gone to Sir *Thomas Gresham,*
according to an agreement in case of survivorship.
Sir *Richard* died first; but the time is unknown.
Sir *Thomas* survived till the year 1579. Sir
Richard had a natural son, whom he sent for from
Antwerp, and settled at *Plâs Clough,* a house he
had built on *Denbigh* green, and which is still possessed by his posterity. An original picture[g], on
board, of this illustrious person, is preserved at
the present residence of the family, *Glanywern.*

---

[f] *Salusbury Pedigree,* 17.
[g] Engraved in Mr. *Pennant's* "Account of London," p. 369. ED.

It is a half length, extremely well painted on
board. His hair is very short, and of a dark
brown; his beard has a cast of yellow. He is
dressed in a close short jacket, black striped with
white; great white breeches. In his right hand is
a glove; his left is on his sword; and on his right
side is a dagger. The arms of the Holy Sepulchre,
which he had assumed, are painted on one side of
the picture. It was probably painted at *Antwerp*,
which, at this period, abounded with artists of the
first merit. Sir *Richard* meditated great things
for the advantage of his country: he designed to
make the *Clwyd* navigable from *Rhuddlan;* to
have introduced commerce; and to have made
the sides of his court the magazines, from which
he was to dispense his imports to the neighboring
parts.

IN front of the house, cross the *Clwyd* on *Pont
y Cambwll,* and turning to the left, cross it again
at *Pont Gryffydd,* in order to search in the parish

VARIS.
of *Bodfari,* for the antient *Varis.* Soon enter the
deep pass, formed by nature in the *Clwydian*
hills, from the vales into the county of *Flint.* But
neither my own examination, or that of some intelligent friends, availed any thing. The sole remaining antiquity is *British;* a post on a hill to
the left, called *Moel y Gaer,* or the hill of the
camp. The beauty of the ride makes amends for
the disappointment. The vale is narrow, fertile,

diversified with groves, and watered by the crystal *Wheeler*. The part about *Maes mynan* is singularly fine, consisting of detached hills, cloathed with timber; a charming extent of meadows; and the lofty mountain *Moel y parc*, skirted with trees, contrasting itself to the softer part of the scenery. This place is at present the property of Sir *Roger Mostyn*, purchased by one of his family from the *Massies*, a name which represented the county of *Flint* as early as the first of queen *Mary*[h]. This place has been called *Llŷs Maes Mynan*, or the palace of *Maes Mynan*, where *Llewelyn ap Gryffydd*, last prince of *Wales*, resided in a house, whose foundations, till within these few years, were to be seen in an adjacent meadow[i]

BUT no part of this vale furnished me with the least vestige of the *Roman* station, *Varis*, mentioned by *Antonine*, in his eleventh *Iter*, and placed at nineteen or twenty-one miles distant from *Conovium*, or *Caer-hên*; for there appears an uncertainty in the reading.

QUIT the turnpike road on the left; ford the *Wheeler*; and, after crossing the *Clwyd*, reach *Lleweni* hall. On this spot is said to have resided, about the year 720, *Marchweithian*, one of the fifteen tribes or nobility of *North Wales*. At present it is the seat of the honourable *Thomas Fitz-*

[h] *Willis's* Not. Parliam. ii. part 2nd. 25.   [i] *Hist. Gwedir.* 28.

maurice[k], brother to the marquis of *Landsdown*,
purchased about ten years ago by him from Sir
Robert Salusbury Cotton, baronet, of *Cumber-
mere-Abby*, in *Cheshire*. That gentleman possessed the place by the marriage of his ancestor
Sir *Robert Cotton*, with *Hester*, sister to Sir *John
Salusbury*, the last baronet of his name, in the time
of *Charles* II. The *Salusburies* were an *English*
family settled here before the time of *Henry* III.
Several of the portraits were transferred with the
estate, to the present owner, and preserved in the
magnificent old hall. Sir *John Salusbury the
Strong*, is represented on board, a half length,
with short dusky hair, beardless, in a yellow
figured jacket, a vast ruff, and one hand on his
sword; dated 1591 æt. 24. He succeeded to
the estate on the execution of his elder brother
Thomas, who suffered in 1586, for his concern in
Babington's plot. A picture, supposed to be his,
is to be seen here; representing him in a grey and
black vest, dark hair, short whiskers, bushy beard,
and with an ear-ring; his bonnet in his hand; his
breast naked.

SIR JOHN SALUSBURY.

I. SIR THOMAS.

SIR HENRY.   SIR *Henry*, the first baronet, is placed sitting
in his shirt; his bosom naked; over one arm is
cast a red mantle; his breeches red, with points at
his knees; his stockings purple; his slippers rich

[k] Now of his only son Viscount *Kirkwall*. ED.

in lace; his beard bushy; his whiskers small; he is seated in a balcony, as if at his toilet. I have seen here a fine picture of his eldest son, Sir *Thomas*, as much distinguished by his pen as his sword. He appears as if on the point of quitting his family, to join the army; for he was a distinguished loyalist in the time of *Charles* I. He is taking leave of his lady and three children; is dressed in a buff surtout, brown boots, with a rich scymetar by his side; attended by two greyhounds, a groom, dressed in a long canvass gown, holding a horse, with the arms of the house on the man's shoulders, by way of badge. This gentleman was educated at *Jesus College, Oxford*, and having, as *Wood*[1] says, a natural geny to poetry and romance, exercised himself much in those juvenile studies; and produced from his pen, the *History of Joseph* in *English* verse, in thirteen chapters. He retired to *Lleweni*, and died in 1643.

II. Sir Thomas.

6 f

I MUST not omit the portrait of a lady, exceedingly celebrated in this part of *Wales*; the famous *Catherine Tudor*, better known by the name of *Catherine* of *Berain*, from her seat in this neighborhood. She was daughter and heiress of *Tudor ap Robert Fychan*, of *Berain:* she took for her first husband *John Salusbury*, heir of *Lleweni*, and on his death gave her hand to Sir *Richard Clough*.

Catherine y Berain.

[1] *Athen. Oxon.* ii. 25.

The tradition goes, that at the funeral of her beloved spouse she was led to church by Sir *Richard*,
and from church by *Morris Wynn*, of *Gwedir*,
who whispered to her his wish of being her second:
she refused him with great civility, informing him,
that she had accepted the proposals of Sir *Richard*, in her way to church, but assured him (and
was as good as her word) that in case she performed
the same sad duty (which she was then about)
to the knight, he might depend on being her third.
As soon as she had composed this gentleman, to
shew that she had no superstition about the number THREE, she concluded with *Edward Thelwall*,
of *Plas y Ward*, esq; departed this life *August*
27, and was interred at *Llanyfydd* on the 1st of
September, 1591.

HER portrait is an excellent three-quarters, on
wood. By the date, 1568, it seems to have been
painted by *Lucas de Heere; the only artist I know
of in that period, equal to the performance. I
was told, that in the locket she wore to the gold
chain, was the hair of her second and favourite
husband.

Lleweni, notwithstanding it lies on a flat, has
most pleasing views of the mountains on each side
of the vale; the town and castle of *Denbigh* form
most capital objects, at the distance of two miles,
and the nearer environs of the place animate the

country by the commercial spirit of their active
master.

THE chief of Mr. FITZMAURICE's improvements is a bleachery of uncommon extent. The
building, in which the operations are carried on, is
in form of a crescent; a beautiful arcade four
hundred feet in extent, with a *loggia* in the centre,
graces the front; each end finishes with a pavillion.
The drying loft is an hundred and eighty feet long;
the brown warehouse and lapping room each ninety feet; and before it are five fountains, a pretti-
ness very venial, as it ornaments a building of
Dutch extraction. But this is without parallel,
whether the magnitude, the ingenuity of the ma-
chinery, or the size of the bleaching ground is to
be considered. The greatest part of the linen
bleached here is sent from the tenantry of his great
estates in *Ireland*, in payment of rent. Much also
is sent by private persons from the neighboring
counties for the mere purpose of whitening[1].

THE vast extent to which Mr. FITZMAURICE
carries this business, is most sensibly felt in his
neighborhood. May the utility of his life effectu-
ally awaken in our gentry a sense of his merit, and
the benefits resulting from his labors, and induce

[1] Since the death of Mr. *Fitzmaurice* in 1793, the activity of the
Bleachery has declined. *Lleweni* is now (1809) advertised for sale.
ED.

them to promote every design of his, calculated
for the public good.

Dafydd, brother of our last *Llewelyn*, makes
great complaints of the havock made by *Reginald
de Grey*, justice of *Chester*, in cutting down his
wood of *Lleweni*[m]; which *Dafydd* probably held as
lord of *Denbigh*.

PONTRIF-
FITH.

OPPOSITE to *Lleweni* is *Pontriffith* bridge, now
rebuilding in an elegant manner: and near it, is a
pretty *ferme ornée* belonging to *Bell Lloyd* esq.
In the house is the head of *William Roberts*, a
venerable *Welsh* prelate, in a close black cap, with
beard and long hair; and in his robes. For his
integrity in discovering church goods to the value
of a thousand pounds, he was promoted, by the
interest of archbishop *Laud*, to the see of *Bangor*
in 1637. During the civil wars, he suffered greatly
for his loyalty, and was ejected out of everything.
On the Restoration, he was restored to his see,
and, after a life of distinguished piety and charity,
died *Aug.* 12th 1665, at his parsonage at *Llandurnog* near *Denbigh*, where he was interred, having
attained his eightieth year.

WHIT-
CHURCH.

ABOUT a mile and a half south of this house,
visit the church of *Whitchurch*, or *St. Marcellus*,
the parish church of *Denbigh*. In the porch, a
small brass shews, kneeling at an altar, *Richard*

m *Powel*, 350.

Myddelton (governor of *Denbigh* castle under *Edward* VI. *Mary*, and *Elizabeth*) who, with *Jane* his wife, was interred beneath. Behind him are nine sons; behind her seven daughters. He died in 1575; she in 1565. His virtues are rehearsed in the following quaint lines:

> In vayn we bragg and boast of blood, in vayne of sinne we vaunte,
> Syth flesh and blood must lodge at last where nature did us graunte.
> So where he lyeth that lyved of late with love and favour muche,
> To fynde his friend, to feel his foes, his country skante had suche.
> When lyff did well reporte his death, whose death hys lyff doth trye,
> And poyntes with fynger what he was that here in claye doth lye.
> His virtues shall enroll his actes, his tomb shall tell his name,
> His sonnes and daughters left behind, shall blaze on Erth his fame.
> Look under feete and you shall fynde, upon the stone yow stande,
> The race he ranne, the lyff he led, each with an upright hand.

SEVERAL of the sons were men of distinguished characters. The third, *William*, was a sea captain, and an eminent poet. His early education was at *Oxford*; but his military turn led him abroad, where he signalized himself as soldier and sailor. By his good conduct our fleet, which was sent in 1591 to the *Açores*, to intercept the *Spanish* galleons, was saved. *Philip* II. by his excellent intelligence, got advice of the design, and sent another, of ten times our force, to frustrate our plan. Captain *Myddelton* kept company with the enemy three days to get acquainted with their force, and left them just time enough to give our admiral,

Lord *Thomas Howard*, notice of their strength, who prudently retired from so unequal a conflict, and certain destruction. Sir *Richard Greenville*, vice admiral, was unavoidably left behind. We are at a loss whether to admire his courage or blame his temerity,

When his one bark a navy did defy.

He[1] fell oppressed by multitudes, leaving to the astonished enemy an immortal proof of his own valour and of *British* spirit. He[2] translated the psalms into *Welsh* metre, and finished them on *Jan.* 4th, 1595, *apud* Scutum *insulam occidentalium Indorum;* which as well as his *Barddoniaeth,* or art of *Welsh* poetry, were published in *London:* the first in 1603, the other in 1593[n]. It is sayed, that he, with captain *Thomas Price* of *Plâsyollin,* and one captain *Koet,* were the first who smoked, or (as they called it) drank tobacco publickly in *London;* and that the *Londoners* flocked from all parts to see them[o]. Pipes were not then invented, so they used the twisted leaves, or *segars.* The invention is usually ascribed to Sir *Walter Raleigh.* It may be so; but he was too good a courtier to

---

[1] The story of Sir *Richard Greenville* has been told by the Poet Laureate in one of his latest poems, *The Revenge, a Ballad of the Fleet.* T.P.

[2] Captain *Myddelton* translated the psalms. T.P.

[n] Athen. Oxon. i. 284.   [o] Sebright MSS.

smoke in public, especially in the reign of *James,* who even condescended to write a book against the practice, under the title of *The Counter-blast to Tobacco.*

Thomas, the fourth son, became lord mayor of *London,* and was the founder of the family of *Chirk-castle.* It is recorded, that having married a young wife in his old age, the famous song of *Room for cuckolds, here comes my lord mayor!* was invented on the occasion[p].

Charles, the fifth son, succeeded his father in the government of *Denbigh* castle.

I NOW speak of the sixth son, *Hugh;* a person whose useful life would give lustre to the greatest family. This gentleman (afterwards Sir *Hugh*) displayed very early his great talents; and began, as we are told by himself, by searching for coal within a mile of his native place. His attempts did not meet with success: his genius was destined to act on a greater stage. The Capital afforded him ample space for his vast attempts: few readers need be told, that he planned, and brought to perfection, the great design of supplying the city with water. This plan was meditated in the reign of *Elizabeth;* but no one was found bold enough to attempt it. In 1608, the dauntless WELSHMAN stept forth, and SMOTE THE ROCK: and on *Mi-*

p *Myddelton Pedigree, MS.*

chaelmas 1613, the waters flowed into the thirsting metropolis. He brought it, in defiance of hills and vallies, reckoning every winding, near thirty-nine miles; conveyed it by aqueducts in some places; in others pierced the high grounds, and gave it a subterraneous course. He was a true proto-type of the later genius of similar works; but he sacrificed private fortune to the public good. Two thousand pounds a month, which he gained from the *Cardiganshire* mines were swallowed up in this river[q]. He received the empty honour of see-ing himself attended by the king, his court, and all the corporation of *London*, among whom was his brother (designed mayor for the ensuing year.) The waters gushed out in their presence, the great archi-tect received their applause, and knighthood; and, in 1622, the title of baronet. His own fair fortune being expended on an undertaking, which now brings in to the proprietors an amazing revenue, he was reduced to become a hireling surveyor, and was eminently useful in every place where draining or mining was requisite. I shall have occasion to speak of some other of his labors in the course of this book. He served in parlement for the borough of *Denbigh* in the years 1603, 1614, 1620, 1623, 1625, and 1628. He presented a silver cup to the corporation of *Denbigh,* and an-other to the head of his family, both of which are

q *Fodinæ Regales,* 32.

still preserved. On that at *Guaenynog* is inscribed,

Mentem non munus.
Omnia a DEO.
Hugh Myddelton.

He died in 1631[r]. Sir([1]) ———— *Myddelton*, the
last baronet of this branch of the family, died a
few years ago. The present representative is a
widow in distressed circumstances: Sir *Hugh* left a
certain number of shares to the *Goldsmith's* company, to be divided among the poor members; but,
as the husband of this poor woman happened not
to be of that company, the representative of the
greatest benefactor *London* ever had, is, I trust
through ignorance of her case, permitted to linger
away her days in cruel penury.

A MURAL monument needlessly attempts to
preserve the memory of that great antiquary,
Humphrey Llwyd. He is represented in a *Spanish*
dress, kneeling at an altar, beneath a range of
small arches; above, a multitude of quarterings
proclame his long descent. He derived himself
from the *Rosendales* of the north, who settled at

HUMPHREY
LLWYD.

[r] *Myddelton Pedigree, MS.*

([1]) A Sir *Hugh Myddleton* is said (see Arch. Camb. 1850) to have
died s.p. in 1756—7. The title does not appear to have been since
assumed; but there is reason to believe that it had not become extinct
in 1792, and very possibly it has not subsequently expired. T.P.

Foxhall, in this neighborhood, in 1297, by marriage
with the heiress of the place. He himself was of
a branch, which fixed at *Denbigh*, a borough he
represented in 1563. He was educated at *Oxford*,
a commoner of *Brazen-nose* college, and master of
arts. He returned to his native place, an accomplished gentleman. He studied at the university
the healing art; but is celebrated as a person of
great eloquence, an excellent rhetorician and
sound philosopher. After the panegyric passed
on him by *Camden*, it would be presumptuous to
add any thing relative to his great skill in the antiquities of our country. He practised, for his
amusement, physic and music. The motto on his
portrait, in possession of his representative *John
Lloyd* of *Aston* esq; expresses his liberal turn of
mind: *Hwy pery clod na golyd;* FAME IS MORE
LASTING THAN WEALTH. In medicine, and the
study of antiquities, he has left several proofs of
his knowledge, which seems to have been quite
unconfined. He made the map of *England*, for
his friend *Ortelius*. For his brother-in-law, lord
Lumley (whose sister he married) he formed a large
collection of useful and curious books; which were
afterwards purchased by *James* I. and now make
the most valuable part of the *British Museum*[a].

BNC

Granger, i. 270. For the History of his works, see *Athen.
Oxon.* i.

In his last letter to the great geographer *Ortelius*[t],
he foresees his own death, which happened soon
after its date, in *August* 1568, aged 41. The very
simple inscription on the monument promises his
character; but instead, appear only three lines of
a psalm tune.

> THE CORPS AND EARTHLY shape doth rest, Here tombd in
>   your sight,
> Of *Humfrey Lloyd*, M[r] of Arte, a famous worthy Wight.
> By fortune's hapye Lore he Espowsyd and take hys wyfe to be
> *Barbara*, second Syster to the noble Lord *Lumle:*
> *Splendian, Hare, Jane,* and *John, Humfrey,* Also a *Lumley,*
> His Children were, of whych be dead *Jane* and eke *Humfrey.*
> His famous Monuments and dedes that lusteth for to see,
> Here in the Epytaph annext set forth at large they Be.

THE tomb of Sir *John Salusbury* is altar-shaped;
his image, and that of his lady are placed in it,
recumbent; he in armour; she with a great ruff.
Nothing is recorded of this good couple, except
that Sir *John* died in 1578; and that ten years
after she erected this monument to his memory,
and I suppose to her own, a blank being left for
the year and day of her departure.

A LITTLE further stands *Denbigh*, placed, like
Sterling, on the slope of a great rock, crowned
with a castle.   Its antient *British* name was
Castell Cled fryn yn Rhôs, or the Craggy Hill in

DENBIGH.

---

[t] Prefixed to his *Commentarioli Britannicæ descriptionis' fragmen-
tum. 4to edit.*

Rhôs, the former name of the tract in which it is seated. The word *Dinbech*, the present *Welsh* appellation, signifies a small hill, which it is, in comparison of the neighboring mountains. The first time I find any mention of it, is in the beginning of the reign of *Edward* I. from whom *Dafydd*, in defiance of his brother *Llewelyn*, chose to hold this lordship, together with the cantred of *Dyffryn Clwyd*[n]. He made it his residence till the conquest of our country: soon after which, he was taken near the place, and carried, loaded with irons, to the *English* monarch at *Rhuddlan*.

THE king politically secured his new acquisitions, by bestowing several of the great lordships on his followers. He gave that of *Denbigh* to *Henry Lacy*, earl of *Lincoln*, who built the castle, and inclosed within a wall the small town he found there. Among other priveleges, he gave his vassals liberty of killing and destroying all manner of wild beasts on the lordship, except in certain parts reserved out of the grant; I suppose for the purpose of the particular amusement of the lord[x]; for I find in the reign of *Henry* VI. the names of five parks in this lordship, viz. *Moylewike*, *Caresnodooke*, *Kylford*, *Bagh*, and *Posey*, of which the king constituted *Owen Tudor*, ranger. On the death of *Lacy*, the lordship passed to *Thomas* earl of

---

[n] *Rotulæ Walliæ*, 66.   [x] *Sebright MSS.*

Lancaster, by virtue of his marriage with *Alicia*, daughter of the last possessor. After the attainder of *Thomas*, *Edward* II. bestowed it on *Hugh D'Espencer*, who proved an oppressive superior, and abridged the inhabitants of the priveleges granted to them by *Lacy*[y]. By the fatal end of that favorite, it fell again to the crown: and was given by *Edward* III. to another, equally unfortunate, *Roger Mortimer* earl of *March*, whose death enabled the king to invest with this lordship *William Montacute* earl of *Salusbury*. He died in 1333: and on the reversal of the attainder of the earl of *March*, it was restored to his family, in the person of his grandson *Roger:* and by the marriage of *Anne*, sister to another *Roger*, last earl of *March*, with *Richard Plantagenet* earl of *Cambridge*, it came into the house of *York*, and so into the crown. Queen *Elizabeth*, in 1563, bestowed it as a most valuable gift, on her unmerited minion, *Robert Dudley* earl of *Leicester;* who soon made the country feel the weight of his oppression. Notwithstanding the tenants made him a present of two thousand pounds at his first entrance into the lordship, he remained unsatisfied; he constrained the freeholders to raise the old rents of 250*l.* a year, to 8 or 900*l.*[z] and at his will inclosed the waste lands, to the injury of the tenants,

---

[y] *Sebright MSS.*

[z] Secret Memoirs of *Robert* earl of *Leicester*, 89.

who, offended at his rapacity, rose, and levelled
his encroachments. This was construed into riot
and rebellion: two hopeful young men of the house
of *Lleweni*, were taken to *Shrewsbury*, tried and
executed there, for the pretended offence.   He
had the insolence even to mortgage the manor to
some merchants of *London*[a]; and, I apprehend,
tricked them for their credulity.   The various disorders which arose from these practices, were so
great, that *Elizabeth* interposed, and by charter
confirmed the quiet possession of the tenants, and
allayed the discontents[b].   They were again excited in the reign of king *William*, by the vast
grant made to the earl of *Portland*.   The same
ferments arose, and the same means were used to
allay them: at present, this, and the other great
manors of *Bromefield* and *Yale*, remain in the
crown, and are peacefully superintended by a
steward appointed by the king.

THE castle and inclosed part of the town, occupied a very considerable space, and were defended
by strong walls and towers: the last are chiefly
GATES.   square.   There are two gates to the outermost precinct: that called the *Burgesses Tower*, is large,
square, and built singularly, with small ashler
stones.   The other was called the *Exchequer Gate*,
in which the lord's court was kept.   Some few

---

[a] *Strype's Annals*, ii. 498.   [b] Baron *Price's* Speech.

houses, with most beautiful views, are at present inhabited in this part. *Leland* says, that there had been divers rows of streets; but in his time there were scarcely eighty householders within these walls. Here stands the chapel, called *St. Hilary's*, formerly belonging to the garrison, now the place of worship for the town. In old times, on every Sunday here were masses for the souls of *Lacy* and *Percy*[c]. Not far from it are the remains of an unfinished church, a hundred and seventy-five feet long, and seventy-one broad, and designed to have been supported by two rows of pillars. This noble building was begun in 1579, as appears by the date on a foundation-stone. It was to this purpose; for at present it is much defaced:

1mo Martii 1579
Et Regni Re: Elizabethæ 22.
W.

ON the other side appeared,

Veritas, vita, via. Duo sunt templa Dei. Unu mudus I. eiu : est Pontifex primogenties ejus verbu Dei. Alterum rationalis anima : cujus sacerdos est verus homo.

G. A. [d]

THIS church was begun under the auspices of CHURCH. *Leicester:* but it is said that he left off his buildings in *Wales*, on account of the public hatred

[c] *Leland* ITIN. v. 61.

[d] Copied from Dr. *Foulk's* Papers, among Mr. *Mytton's* MSS.

he had incurred by his tyranny[e]. A sum was afterwards collected, in order to complete the work; but report states, that when the Earl of *Essex* passed through *Denbigh,* on his *Irish* expedition, he borrowed the money destined for the purpose, which was never repayed; and by that means the church was left unfinished[f]

CASTLE.   THE castle crowns the summit of the hill, one side of which is quite precipitous. The entrance is very magnificent, beneath a gothic arch, over which is the statue of *Henry Lacy,* sitting in stately flowing robes. On each side of the gate-way stood a large octagonal tower. The breaches in it are vast and awful: they serve to discover the antient manner of building: a double wall appears to have been built, with a great vacancy between, into which were poured all sorts of rubbish, stone and hot mortar, which time consolidated to a stony hardness. This part, as *Leland* says, was never completed, the work having been deserted by the earl, on the loss of his eldest son, who was accidentally drowned in the well, whose opening is still to be seen in the castle-yard. *Charles* I. lay here on the 23d of *September,* 1645, after his retreat from *Chester,* in a tower still called *Siamber y Brenhin,* or the *King's Tower.*

THE prospect through the broken arches is ex-

---

[e] *Memoirs.*   [f] Dr. *Foulk's* Papers.

tremely fine, extending in parts over the whole vale, and all its eastern hills, from *Moel Fenlli*, to *Diserth* rock; a rich view, but deficient in water: the river *Clwyd* being usually too small to be seen; and in great rains so furious, as to overflow a vast extent of the meadowy tract.

LELAND relates a particular of this fortress, which I do not find in any other historian; he says, that *Edward* IV. was besieged in it: and that he was permitted to retire, on condition that he should quit the kingdom for ever. The only time in which that prince was constrained to abdicate his dominions, was in 1470, when he took shipping at *Lynn;* not by reason of any capitulation with his enemies, but through the desperate situation of his affairs at that period.

Jasper Tudor, earl of *Pembroke,* had, in the year 1459, possessed this place, and several others in the principality, in behalf of his weak half-bro- ther *Henry* VI.[g] but they were wrested from him by the *Yorkists* in the following year. In 1468 he returned, was joined by two thousand *Welsh,* and burnt the town[h]; meditating revenge rather than conquest.

IN the beginning of *November* 1645, the parle- ment army obtained, near this town, a most im-

[g] *Dugdale Baron.* ii. 241.   [h] *Carte,* ii. 775.

BATTLE. portant victory over the royalists. The latter, under the command of Sir *William Vaughan*, had formed a considerable body of forces, *Welsh* and *Irish*, with a design of marching to the relief of *Chester*, then besieged; Sir *William Brereton* had notice of the design, and immediately detached that able officer *Mytton*, and under him colonel *Jones* and colonel *Louthian*, with one thousand four hundred horse, and a thousand foot, to frustrate the plan. *Mytton* did his duty, attacked the royalists with vigor, and after several hot engagements totally routed them, took five hundred horse and four hundred foot, killed one hundred, and so entirely dispersed them, as not to leave a hundred together in one place[i].

SIEGE. IN 1646, we find the castle garrisoned by the loyalists: its governor was colonel *William Salusbury*, of *Bachymbyd*, commonly called *Salusbury Hosanau gleision*, or *Blue Stockings*. The siege was begun under the conduct of major-general *Mytton*, about the 16th of *July*[k]; but such was the gallant defence of the besieged, that it was not surrendered till the 3d of *November*, and then only on the most honourable conditions[l]. It is very remarkable, that notwithstanding the orders of fallen majesty, in *June*, for the general surrender

[i] *Whitelock*, 179.   [k] The same, 216.
[l] The same, 226. For the Articles of Capitulation, see *Appendix*.

of every garrison in *England* and *Wales*, on fair
and honourable terms, yet the first which yielded
in *North Wales*, held out above two months
longer than the last *English* castle.

THE priory of *Carmelites*, or *White Friars*,   PRIORY.
stood at the bottom of the town.   It was founded
by *John Salusbury* of *Lleweni*, who died, as appeared from a mutilated brass, found in the conventual church, on the 7th of *March*, 1289[m].
Speed ascribes the building to one *John de Sunimore*,
in 1399; but the inscription fixes the honor on
Salusbury.   On the dissolution, this house was
granted to *Richard Andreas* and *William L'Isle*.
The church, now converted into a barn, is the only
remaining building: it was the burying-place of the
family of the founder, till the reformation; some
of their tombs were to be seen here within memory
of man.

THE present town covers great part of the slope
of the hill, and some streets extend along the
plain.   Its manufactures in shoes and gloves are   TRADE.
very considerable; great quantities are annually
sent to *London*, to the great warehouses of the
Capital, and for the purposes of exportation.

THE constitution of this borough, and its origin,
will be fully explained by the following transcript,
communicated to me by one of its burgesses.   It

[m] *Collins's Baronets*, Edit. 1720, i. 82.

CHARTER. begins by citing the last charter, which is that
granted by king *Charles* II. which recites letters
patent granted by queen *Elizabeth,* and dated at
Westminster the 20th of *June,* in the thirty-ninth
year of her reign; in which the said queen recites,
" That seeing *Edward* I. by his letters patent,
dated at *Northampton* the 29th of *August,* in the
eighteenth year of his reign, hath granted to *Henry
de Lacy,* earl of *Lincoln,* that all his men, then
inhabiting his town of *Denbigh,* or that should for
ever inhabit it, through all his territories, formerly
belonging to the king of *Wales,* and also through
the counties of *Chester, Salop, Stafford, Glouces-
ter, Worcester,* and *Hereford,* should be free and
acquitted for ever from all toll, stallage, payage,
panage, murage, pontage, and passage; and seeing
also king *Edward* III. by his letters patent, dated
at *York* the 27th of *October,* in the sixth year of
his reign, hath, for himself, and his heirs, and successors, then inhabiting, and afterwards to inhabit
the said town, should, through the kingdom and
dominions, be free and acquitted from all such toll,
stallage, payage, murage, pontage, and passage;
and seeing also that *Richard* II. by his letters
patent, dated at *Westminster* the 22d of *February,*
in the second year of his reign, granted to the above-
said men, that the aforesaid town of *Denbigh,* and
half a mile compass about the town, should be a free
borough, and that the men inhabiting, and after-

wards to inhabit, should be free burgesses; and seeing also that *Richard* III. by his letters dated at *Westminster*, the 10th of *December*, in the second year of his reign, confirmed the aforesaid grants, and by his said letters patent did grant unto the said burgesses, their heirs and assigns, being *Englishmen*, common of pasture for all manner of cattle, at all times in the year, in the common pasture of the town and forest of *Lleweney;* and that the burgesses aforesaid, and their heirs and assigns, should be free and acquitted in all his dominions and territories in *England* and *Ireland,* soc, sac, toll, and them, lastage, stallage, payage, pannage, pontage, murage, and other customs whatsoever. And the aforesaid queen *Elizabeth*, by her said letters patent, did ordain, constitute, grant, and confirm, that the town and borough of *Denbigh* may extend, on every side, one mile and a half, according to the common acceptations of that place, from the high cross standing in the market-place of the said town; and that the said town and borough of itself, and the burgesses of the said borough, now and hereafter in being, be, and shall be for ever hereafter, one body corporate and politick, in things, fact, and name, by the name of "The ALDERMEN, BAILIFFS, and BURGESSES of the borough of *Denbigh;*" and it is also ordained, that there be a common seal for transacting of any causes or businesses; and also ordained, that there be two aldermen, two bailiffs, and two coroners, and twenty-five of the better sort and best reputed of the burgesses, to be capital burgesses and counsellors of the said borough."

"THE aldermen and bailiffs are elected and nominated upon *Michaelmas-day*, yearly. There are two other officers, called serjeants at mace (or mace-bearers) for the execution of processes and mandates issuing out of the court of the said borough; they are appointed by the bailiffs of the said borough for the time being.

"THERE is also a recorder of the said borough, who is appointed by the aldermen, bailiffs, and capital burgesses.

"CONSTABLES, leavelookers, and other inferior officers, are likewise appointed by the aldermen, bailiffs, and capital burgesses.

"THERE is a council chamber, or guild, within the said borough, for the purpose of holding and sitting courts of convocation, before the aldermen, bailiffs, and capital burgesses.

"THERE is a court of record, to be held every other *Friday* through the year, before the bailiffs of the said borough, or one of them; and in that court, by complaint made in it, they may hold all and all manner of pleas, actions, suits, demands of all sorts of transgressions *vi et armis*, or otherwise; and also all and all manner of debts, accounts, bargains, frauds, detaining of deeds, writings, muniments, and taking and detaining of beasts and cattle, or goods; and all contracts whatsoever, arising within the said borough; and that such pleas, suits, and actions be heard and terminated before the bailiffs, or one of them.

"THE aldermen are justices, and hold quarter sessions, in the same manner as county sessions are held by statute, to hear and determine causes; but not to proceed in case of death, or loss of life or limb.

"No country justice to intermeddle with any matters or things whatsoever, appertaining to the office of justice of the peace, which shall arise or happen within the borough.

"RESIANT burgesses are to serve upon jury at the sessions.

"THE aldermen and bailiffs are commissioners of array.

"THE resiant burgesses are voters for a member for the borough."

I CANNOT but record the virtue of those of the year 1572, who had the courage to withstand the insinuations, the promises, and the threats, of as unprincipled a lord as this kingdom was ever afflicted with; who had power to inflict, and will to execute, any vengeance that opposition to his arbitrary inclinations might excite. In that year it was his pleasure that one *Henry Dynne* should represent this borough in parlement; the burgesses were refractory, and chose another person, which gave rise to the following letter, which I print, as a *sans pareille.*

A L^{re} sent from the earle of *Leicester* to the bay-liffe, aldermen, and burgesses, greatlie blaminge them for making choice of the burges of the parliament without his lordship's consente, and commanding them to allter their electione, and to chose *Henrie Dynne.*

I HAVE bene latlie advertised how small consideration youe have had of the L^{re} I wrote unto you, for the nomynasion of yor burgess, wherat as I cannot but greatlie mervayle (in re-spect I am yor L. and you my-Tenaunts, as also the manie good tournes and comodities wch I have bene allwayes willinge to procure youe, for the benefitte of yor whole state) so do I take the same in so ——, and vill yte so unthankfullie, as yf youe do not uppon receite hereof presentlie revoke the same, and appointe suche one as I shall nominate, namelie, *Henrie Dynne,* be ye well assured never to loke for any ffrienshipe or favo^r at my hande, in any yor affayres herafter; not for any great accompt I make of the thinge, but for that I would not it shou'd be thought that I have so small regard borne

me at yor hands, who are bounden to owe (as yor
L.) thus much dutie as to know myne advice and
pleasure; that will haplie be aleadged, that yor
choice was made before the receipt of my L^{res} (in
relie I would litle have thoughte that youe would
have bene so forgetfull, or rather carelesse of me,
as before yor elecion not to make me privie therto,
or at the least to have some desire of myne advise
therein (havinge tyme ynoughe so to do) but as you
have of yor selfes thus rashlie proceded herein,
without myne assent, soe have I thought good to
signifie unto youe, that I mean not to take it in any
wise at yor hands, and therefore wysh you more
advisedlie to consider hereof, and to deale with me
as maye continue my fav^r towards you, otherwise
loke for no fav^r at my hands; and so fare ye well.
From the Court, this last day of *Aprill*, 1572.

R. LEYCESTER.

THIS doughty letter had no effect: the burgesses
adhered to their own choice, and *Richard Candishe*, gent. stands as member for *Denbigh* in that
year[n]. Mr. *Candishe* appears to have been a gentleman that did honour to the election of the burgesses. He was the son of *Richard Candishe* esq;
of a good family in *Suffolk*, and an inhabitant of
Hornsey, near *London*, where he died. A neat

[n] *Willis Notitiæ Parliam.* iii. 98.

monument was erected to his memory in *Hornsey*
church: it is in form of a pyramid; *promised and
raised* (as the inscription imports) *by* MARGARET
Countess of CUMBERLAND, 1601: above this is a
goat, the crest of the house of *Bedford*, and above
that a coronet°. The reason does not appear,
but possibly it was on the account of his merit,
which the epitaph records to have been of most
uncommon magnitude.

An epitaph upon the death of the worshipfull and
rarely accomplished master *Richard Candish*,
of *Suffolk*, esq;

> *Candish* derived from noble parentage,
>   Adorn'd with virtuous and heroicke partes;
> Most learned, bountifull, devout, and sage,
>   Graced with the graces, muses, and the artes.
> Deer to his prince, in English court admir'd,
>   Belov'd of great and honourable peeres:
> Of all esteem'd, embraced, and desir'd,
>   'Till death cut off his well employed yeares.
> Within this earth, his earth entombed lies,
>   Whose heavenly part surmounted hath the skies.

Such a man was by no means a likely object of the
patronage of this worthless favourite. *Leicester*
did but copy his mistress in his contempt of privelege of parlements: *Elizabeth* thought them the
mere instruments of giving sanction to her will: for

° Mr. *Candishe*'s arms are on one side of the pyramid; three piles
wavy gules in a field argent; the crest a fox's head erased azure.

if they once presumed to oppose it, she without ceremony informed them of her displeasure. *Peter Wentworth*, for the simple proposition ' that a ' member of parlement might, without controlment ' of his person, or danger of the laws, by bill or ' speech, utter any of the griefs of this common- ' wealth whatsoever, touching the service of GOD, ' the safety of the prince, and this noble realm,' was sent to the tower; and to the petition of the house for his release, an answer was returned, that it *was very unfit for her majesty to give any account of her actions.* Her prerogative was the rule of government: the great council was expressly forbidden to meddle in matters of state, or in causes ecclesiastical[p]: and this was the GOLDEN REIGN of ELIZABETH!

LACY, earl of *Lincoln*, brought with him several *English* families, who settled here; such as the *Lathams, Knowsleys, Curthose, Pigots, Heitons,* and *Peaks:* the two last left posterity which continue to this day. The *Pigots* purchased land in the parish of *Llanyfydd*, and left to the house the name of *Plâs Pigot.* The *Chambers* were another family settled in *Wales* at the same time: the first was chamberlain to the great earl, as appears by this memorandum: *Henricus de Lacy,* comes *Lincoln* constablarius *Cestriæ* D. de *Roos* et *Reweiniok,* concessit *John. de la Chambre camerario* pro ho-

p *Drake's Parliam. Hist.* iv. 396.

magio et servitio suo duas carucutas terræ cum per-
tinentiis in *Lewenny.* The old mansion, called
Plâs Chambres, stands near *Denbigh Green.* *John*
Chambres, esq; the last owner of that name, died
within memory of man.

GWAENYNOG. FROM *Denbigh* I went to the hospitable house
of *Gwaenynog,* about two miles distant, fronted by
the most majestic oaks in our principality[q]. The
fine wooded dingles belonging to the demesne are
extremely well worth visiting: they are most judiciously cut into walks by the owner, *John Myddel-*
ton esq; and afford as beautiful scenery in their kind,
as any we have to boast. *Moel Famma* superbly
terminates one view; and the ruins of *Denbigh*
Castle burst awfully at the termination of the concluding path.

IN rummaging over the family papers of this
house, I met with an anecdote of it, too singular to
be suppressed. It will prove at lest that private
morals, and respect to the laws, were in that distant
period but in a very low state; for no notice seems
to have been taken of so atrocious an offence.
The criminal enjoyed the favor of the crown, in
common with others its peaceful subjects.

David Myddelton, who is styled receiver of
Denbigh in the nineteenth of *Edward* IV. and

---

[q] Age and the axe have nearly destroyed the whole of these venerable trees, and of the adjacent woods. *Gwaenynog* now belongs to
the Reverend Dr. *Myddelton.* ED.

Valectus Coronæ D^u Regis, in the second of
Richard III. made his addresses to *Elyn,* daughter
of Sir *John Done,* of *Utkinton,* in *Cheshire,* and
gained the lady's affections; but the parents preferred their relation, *Richard Done,* of *Croton.*
The marriage was accordingly celebrated; which
David having notice of, watched the groom leading
his bride out of church, killed him on the spot, and
then carried away his mistress, and married her
the same day; so that she was a maid, widow, and
wife twice, in one day. From *Roger,* the eldest
son of the match, descended the *Myddeltons* of
this place.

I MENTION *Thomas Myddelton,* another of his
progeny, only to prove, that the custom of the
Irish howl([1]), or *Scotch Coranich,* was in use
among us; for we are told he was buried *cum
magno dolore et clamore cognatorum et propin-
quorum omnium.*

IN this house is a head of *George Griffith,*
bishop of *St. Asaph,* consecrated, October 28th
1660, to this see, in reward for his piety and great
sufferings in the royal cause. He was of the house
of *Penrhyn,* in *Caernarvonshire,* to which he added
fresh lustre by the excellency of his conduct. He
is dressed in a square cap, a turnover, and in his

([1]) This is borne out by the Mabinogi of the Lady of the Fountain;
see *Guest's Mabinogion,* i. 16, 57. J.R.

robes. He died exactly six years after his conse
cration, and was interred under a plain stone in his
own cathedral.

HENLLAN.

HAVING made *Gwaenynog* my head quarters
for this neighborhood, I one day visited from thence
Henllan, the parish church of these parts; remarkable for the schism between church and steeple:
the first having retreated into the bottom, the last
maintains its station on the top of the hill. The
church is covered with shingles; a species of roof
almost obsolete. *St. Sadwrn,* or *St. Saturnus,*
cotemporary to *St. Wenefrede,* has it under his
protection. Here was interred Sir *Peter Mutton,*
knight, descended from *Richard Mutton, of Rhuddlan,* and *Elen,* daughter to *John (Aer Hên) Conway, of Bodrhyddan.* Sir *Peter,* as his epitaph
informs us, was chief justice of *North Wales,* a
master in chancery, prothonotary, and clerk of the
crown. He died *November* the 4th, 1637. He
had the honor of representing the borough of *Caernarvon;* and once occasioned much diversion to
the house, by asserting, in one of his speeches,
" that he remembered fourteen years *before* he
was born, &c. &c." But he was a good judge, and
made a fair fortune, and acquired the estate of
Llanerch, by purchase from *Edward Gryffydd*
esq; his mother's elder brother, which passed
with his daughter to *Robert Davies, of Gwysaney,*
esq.

LLANERCH stands most advantageously in a LLANERCH·
small but beautiful park, with a fine piece of water
at the bottom, and commanding a rich view of the
vale, and a long extent of the *Clwydian* hills, with
their fertile sides terminating in heathy summits.
The venerable old house, particularly the respectable antient hall, is spoiled by modern alteration,
and frittered into an errant villa. The former
gardens were made by *Mutton Davies* esq; on
his return out of *Italy*, in the last century, and
were fine in that sort of style, decorated with water-
works and statues, emitting water from various
parts, to the astonishment of the rustic spectators.
On the death of *John Davies* esq; on *March* 8th,
1785, the place, and considerable estates, fell to
his two sisters[q], *Lætitia*, since married to *Daniel
Leo* esq; of the kingdom of *Ireland*, and *Mary*,
relict of *Philip Puleston* esq; of *Havod y wern*,
near *Wrexham*.

IN this parish is *Foxhall*, the antient seat of the FOXHALL.
Rosyndales, of *Rosyndale*, in the north, who came
into this country in 1297, but soon changed their
names to *Lloyd:* It is to this day the property of one

[q] Both deceased.—The estates were divided; Mrs. *Leo* bequeathed
her portion to her husband's son, who now possesses *Llanerch ;* Mrs.
Puleston's share descended to her only daughter, the wife of *Bryan
Cooke* esq. of *Owston*, in *Yorkshire*. On the death of Mr. *Leo* in *March*
1810, the *Llanerch* estates reverted to the family which had so long
possessed them, most happy in its representative the reverend *White-
hall Davies*. ED.

of their descendants, the Reverend Mr. *Lloyd*, of *Aston*, in *Shropshire;* near it upstarted a new *Foxhall*, part of a magnificent design conceived by Mr. *John Panton*, recorder of *Denbigh*, and member for the borough in 1592 and 1601. One wing only was built. The ambition of the founder was to eclipse the other *Foxhall:* but he became bankrupt, and was obliged to sell the unfinished house, and the little estate which belonged to it, to the very neighbor whom he wished to outshine. He died in 1614, and was buried at *Henllan*.

Not far from *Henllan* church, in the parish of *Llanyfydd*, on the bank of the brook *Meirchion*, are the remains of a seat of *Meredydd ap Meirchion* or *Merach y Meirch*, lord of *Isdulas*. Part is now standing, particularly the chapel, which serves for a farm-house; but some very extensive foundations shew its former importance.

From hence, after a ride of a few miles, I reached *Dyffryn Aled*, or the vale of the river *Aled*, a very narrow tract bounded by high hills. The old house of *Dyffryn Aled* stood in the bottom: it had been for many generations the seat of the *Wynnes*, descended from *Marchudd*, one of the XV tribes of *North Wales*, lord of *Brynffanigl*, near *Abergeleu*. *Diana Wynne*, daughter and sole heiress to *Pyers Wynne* esq; the last male heir, married first *Ridgeway Owen Meyric* esq;

Dyffryn
Aled.

of   in *Yorkshire*, afterwards *Phillip Yorke* esq; of *Erddig*, in *Denbighshire*[r]. During her widowhood she built a new house, in a most elegant and magnificent manner, on the side of the hill opposite to the antient mansion, and cased it with stone brought from the quarries near *Bath*. The very day after the masons had finished their work, almost the whole casing fell down, which occasioned a vast expence in the repair.

AT the head of the valley stand the village and church of *Llansannan*, dedicated to *St. Sannan*, confessor and hermit; descended (for our very saints boast of their pedigree) from antient parentage, near the territory of the father of *St. Wenefrede*, with whom he maintained strict friendship. Their remains were both interred at *Gwytherin;* to which place, though unworthy, I resolved on an immediate pilgrimage.

IN my way, I descended a very steep wooded dell, in the township of *Penared*, to visit the gloomy cataract of *Llyn yr ogo*, where the *Aled* tumbles into a horrible black cavern, overshaded by oaks. Somewhat higher up is another, exposed to full day, falling from a vast height, and dividing the naked glen. *Llyn Aled*, the lake from which the river flows, lies at a small distance, amidst black

LLAN-SANNAN.

LLYN YR OGO.

[r] *Dyffryn Aled* now belongs to *Pyers Wynne Yorke* esq. the eldest son of the worthy persons above-mentioned. ED.

and heathy mountains, through which runs much
of the road to *Gwytherin.*

GWYTHERIN. THAT little village and church stand on a bank,
at the head of a small vale, near the rise of the
Elwy. The church is celebrated for the honor of
ST. WENE- having first received the remains of St. *Wenefrede,*
FREDE. after her second death. On the decease of *St.
Beuno,* she was warned by a voice to call on *St.
Deifer,* at *Bodfari;* by *St. Deifer* she was directed
to go to *St. Saturnus,* at *Henllan;* and by *St.
Saturnus,* to seek a final retreat with *St. Elerius,*
at *Gwytherin.* Hither she repaired, found a convent of nuns, received the veil from the saint, and,
on the death of the abbess *Theonia,* succeeded to
the high charge. *St. Wenefrede* died on the third
of *November,* and rested here in quiet, near the
body of her predecessor, for the space of five hundred years. By reason of a miracle, wrought, as
was supposed, by her intercession, on a monk of
HER *Shrewsbury,* the abbot determined on the trans-
REMAINS
TRANSLATED. lation of her remains to their monastery. Seven
holy men were deputed: the inhabitants of *Gwytherin* refused to part with such a treasure: visions
determined the former to persist in their request:
and at length, on the declaration of the will of
heaven, by another vision, to the parson of *Gwytherin,* who declared to his flock the impiety of
farther resistance, the reliques were delivered up,

and carried in triumph to their place of destination[s]. The prior at this time was *Robert.* Mr. *William Mytton*[t] calls him *Pennant.* If he was of the neighborhood of *Holywell,* I do not wonder he was so anxious about the remains of his countrywoman, which he knew could not fail enriching his house, by virtue of the miracle-craft so frequent in that age.

In the church is shewn the box in which her reliques were kept, before their removal to *Shrewsbury.* Here is also an antient grave-stone, with a flowery cross and chalice (the last denoting the priestly profession of the deceased) with *Hic jacet Lowarch Mab Cadell,* inscribed on the cross.

THE Saint's Chapel, *Capel Gwenfrewi,* is now totally destroyed: it stood on the south side of the church; but nothing remains, except some slight ditches and foundations. In this chapel was a tomb-stone with a singular cross engraven on it, and by the cross an antient battle-axe, the usual weapon of the deceased. I have a copy of the drawing, taken from the original by Mr. *Edward Llwyd,* in the *Sebright* collection.

ON the north side of the church-yard stand four rude upright stones. On one is roughly cut an

[s] This, and much more, may be seen in the Life of *St. Wenefrede,* pp. 88, &c.

[t] Antiquities of *Shropshire,* folio MS.

inscription, for which I refer to the supplemental plates.([1])

IN my return, I followed the course of the *Elwy*, by *Havodynos*, the seat of *Howel Lloyd*[t] esq; by the church and village of *Llangerniew;* by *Garthewin*, the seat of *Robert Wynn* esq; commanding a most lively view of a fertile little valley, bounded by hills, covered with hanging woods; and by *Llanfair Dólhaearn*([2]), a village and church at a small distance above the conflux of the *Elwy* and *Aled.* Mr. *Wynn* is descended from *Gronou Llwyd*, surnamed *Penwyn*, of *Melay*, in this neighborhood, a branch of *Marchudd*, but with different arms. In this parish, above the *Elwy*, was one of the residences of *Hedd Molwynog*, descended from RODERICK THE GREAT, king of all *Wales.* A large moat called *Yr Hên Llys*, marks the place; as the field styled *Maes y Bendithion*, does the spot where the poor received his alms[u]. *Molwynog* was chief of one of the fifteen tribes of *North Wales;* was cotemporary with *Dafydd ap Owen Gwynedd*, and assisted that prince to carry

(margin notes:) LLAN-GERNIEW.

YR HEN LLYS.

([1]) The "supplemental plates" here referred to, were, on examination, found too much worn to supply impressions for this work. ED.

　　　　[t] Now of his son, *John Lloyd* esq. ED.

([2]) This *is* now called *Llanfair Talhaearn*: what authority there is for *Dolhaearn*, I do not know; but writers of Pennant's time never felt themselves in the least bound to give place-names as they found them, if they happened to have a theory of their own as to their etymology. J.R.

　　　　[u] *Llwyd's Itin.* i. 14. MS.

fire and sword through *England,* even to the walls of *Coventry.* A descendant of his third son, *Gwrgi,* peopled *North Wales* with *Llwyds;* for *Bleyddyn,* the son of *Bleyddyn Fychan,* assuming the addition of *Llwyd,* or the *Grey,* founded the house of *Havodynos.* Among his good deeds must be told, that to him is owing the stone bridge at *Llansannan.*

I HOPE my countrymen will not grow indignant when I express my fears, that in very early times we were as fierce and savage as the rest of *Europe:* and they will bear this the better, when they reflect, that they keep pace with it in civilization, and in the progress of every fine art. We cannot deny but that we were, to the excess,

> Jealous in honor, sudden and quick in quarrel.

Two gentlemen of this house exemplify the assertion. *Meiric ap Bleyddyn,* resentful of the injuries which he and his tenants received from the *English* judges and officers, slew one of the first, and hanged several of the latter on the oaks of his woods; by which he forfeited to the crown the lands, still known in these parts by the name of *Tir Meiric Llwyd,* or the estate of *Meiric Llwyd*[x] As to his person, he secured it within the sanctuary at *Halston*[y]; and marrying, founded in that neighborhood the house of *Llwyn y Maen.*

---

[x] *Llwyd's Itin.* i. 16.   [y] See vol. i. p. 305, of this work.

VOL. II.   N

Bleyddyn Fychan, another of this race, fell out with his tenants, and in a fit of fury, chased them from his estate, and turned it into a forest[z]; a pretty picture of the manners of the times! The place lies in the parish of *Llansannan*, and bears the name of *Forest* to this day.

LLAN-
RHAIADR.

RETURNED to *Gwaenynog*, and passing beneath *Denbigh Castle*, visit *Llanrhaiadr*, a village in the middle of the vale, remarkable for an east window of good and very entire painted glass, expressing a favorite subject of the time, the root of *Jesse*. The patriarch is represented sprawling at the bottom, with a genealogical tree issuing out of him, containing all the kings of *Israel* and *Juda*, up to our SAVIOUR. The branches around the kings are in very beautiful foliage; at the top is a rose of *Lancaster*, and another with an eye in glory within it; the window being done in 1533, after the accession of that house. Here, in a vast monument of *Maurice Jones*, of *Llanrhaiadr*, esq; may be seen

Eternal buckle take in *Parian* stone.

His figure is lying down, leaning on his arm, in his gown, with his wig in excellent curl, and surrounded by weeping *genii*, and much funebrial absurdity.

[z] *Llwyd's Itin.* i. 15.

IN the church-yard is a common altar-tomb of a gentleman, who chose to build his fame on the long series of ancestors which distinguished his from vulgar clay. It tells us, that

HEARE LYETH THE BODY OF
JOHN, AP ROBERT, OF PORTH, AP
DAVID, AP GRIFFITH, AP DAVID
VAUCHAN. AP BLETHYN AP
GRIFFITH, AP MEREDITH,
AP JERWORTH, AP LLEWELYN,
AP JERORH, AP HEILIN, AP
COWRYD, AP CADVAN, AP
ALAWGWA, AP CADELL, THE
KING OF POWYS, WHO
DEPARTED THIS LIFE THE
XX DAY OF MARCH, IN THE
YEAR OF OUR LORD GOD
1642, AND OF
HIS AGE XCV.

OPPOSITE to the church is the house of *Llan-rhaiadr*, partly antient, partly rebuilt by *Richard Parry* esq; the late owner, who, within these three years, disposed of it to *Richard Wilding*, esq; of *Leverpool*. It originally belonged to the *Salusburies;* it was conveyed to *John Lloyd* esq; of *Bodidrys*, by his marriage with *Catherine,* daughter of *Henry Salusbury* esq. Sir *Evan Lloyd* bart. of *Bodidrys*, sold it to the above *Maurice Jones*, and from him it descended to *Robert*, father of the late owner.

ON an eminence to the north-west of the church,

called *Cader Gwladus,* or *Gwladus's*[a] *Chair,* is an
extremely beautiful view of the vale between *Den-*
bigh and *Ruthin,* and the whole breadth chequered
with wood, meadows, and corn-fields; and almost
the whole range of the eastern limits soaring far
above it. *Denbigh* Castle from hence shews itself
to great advantage, with its walls and towers extending along the precipitous base.

AT the foot of this rising is *Ffynnon St. Dyfnog,*
a fine spring dedicated to *St. Dyfnog,* one of our
long pedigreed saints; formerly much resorted to
by votaries. The fountain is inclosed in an angular wall, decorated with small human figures; and
before is the well for the use of the pious bathers.

NEAR this are some comfortable alms-houses
for eight widows, founded by Mrs. *Jones,* of *Llan-*
rhaiadr (a *Bagot*) in 1729: each has her garden,
and two shillings a week.

HERE the diocese of *Bangor* encroaches on that
of *St. Asaph,* and takes out of it the beautiful parish
of *Llanrhaiadr,* and all the upper end of the vale.

NEAR the road to *Ruthin* is *Bachymbyd,* a seat
and estate belonging to Lord *Bagot,* which came
into the family by the marriage of his great grandfather Sir *Walter Bagot,* with *Jane,* daughter and
sole heiress to *Charles Salusbury* esq. Near the

---

[a] A common *Welsh* name.

side of the road are to be seen some very fine ches- nut([1]) trees; one of which is near twenty-four feet in circumference. The reader need not be told, that this species of tree is not a native of *Great Britain*, nor even of *Europe*. We are indebted for it to the *Romans*, who probably first planted it in *Kent*, where it has been so fully naturalized, as to form, in certain tracts, great woods; in other parts of the kingdom, it every where appears cultivated; as sparingly as it might have been originally in *Italy*, after it had been brought from *Lydia*, its native place[b]

REACH *Ruthin*([2]), and enter under *Porth y Dwr*, its only remaining gate. The town is pleasantly seated, on the easy slope and summit of a rising ground. The castle stood on the south side, and in part sunk beneath the earth: its poor remains impend over the fall of land fronting the west, where a fragment or two of a tower are still to be seen, mixed with the native rock, which in parts serves as a facing to the fortress, whose base was formed out of it; a very deep foss, hewn out of the live stone, with a portal at each end, divides

---

([1]) They are *Spanish* ones. T.P.

[b] *Sardibus eæ* provenere primum. Ideo apud *Græcos, Sardianos balanos* appellant. *Plin. Hist. Nat.* lib. xv. c. 23.

([2]) *Ruthin* is pronounced in *Welsh* Rhuthin, and seems to mean *Rhudd-ddin*, or red fort, as indicated by the other name of *Castell Coch*, not to mention that the castle now certainly is red. J.R.

it breadthways. Honest *Churchyard*, with great
truth and simplicity, thus describes the work:

> This castle stands on rocke much like red bricke,
>   The dykes are cut with toole throughe stonie cragge;
> The towers are hye, the walles are large and thicke,
>   The worke itself would shake a subject's bagge.

A DRAWING I discovered in the *British Museum*, shews that it soared high above the ground,
and that its numerous towers well merited the
poet's praise.

THE views from the summit of the ruins, are
very well worthy of the traveller's attention. If
he is fond of a more aerial one, I would by all
means have him ascend the heights of *Bwlch pen y
Barras*, from whence is a full prospect of our
boasted vale, and the remote hills of our *Alpine*
tract.

THE *Welsh* name of the fortress is *Castell Gôch
yn Gwernvor*[c]. Possibly our countrymen had
here a strong-hold before the time of *Edward* I.
who built the castle whose ruins we survey[d], and
bestowed it, in 1281, with the cantred of *Dyffryn
Clwyd*, on *Reginald de Grey;* for which he, in 1301,
did homage, at *Chester*, to *Edward* of *Caernarvon*,
then prince of *Wales*. The king added at the
same time the townships of *Maesmynnan, Penbedw,*

c *Llwyd's Itin.* MS. iii. 61.   d *Rotulæ Walliæ*, 66.

and *Blowite*, as dependencies on the castle; and I ought to add the land of *Wenchal de Lacy*. Out of this antient cantred was formed the present lordship of *Ruthin*, which comprehends several parishes. It remained in the family of the *Greys* till the time of *Richard* earl of *Kent*, who having dissipated his fortune by gaming, sold it to *Henry* VII. Queen *Elizabeth* bestowed it on *Ambrose Dudley*, earl of *Warwick*; and it is now in possession of *Richard Myddelton* esq; of *Chirk Castle*. I must observe, that this lordship was directed by *Edward* the Second, to contribute two hundred foot soldiers for his *Scottish* expedition, in 1309; but, in 1325, only one man at arms and thirty footmen were required[e].

THE inhabitants, united with those of *Denbigh* and *Holt*, send a representative to parlement.

THE town of *Ruthin* was burnt by *Owen Glyndwr*, on *September* the 20th, 1400. He took the opportunity of surprising it during the fair, enriched his followers with the plunder, and then retired to his fastnesses among the hills.

BURNT BY GLYNDWR.

IN the seventeenth century, the castle was garrisoned by the loyalists, and sustained in 1646, a siege, from *February* to the middle of *April*; when it surrendered, with two months provisions,

[e] *Rymer*, iii. 157. iv. 137.

to general *Mytton*[f]; who received the thanks of
the house for his services; the commons ordered
Mr. *Fogge*, his chaplain, fifty pounds for bringing
the news, and confirmed the general's appointment
of lieutenant-colonel *Mason* to the government of
the new conquest[g]. The fortress was afterwards
demolished by an order of the house.

THE church is large, yet only a chapel to *Llanruth*. The roof prettily divided into small squares,
ornamented with sculpture, and marked with the
names of the workmen. The only monument of
any note, is that of Doctor *Gabriel Goodman*, dean
of *Westminster* in the time of queen *Elizabeth*,
whose figure is represented by a bust. This illustrious divine was a native of *Ruthin*, and was
greatly distinguished by his various merit. As a
churchman, he acquired great fame by his trans-

[f] General *Mytton*, in the preceding year, issued his protections in
the following form: the original of which is in the possession of
Paul Panton esq. of *Plasgwyn*.

"These are to require You nott to molest or trouble Mr. *John
Price* of *Derwen* in (ye Country of *Denbigh* in his pson, horses, estate, or offering any other violence to him without speciall orders
from me, or the Committee of *North Wales*—Dated ye 16th off *February* 1645.)

THO. MYTTON.

To all Commanders officers and
   souldiers in the service
   of the kinge and pliamt within
   ye Six Countyes of *North Wales*.   ED.

[g] *Drake*'s Parlement. Hist. xiv. 355.

lation of the epistle to the *Corinthians*, being an assistant in the version of the bible into *English:* as a philanthropist, his foundation for a hospital for twelve poor people, and a warden (who is the clergyman of the place) perpetuates his benevolent turn: and his affection to learned men is evident, not only by his establishing here a free school for this parish, and that of *Llan-Elidan*, with a stipend to the master of half the tithes of the parish of *Llan-Elidan*, now amounting to above a hundred and twenty pounds a year; but by his being the patron of the great *Camden*[h], whom he enabled to take those travels, which produced the finest collection of provincial antiquities ever extant.

THE church was originally conventual, and belonged to a house of *Bonhommes*[i], a species of *Augustins*, introduced into *England* in 1283: but the time of their continuance here could be but very short; for, in 1310, *John*, son of *Reginald de Grey*, made it collegiate, and established seven regular priests, with an endowment of two hundred and five acres of land, in *Rhosmeryon* and *Rue*, besides other lands, and woods, a mill, pasture for twenty-three cows and a bull; and *pannage*, or the free keeping of sixty hogs in the woods of the lordship[k]. For these, and several other good

---

[h] *Camden Middlesex*, i. 385.   [i] *Leland Itin*. iii. 135.
[k] *Dugdale's Monast*. iii. pars ii. 57.

things, the said priests were for ever to celebrate
daily a solemn mass, for the souls of *Edward* I.
queen *Eleanor, Reginald de Grey,* and *Matilda*
his wife, the founder and his wife, all their friends
and relations, and of all the benefactors to this
church[l].

John de Grey was possibly buried here; and his
might be the tomb, which *Churchyard* calls that of
an earl of *Kent:* it stood in the chancel, and in his
days was placed on the right side of the choir.

THE apartments of the priests were joined to the
church by a cloister; part of which is built up, and
serves as the mansion of the warden. When *John
de Grey* undertook this work, he obtained the consent of Sir *Hugh,* then rector of *Llanruth;* to
whom he allows this to have been subordinate, by
custom as well as right[m]

IN 1583, here were left in charge four incum-
bents, with pensions from six pounds to one pound
six shillings and eight-pence each[n].   The lands
were granted by *Edward* VI. to *William Winlove*
and *Richard Fyld*[o].

Ruthin, and several other parishes, which formerly composed the cantref of *Dyffryn Clwyd,*
form a deanery in the diocese of *Bangor,* bearing
the antient name.

[l] *Dugdale's Monast.* iii. pars ii. 57.   [m] The same.
     [n] *Willis Abbies, ii.* 311.   [o] *Tanner,* 708.

Leland mentions a house of white friers[p] in this town, but gives no particulars. It possibly stood in the street, to this day called *Prior's Street.*

Reginald de Grey settled in this country several of his followers, such as the *Thelwalls, Goodmans, Moyles, Jervises, Towerbridges,* and *Alsbels;* which last, corrupted to *Ashpool,* remained at a house called *Plâs Ashpool,* in the parish of *Llandurnog,* in the lower end of the vale of *Clwyd,* within my memory. The last of the line, an amiable young lady, in a deep decay, married an *Irishman* of the name of *Uniack,* and died in a very few weeks after marriage.

THE new jail does much honor to the architect, JAIL. Mr. *Joseph Turner,* being planned with attention to all the requisites of these seats of misery; security, cleanliness, and health. The debtors are separated from the criminals by a very lofty wall, dividing their respective yards, which are airy and spacious, and are supplied with baths. The condemned cells on a level with the ground, are dry, light, and strong; an excellent contrast to the sad dungeons of antient prisons.

FROM *Ruthin,* I visited the neat little mother church of *Llanruth,* dedicated to *St. Meugan,* a great astrologer, and physician to king *Vortigern.* In it is the monument of *John Thelwall* esq; of THE THEL-WALLS.

[p] *Itin.* v. 45.

Bathafarn, and his wife, kneeling at an altar: behind him are ten sons; behind her, four daughters.
Of the sons, Sir *Bevis* is armed; the rest are in
gowns; and three carry in their hands a skull, to
denote their early departure. Sir *Bevis* was page
of the bedchamber to *James* I. and seems to have
had in him a strong spirit of project. He bought
from one *Gibbs* a share of certain lands, which
were to be recovered from the sea, in *Brading
haven*, in the *Isle of Wight*, and admitted as partner his countryman, the famous Sir *Hugh Myddelton.* Sir *Hugh* procured a number of *Dutchmen*
to inclose and recover the haven from the sea; but
after expending seven thousand pounds, Sir *Bevis*
and he were obliged to retire, and submit to their
loss[q]. The other seven sons lived to advanced life,
and flourished cotemporaries in the several profes-
sions they had embraced.

John, the eldest, died aged 97, and left a posterity, amounting to between two hundred and forty
and two hundred and sixty.

Sir *Eubule* became principal of *Jesus College*,
Oxford. I will not tire the reader with the whole
family history; but must not omit *Ambrose*, the
ninth son, who began life with being servant to Sir
Francis Bacon; and so great a favorite was he,
that in order to reward him, Sir *Francis* moved

[q] *Worsley's* Hist. Isle of *Wight*, p. 196.

his royal master to knight all the masters in chancery; for which *Ambrose* was to have a gratuity of one hundred pounds a man. The affair was done, and the money paid, except by his brother, Sir *Eubule*, then one of the masters, to whom he remitted the fees.

THERE is in the church a monumental bust of *Ambrose* admirably cut: his hair short; beard, peaked; and ruff, flat.

THIS family came from *Thelwall* in *Cheshire*, and took their name from the place. The founder was a follower of *Reginald de Grey*, and made a settlement in these parts. Notwithstanding the numerous offspring of the family, and the other branches, only two remain of the name, the reverend *Edward Thelwall*, of *Llanbedr*[r], a most beautiful situation, high on the side of the hills, two miles east of *Ruthin;* and *Simon Thelwall* esq; of *Blaen-yâl.*

OTHER branches were the *Thelwalls* of *Bathafarn*, antiently a park of the lord *Grey*'s of *Ruthin*, finely seated near the foot of *Moel Fenlli.* The grounds rise with rich cultivation from the house, and are delightfully varied with hanging woods. In the house are the portraits of seven of the sons of *John Thelwall* above mentioned. Here is also another portrait of a *John Thelwall*, a barrister

---

[r] Now the property, by purchase, of *Robert Ablet* esq. ED.

learned in the law, in physic, and the humane
sciences. He died in 1686, and was buried at
Llanruth. He is represented in half length, long
white hair, a cravat, and brown night-gown, aged
sixty-seven: it is well painted by *Randle Wilcock,*
in 1675. On board is the head of Sir *James Dyer,*
chief justice of the king's bench in the reign of
queen *Elizabeth.* On his head is a square cap; he
is dressed in a red gown, with a rich gold chain, a
small ruff, and with a small white beard. He was
author of a book of reports in *French,* which went
through several editions; his head is prefixed to
it[s]. He died *March* 29th, 1581-2, aged 72.

ANOTHER branch was of *Plâs y ward,* which
came into the family by the marriage of a *John
Thelwall* with *Felice,* daughter and heiress of
Walter, alias *Ward*[t] of that place. Of this house
was the *Edward Thelwall* esq; with whom lord
Herbert of *Cherbury* was placed in his younger
days, to learn *Welsh,* and of whom he gives the
highest character[u]

THE *Thelwalls* of *Plâs Coch,* and of *Nantclwyd*
(all of these places are not remote from each other)
were the sum of this flourishing family. *Bathafarn* is now possessed by the Reverend Mr. *Carter*[x],

[s] *Granger,* i. 235.   [t] *Salusbury Pedigree,* 33. b.
[u] Life of Lord *Herbert,* pp. 23, 24.
[x] Whose daughter and sole heiress (now deceased) conveyed it by

and *Nantclwyd* by *Richard Kenrick* esq ; the latter descended by the female line from the *Thelwalls*.

From *Llanruth* the vale grows very narrow, and almost closes with the parish of *Llanfair*. If I place the extremity at *Pont Newydd*, there cannot be a more beautiful finishing; where the bridge, near the junction of the *Clwyd* and the *Hespin*, and a lofty hill, with its back cloathed with hanging woods, terminate the view.

Go over part of *Coed Marchan*, a large naked common', noted for a quarry of coarse red and white marble. Descend into the narrow vale of *Nantclwyd;* and for some time ride over dreary commons. On one is a small encampment, with a single foss, called *Caer Senial*. Near this place, enter

MEIRIONEDDSHIRE.

And, within sight of the former, visit *Caer Drewyn*, another post, in full view of the beautiful vales of *Glyn-dwrdwy* and *Edeirnion*, watered by the *Dee*. It lies on the steep slope of a hill; is of a circular form, and about half a mile in circumference; and the defence consists of a single wall, mostly in

British Post.

marriage to Lord *William Beauclerk*, who recently sold it to the reverend *Roger Butler Clough*, of *Ereiviat*. Ed.

' Now enclosed. Ed.

ruins; yet in some parts the facings are still apparent: in the thickness of the walls are evident remains of apartments.   It had two entrances.   Near
the north-eastern is an oblong square, added to the
main works; and as the ground there is rather flat,
it is strengthened with a great ditch, and a wall:
within are the foundations of rude stone buildings;
one of which is circular, and several yards in diameter: the ditch is carried much farther than the
wall; and seems part of an unfinished addition to
the whole.   It is conjectured, that *Owen Gwynedd*
occupied this post, while *Henry* II. lay encamped
on the *Berwyn* hills, on the other side of the vale.
Owen Glyndwr is said also to have made use of this
fastness, in his occasional retreats.

NOT far from hence, near *Gwyddelwern*, is a
place called *Saith Marchog*, from the circumstance[1]
of *Owen* having there surprised *Reginald de Grey*,

SAITH
MARCHOG.
and *seven* knights *(Saith Marchog)* in his train.[z]
A family from antient times took a name similar
to this, *Saeth Marchog*, or the *Shot* of the *Knight*;
and bore arms, a lion rampant argent, in field azure,

[1] This is a mistake, for the name existed when the Mabinogi of
Branwen, daughter of *Llyr*, was written; and if the reader will take
the trouble to turn to Guest's Mab. iii. 92, he will find another set
of seven knights mentioned: the passage is grossly mistranslated at
p. 116, where one reads "And for this reason were the seven knights
placed in the town:" it should be—And for that reason the town
was called *Saith Marchog*, or Seven Knights. J.R.

[z] Mr. *Thomas*'s MSS.

upon a canton argent, an arrow's head gules. *Lowry*, heiress of the family, married *Thomas Myddelton*, of *Garthgynan*[a].

THIS post or fastness of *Caer Drewyn*, is but one of the chain which begins at *Diserth*, and is continued along the *Clwydian* hills into the mountain of *Yale*; for on the last are others; one on a *Moel y Gaer*; and another on *Moel Forfydd*; and *Bryn Eglwys* church seems to have been placed in the area of a third. These were the temporary retreats of the inhabitants in time of war, or sudden invasions: here they placed their women, their children, and cattle, under strong garrison; or perhaps a whole clan or nation might withdraw into them, till the retreat of the enemy, who could never subsist long in a country, where all the provisions were in this manner secured. It is also equally certain, that the inhabitants themselves could not remain here for any long space, as most of these fastnesses are destitute of water[b].

DESCEND, and finding the usual ford of the *Dee* to *Corwen* impassable, get again into the *Ruthin* road, on a common marked with Tumuli, the frequent signs of slaughter. These appear to me to have been the graves of the slain in some skirmish which the *Welsh* had with the *English* about the year 1255; when *Llewelyn ap Gryffydd*,

[a] *Salusbury Ped.* 25. b.   [b] See p. 61 of this volume.

collecting all his power, recovered the inland part of *North Wales,* and all *Meirioneddshire,* from the usurpation of *Henry* III[c]

Rug. PASS near the house of *Rûg.* This place is memorable for the treacherous surprizal of *Gryf-fydd ap Cynan,* king of *Wales,* soon after his victory at *Carno,* in the year 1077; having been enveigled hither by the treason of one *Muriawn Goch.* The mount on which the castelet stood, is still to be seen in the garden. Notwithstanding his eminent success, he fell into a long captivity, being here betrayed into the hands of *Hugh Lupus* earl of *Chester,* and *Hugh Belesme* earl of *Shrewsbury,* and was conveyed to the castle of *Chester,* where he endured a twelve years imprisonment. At length he was released by the bravery of a young man of these parts, *Cynwric Hîr;* who, coming to *Chester* under pretence of buying necessaries, took an opportunity, while the keepers were feasting, to carry away his prince, loaden with irons, on his back, to a place of security[d].

IN after-times, this place became the property of *Owen Brogyntyn,* natural son of *Madog ap Meredydd,* a prince of *Powys.* Such was the merit of *Brogyntyn,* that he shared his father's inheritance equal with his legitimate brethren. His dagger, curiously wrought, is, I am told, still

c *Powel,* 320.   d *Life of Gr. ap Cynan. Sebright* MSS.

preserved in the house. *From* the marriage of *Margaret Wenn*, daughter and heiress of *Jevan ap Howel*, a descendant of *Brogyntyn*, with *Pyers Salusbury*, of *Bachymbyd*ᵉ, were derived the *Salusburies* of *Rûg;* a name existing in the male line till the present century[f].

I MAY mention here, as a sequel to the life of *Owen Glyndwr*, that on his attainder, *Henry* IV. sold the lordship of *Glyndwrdwy* to *Robert Salusbury*ᵍ of *Rûg*.

CROSS the *Dee*, on a very handsome bridge of six arches, from which the river shows itself to vast advantage, above and below, in form of two extensive channels, bordered by trees, and fertilizing a verdant tract of meadow.

REACH *Corwen*, whose church and small town, CORWEN. seated beneath a vast rock at the foot of the *Berwyn* hills, form a picturesque point of view, from various parts of the preceding ride.

Corwen is celebrated for being the great rendezvous of the *Welsh* forces under *Owen Gwynedd*[h], who from hence put a stop to the invasion of

---

ᵉ *Salusbury Pedigree*, 14.

[f] The name of *Salusbury* was re-assumed by *Edward*, the second brother of Sir *Robert Vaughan* bart. to whom the property was bequeathed, and whose premature death in *Sicily*, in 1807, while in the service of his country, occasioned the deepest and most general regret. He rebuilt the house at *Rûg*. ED.

ᵍ *Powel*, 214.　　　ʰ Lord LYTTELTON, iv. 99.

Henry II. in the year 1165. The place of encampment is marked, as I am told, by a rampart of earth, above the church southward; and by the marks of the sites of abundance of tents from thence to the village of *Cynwyd*.

THE church is built in form of a cross. Within is the tomb of one of its vicars, *Jorwerth Sulien*. His figure, holding a chalice in his hand, is represented as low as his breast, over which the inscription, "*Hic jacet Jorwerth Sulien, Vicarius de Corvaen, ora pro eo*," is continued. The whole is a very elegant piece of engraving, upon the coffin-lid, I fear not old enough to make it the tomb of *St. Julien*, archbishop of *St. David;* the godliest man and greatest clerke in all *Wales*[1]: yet that saint has his well here, and is patron of the church.

ON the south side of the church wall is cut a very rude cross, which is shewn to strangers as the sword of *Owen Glyndwr*. A most singular cross in the church-yard merits attention: the shaft is let into a flat stone, and that again is supported by four or five rude stones, as if the whole had been formed in imitation of, and in veneration of the sacred *Cromlechs* of very early time.

A MONUMENT of our superstition remains in the *Carreg y Big yn y fach Rewlyd*, a pointed

[1] He died in 1089.

rude stone, which stands near the porch. We are told that all attempts to build the church in any other place, were frustrated by the influence of certain adverse powers, till the founders, warned in vision, were directed to the spot where this pillar stood.

IN the church-yard is a building, founded by *William Eyton*, of *Plâs Warren*, in *Shropshire*, who in 1709, left by will a sum for the support of six widows of clergymen of the county of *Meirion-edd* only; and for the erecting of six houses for them to live in. In consequence, this building was finished, and lands, amounting at present to sixty pounds a year, bought, which is equally divided among the widows resident there.

LEAVE *Corwen*, and return as far as the bridge on the way I came. The vast *Berwyn*([1]) mountains are the eastern boundary of this beautiful vale. Their highest tops are *Cader Fronwen*, or *The White Breast*, and *Cader Ferwyn*. On the first is a great heap of stones, brought from some distant part, with great toil, up the steep ascent; and in their middle is an erect pillar. Of him, BERWYN MOUNTAINS.

([1]) *Berwyn* might mean either the mountain with the white top, or the man with the white or fair head: judging from *Cadair Fer-wyn* and *Cadair Fronwen*, it was first a personal name, as used elsewhere; so that *Cadair Ferwyn* would mean the Chair of Berwyn, who was perhaps a personage of the same mythical character as *Bronwen* and *Idris*. J.R.

whose ambition climbed this height for a monument, we are left in ignorance.   Under their sum-

FFORDD
HELEN.

mit is said to run an artificial road, called *Ffordd
Helen*, or *Helen's Way;* a lady, of whose labours
I shall soon have occasion to speak further.

CLOUD
BERRIES.

ON these hills, particularly about *Cader Fronwen*, is found the *Rubus Chamæmorus, Cloud
Berries*, or *Knot Berries.   Llwyd*[k] says, that the
Welsh call it *Mwyar Berwyn, Mora Montis Berwyn.*   They are frequently used for the making of
tarts; and the *Swedes* and *Norwegians* reckon the
berries to be excellent antiscorbutics, and preserve great quantities in autumn, for culinary purposes.   The *Laplanders* bruise and eat them as a
delicious food, in the milk of rein-deer; and to
preserve them through the winter, bury them in
snow, and at the return of spring, find them as
fresh as when first gathered[l].   I have seen them
in the *Highlands* of *Scotland*, brought to table as
a desert.

CYNWYD.

REACH *Cynwyd*, a small village, formerly noted
for the courts kept here by the great men of the
neighborhood to settle the boundaries of their
several clames on the wastes and commons, and to
take cognizance of the encroachments; but they
have been long discontinued, and the records destroyed.

[k] In *Camden's Br.* ii. 835.
[l] *Flora Scotica,* i. 267. tab. xiii.

VISIT from this place *Rhaiadr Cynwyd*, or the fall of *Cynwyd*, which finely finishes the end of the dingle that extends about half a mile from the village. The water of the river *Trystion* bursts from the sides of the hill, through deep and narrow chasms, from rock to rock, which are overgrown with wood. The rude and antient stocks, that hang in many parts over the precipices, add much to this picturesque scene; which is still improved by the little mill, and its inhabitants, in this sequestered bottom.

PURSUE the journey to *Bala*. Go by the little church of *Llangar*. Observe somewhat farther on the left, in a field called *Caer Bont*, a small circu- lar entrenchment, consisting of a foss and rampart, with two entrances, meant probably as a guard to this pass. My fellow-traveller, the reverend *John Lloyd*, informed me, that in another tour, he had ascended a hill, above this place, called *Y. Foel*, on whose summit was a circular coronet, of rude pebbly stones, none above three feet in height; with an entrance to the east, or rising sun. The diameter of the circle is ten yards. Within was a circular cell, about six feet in diameter, sunk a very little below the surface; and about a hundred yards distant, facing this, were the reliques of a great *Carnedd*, surrounded by large stones. The whole of this formed a place of worship among the antient *Britons*, and probably was surrounded with a grove. But what I have to say on the subject of *Druidism*, is reserved till I reach *Anglesey*, its principal seat.

LLANDRILLO. PROCEED to *Llandrillo*, a village with a church dedicated to *St. Trillo.* It is seated on the tor-rent *Ceidio*, at the mouth of a great glen, which extends upwards of two miles, embosomed in the *Berwyn* mountains, and leads to the noted pass through them, called *Milltir Gerrig*, into the county of *Montgomery.*

ABOUT a mile distance from *Llandrillo*, I again PONT GILAN. crossed the *Dee*, at *Pont Gilan*, a bridge of two arches, over a deep and black water. Beyond this spot, the valley acquires new beauties, espe-cially on the right; it contracts greatly: the road runs at the foot of a brow, of a stupendous height, covered with venerable oaks, which have kept their stubborn station[1], amidst the rudest of rocks, which every now and then shew their grey and broken fronts, amidst the deep verdure of the foliage of trees, which so strangely find nutriment amongst them. The growth of the oak, in forcing its root downward, frequently rends these vast strata, whose fragments often appear scattered at the base, of most amazing sizes. The whole scenery re-quires the pencil of a *Salvator Rosa;* and here our

[1] A station, alas! they no longer occupy. ED.

young artists would find a fit place to study the manner of that great painter of wild nature.

A LITTLE beyond the extremity of this romantic part, in an opening on the right, stand the church and village of *Llan Dderfel:* the first was dedicated to *St. Derfel Gadarn,* and was remarkable St. DERFEL. for a vast wooden image of the saint, the subject of much superstition in antient times. The *Welsh* had a prophecy, that it should set a *whole forest on fire.* Whether to complete it, or whether to take away from the people the cause of idolatry, I cannot say; but it was brought to *London* in the year 1538, and was used as part of the fuel which consumed poor frier *Forest* to ashes, in *Smithfield,* for denying the king's supremacy. This unhappy man was hanged in chains round his middle to a gallows, over which was placed this inscription, allusive to our image:

> David Darvel Gutheren,
> As sayth the *Welshman,*
> Fetched outlawes out of Hell.
>
> Now is he come with spere and sheld,
> In harnes to burne in *Smithfeld,*
> For in *Wales* he may not dwel.
>
> And *Foreest* the freer,
> That obstinate lyer,
> That wylfully shalbe dead.
>
> In his contumacye,
> The gospel doeth deny,
> The kyng to be supreme heade.[m]

> [m] *Halle's Chr.* ccxxxiii.

THE prophecy was fulfilled, the image burnt, and
the Forest consumed, to the great content of the
lord mayor, the dukes of *Suffolk* and *Norfolk*,
the lord admiral, and lord privy seal, and divers others of the nobility, who honored this *auto
de fe* with their presence[n]; but unfortunately, the
frier not having the insensibility of our wooden
saint, on the touch of the flames shewed the natural
horrors at the approach of an agonizing death,
and payed very little respect to the arguments of
the pious *Latimer,* who was placed opposite to the
sufferer, in a pulpit, to preach him into a sense of
the crime of differing in opinion with his sovereign in religious matters; for which the prelate
himself suffered in a succeeding reign. *Forest*
.thought fit to deny that *Henry* was head of
the church; and *Latimer* would force that honor
upon *Mary,* who chose to cede it to the Pope.

OPPOSITE to this church is *Llandderfel* bridge,
of four arches. At some distance from it, the
vale almost closes; and at *Calettwr* finishes nobly
with a lofty wooded eminence, above which soars
the vast mass of the *Arennig* mountains, notwithstanding they appear immediately after to be very
remote. And I here stop a moment, to recommend to the traveller, who does not chuse precisely
to pursue my steps, to follow the course of the *Dee*
from *Bangor,* through the delicious tract it waters

n *Stow's Annals,* 573.

RHIWAEDOG.

Glyndwrdwy to *Corwen,* and thence, through the
matchless vale of *Edeirnion,* to this spot, where,
for a small space, it passes through a flat, an un-
pleasant contrast to the preceding ride.

ON the left lies *Rhiwaedog,* or *The Bloody Brow,* RHIWAEDOG.
noted for a battle between *Llowarch Hên* and the
Saxons, in which he lost *Cynddelw,* the last of his
numerous sons.   A spot not far from hence, called
Pabell Llywarch Hên, or the tent of that monarch,
is supposed to have been the place where he rested
the night after the battle, and where he finished
that pathetic elegy, in which he laments the loss of
all his sons.   In it he directs the last to defend
the brow of that hill, indifferent to the fate of the
only survivor.

> CYNDDELW cadw dithau y Rhiw
> Ar a ddêl yma heddiw
> Cudeb am ũu mab nid gwiw.[o]

"CYNDDELW, defend thou the brow of yonder hill. Let the event of
"the day be what it will: when there is but one son left, it is vain
"to be over-fond of him."

THE house and estate of *Rhiwaedog* is now
owned by Mr. *Dolben,* descended by his mother
from the *Llwyds,* the very antient possessors.
Eineon ap Ithel, of this place, a valiant ancestor
of his, articled with *John* duke of *Lancaster,* in

[o] *J. D. Rhys's* Grammar, 103.

1394, to attend him for a year in his expedition to *Guyenne*, with one man at arms and one archer; for which the duke rewarded him with twenty marks, issuing out of his manor of *Halton*[p].

RHIWLAS. Pass by the village and church of *Llanfawr*, and cross the torrent *Troweryn*, beneath *Rhiwlas*, the antient seat of the *Prices*. In the house are the portraits of some of the family: among others, that of *William Price* esq; member for the county in the long parlement, but soon displaced for his adherence to the king.

BALA. Reach *Bala*, a small town in the parish of *Llanyckil*, noted for its vast trade in woollen stockings, and its great markets every *Saturday* mornings, when from two to five hundred pounds worth are sold each day, according to the demand. Round the place, women and children are in full KNITTING. employ, knitting along the roads; and mixed with them *Herculean* figures appear, assisting their *Omphales* in this effeminate employ. During winter the females, through love of society, often assemble at one another's houses to knit; sit round a fire, and listen to some old tale, or to some antient song, or the sound of the harp; and this is called *Cymmorth Gwau*, or, the knitting assembly.

Much of the wool is bought at the great fairs at *Llanrwst*, in *Denbighshire*.

[p] Mr. *Evan Evans's* Notes.

CLOSE to the south-east end of the town, is a great artificial mount, called *Tommen y Bala,* in the summer time usually covered in a picturesque manner with knitters, of both sexes, and all ages. *F*rom the summit is a fine view of *Llyn-tegid,* and the adjacent mountains. On the right appear the two *Arennigs, Fawr* and *Fach;* beyond the farther end, soar the lofty *Arans,* with their two heads *Aran Mowddwy* and *Penllyn;* and beyond all, the great *Cader Idris* closes the view.

THIS mount appears to have been *Roman,* and placed here, with a castelet on its summit, to secure the pass towards the sea, and keep our mountaineers in subjection. The *Welsh,* in after time, took advantage of this, as well as other works of the same nature.

THE town is of a very regular form: the principal street very spacious, and the lesser fall into it at right angles. I will not deny, but that its origin might have been *Roman.*

THE mounts form a chain. I have observed one within sight of this, on the mountain road to *Ruthin,* which is called *Tommen y Castell; Caer Crwyni* is a small entrenchment, not remote from it, overlooking the vale of *Edeirnion;* the mount in the garden of *Rûg* is another; a third, much more considerable, lies within sight of this, on the road to *Gwyddelwern;* and farther on, in the parish

of *Bettws*, is a fourth, which goes under the usual
name of *Tommen y Castell.*

Bala takes its name from its vicinity to the place
where a river discharges itself from a lake. *Balloch*
in the *Erse* language signifies the same. I know
little more of its antient history, than that it seems
to have been dependent on the castle of *Harlech;*
and that, in the reign of *Edward* II. it was committed to the care of *Einian de Stanedon,* constable of that castle[q]; and that in the time of *Edward*
III. his great general, *Walter de Manni,* was
rewarded with the fee-farm of *Bala* and *Harlech;*
and was made sheriff of this county for life[r]. I
may add incidentally, that *Edward* I. gave one
Hugo de Turbervill liberty of hunting through
Meirioneddshire all kinds of wild beasts[s], while
probably the subdued natives were only his
Chasseurs.

LAKE.   *Bala Lake, Pimble Mere,* or *Llyn-tegid,* lies at a
small distance from the town; and is a fine expanse
of water, near four miles long, and twelve hundred
yards broad in the widest place: the deepest part
is opposite *Bryn Golen,* where it is forty six yards
deep, with three yards of mud; the shores gravelly;
the boundaries are easy slopes, well cultivated,

q *Sebright MS.*   r *Dugdale Baron.* ii. 149.

s *Rotulæ Walliæ,* 98. In p. 97 is an order for him to have six
stags out of the forest of *Meirionith.*

and varied with woods. In stormy weather, its billows run very high, and incroach greatly on the north east end, where, within memory of man, numbers of acres have been lost. It rises sometimes nine feet, and rains and winds jointly contribute to make it overflow the fair vale of *Edeirnion*.

ITS fish are pike, perch, trout, a few roach, and abundance of eels; and shoals of that *Alpine* fish, the *Gwyniaid*, which spawn in *December*, and are taken in great numbers in spring, or summer. Pike have been caught here of twenty-five pounds weight, a trout of twenty-two, a perch of ten, and a gwyniaid of five. Sir *Watkin Williams Wynn* clames the whole fishery of this noble lake. It had been the property of the abby of *Basingwerk*; for *Owen de Brogyntyn* made a grant to GOD, *St. Mary*, and the monks of that house, of "a certain " water in *Penthlinn*, called *Thlintegit*, or *Pem-* " *belmere*, and all the pasture of the said land of " *Penthlinn*." This was witnessed by *Reiner* (who was bishop of *St. Asaph* from 1186 to 1224) and by *Ithail*, *Owen's* chaplain[t].

THE waters are discharged under *Pont Mwnwgl y Llyn*, a bridge of three arches. They seem inconsiderable in respect to the size of the streams which feed the lake; for the *Dee* does not make in dry seasons the figure I expected. Salmon come

[t] *Sebright MSS.*

in plenty to this place; but neither do they trespass into the lake, nor the gwyniaids, except rarely, into the river. Report says, that the *Dee* passes through the lake from end to end, without deigning to mix its waters; as the *Rhone* is fabled to serve the lake of *Geneva*. But, in fact, the *Dee* does not assume its name till it quits its parent.

NEAR the west side, close to the bridge, and just opposite to *Tommen y Bala*, stood another castelet; not so high, but of a greater extent than that mount. It is now broke through by a public road, but is very apparent on both sides; the mount, or keep, was on the lower, immediately above the river; and the vestiges of a wall are still evident. This was subservient to the same purposes as the others; for there must have been, from the nature of the ground, a travellable road on both sides of the lake. This I apprehend to have been the castle of *Bala*, which *Llewelyn ap Jorwerth* founded in 1202[u]. Possibly there might have been, prior to this, a more antient castelet; for in a certain manuscript it was called *Castell Gronw Befr o Benllyn*, which *Gronw*, according to the *Triades*, was supposed to live about the time of king *Arthur*.

THE DEE SACRED. THERE is no river in *England* which has been so much celebrated by our poets, for its sanctity,

[u] *Powel*, 258.

as the *Dee*. Most countries had a stream which they held in peculiar veneration. The *Thessalians* paid divine honors to the *Peneus*, on account of its beauty: the *Scythians* worshipped their *Ister*, on account of its size: the *Germans* the *Rhine*, because it was the judge whether their offspring was legitimate; for the spurious sunk, the lawful floated[x]: and let me add to the list, the *Ganges*, out of whose waters no *Indian* of a certain sect would willingly yield his last breath. Our river foretold events by the change of its channel[y]; and it often seemed miraculously to *increase*, without the usual intervention of rains; therefore, in all probability, derived its name, not from *Ddu*, or black, because its waters are not so, except in parts, by reason of the depth; nor from *Dwy*, two, because it does not appear to flow from any two particular fountains; but from Duw, *divine*, by reason of its wondrous attributes. Our original stock, the *Gauls*, deified fountains, lakes, and rivers. They even had one which in theirs, our primitive tongue, bore the same name, and was Latinised into *Divona*([1]).

---

[x] *Cluverius Germ. Antiq.* lib. i. 185.

[y] *Girald. Camb. Itin.* c. xi.   Sir *Richard Hoare* Ed. vol. ii. p. 165.

([1]) This is quite right, the Welsh name being in full *Dyfrdwy*, for the still older ones of *Dyfrdwyf*, and *Dubrduiu*, all of which occur—they mean the Divinity's Water, and as *dwfr* is reduced to *dwr* in the colloquial, the great Owen is called of *Glyndwrdwy*, or more briefly *Glyndwr*, while such forms as Glendower are partly Gaelic

Salve fons ignote ortu, sacer, alme, perennis
Vitree, glauce, profunde, sonore, illimis, opace.
Salve urbis GENIUS, medico potabilis haustu,
DIVONA *Celtarum* lingua, fons addite divis[z].

Giraldus, who travelled through our country in
1188, gives the first account of the prophetic quality of the *Dee;* and the notion was continued to
many ages after his.   *Spenser* introduces it among
the rivers attendant on the marriage of the *Thames*
and the *Medway*[a]:

And following *Dee,* which *Britons* long ygone
Did call DIVINE, that doth by *Chester* tend.

BUT *Drayton* is still more particular, and adds
many of its presaging qualities, delivered down to
him from the more antient times.

Again *Dee's* holiness began
By his contracted front and sterner waves to show,
That he had things to speak that profit them to know:
A brook that was suppos'd much business to have seen,
Which had an antient bound 'twixt *Wales* and *England* been,
And noted was by both to be an ominous flood,
That changing of his fords, the future ill or good
Of either country told; of cither's war or peace;
The sickness or the health, the dearth or the increase[b].

WELL, therefore, might the sacred rivers be
called URBIS GENII; and that ours was as de-

and partly gibberish. In spite of Pennant, charlatans to this day
delight in talking nonsense about the name of this river. J.R.

[z] *Ausonius* Clæræ Urbes, lin. 29.
[a] Stanza 39, cant. xi. lib. iv.   [b] Song x.

serving as the best of them of that title, is evinced from the above. *Finally, Milton*, in the following line, beautifully alludes to the interpreters of the presages among the *Britons,* the antient *Druids,* who dwelt upon its banks:

Nor yet where DEVA spreads her wizard stream[c].

IT was long before we got clear of these superstitions. They were very prevalent in the time of *Gildas,* in the sixth century, when our ancestors strongly retained the idolatry of the *Druids* among their *Christian* rites: and, notwithstanding the fulmination of many a monarch[d], it kept its ground, and hydromancy is still practised among us; of more than one kind of which I shall have occasion to speak.

I FOUND that I could here, with greater ease than from any other place, digress to *Kerrig y Druidion*([1]) a parish a few miles to the north, in the county of *Denbigh,* noted for certain *Druidical* remains, which gave name to the place. After a dreary ride, I found myself disappointed; these sacred reliques having heen profanely carried away, and converted into a wall. It is therefore from

KERRIG Y
DRUIDION.

---

[c] *Lycidas.*   [d] *Edgar* and *Canute.*

([1]) The name is *Cerrig y Drudion:* it means nothing more or less than the Stones of the Heroes. There is a place also called *Cerrig y Drudion* in Anglesey; but it is less known, and the Anglesey people have not yet spelled the druids into it, so far as I know. J.R.

the annotator on *Camden*[*], and the drawings preserved by him among the *Sebright* MSS. that I
must form my description.

THE largest was a fine specimen of the *British
Kist vaen,* or stone chest. It consisted of one
stone at top, placed inclining to the north, and was,
when measured by Mr. *Llwyd,* ten feet long, supported by a stone on each side about seven feet
long, and near two and a half broad. Under one
end was a stone, three feet long; at the other, one
of the length of two feet. The hollow beneath
was only seven feet long, three and a half broad,
and only two and a half high; which sufficiently
shews, that these monuments had not been the
cells of *Druids;* their uses, therefore, must have
been sepulchral, according to the conjecture of
Doctor *Borlase.* The antient natives of our isle
did not always burn their dead. Skeletons have
been discovered in similar *Kist vaens,* at full
length: in such as this, they might lie commodi-
ously, with all the parade of arms, often buried
with them. Around this, was a circle of stones,
inclosing an area of about forty paces in diameter;
and the precinct might be formed with the intent
of keeping people at a respectable distance from
the remains of perhaps some mighty chieftain.
This monument went by the name of *Carchar*

[*] II. 813.

Cynric Rwth;([1]) not that it ever was used as a
prison originally; but there is a tradition, that in
after times, a little tyrant of that name, in the
neighborhood, was wont to cram those who offended
him, into the hollow of these stones; which might
serve for the purposes of torment as well as the
little case in the tower of *London,* or the iron cages
of the *Bastille.*

THE other *Kist vaen* was nearly similar to the
first; but no mention is made of the circle of stones:
probably they were taken away before Mr. *Llwyd*
visited the place.

AT *Giler,* in this parish, was born that upright
and able judge, *Robert Price* esq; baron of the
exchequer, and finally justice of the common pleas.
His famous speech in the house of commons,
against the grant of the great *Welsh* lordships to
the earl of *Portland,* will ever testify his love to
his country. His speedy promotion by king *William,* does equal credit to his majesty, and Mr.
Price; since the former, howsoever grievous to him
might be the opposition to his will, yet no consideration could induce him to permit his subjects

BARON
PRICE.

([1]) *Cynric Rwth* was a sort of a she-Polyphemus, who delighted to
feed on babies' flesh: she is called *Cynrig Bwt* at *L*lanberis, and had
her abode under a huge stone called *Y Gromlech,* near the way to
the *L*lanberis Pass. There was one also in the neighbourhood of
Llangollen: see The *Cymmrodor,* vol. ii. pp. 33—39. J.R.

to lose the benefit of a magistrate capable and honest, as he knew our countryman to be.

RETURN to *Bala,* and continue my journey on the south side of the lake, a most beautiful ride. LLANYCKIL. Pass by *Llanyckil* church, dedicated to *St. Beuno:* and see, on the opposite side, *Llangower,* dedicated to *St. Gwawr,* mother of the *Cambrian* bard *Llowarch Hên.* Beneath flows *Afon Gwawr,* the only feed of the lake on that side.

GLAN Y LLYN. Go by *Glan y Llyn*[t], an old house near the water edge; which, as well as the following, had been the property of the *Vaughans.*

LEAVE on the right another antient seat, *Caer* CAER GAI. *Gai,* placed on an eminence. *Camden* says it was a castle, built by one *Caius,* a *Roman;* the *Britons* ascribe it to *Gai,* foster-brother to king *Arthur.* It probably was *Roman,* for multitudes of coins have been found in different parts of the neighborhood; and it is certain, that it had been a fortress to defend this pass, for which it is well adapted, both by its situation, and the form of the hill.

I PROCEEDED about two miles farther, to visit another fortress, seated a mile from the *Dolgelleu* CASTELL road, on the summit of a high rock, which bears CORNDO- the name of *Castell Cordochon,* the origin of which CHAN.

---

[t] The old house is converted into offices; a new one has been erected near it by Sir *W. W. Wynn,* which is backed by flourishing plantations. ED.

we are equally ignorant of. Two sides of the rock are precipitous. In front of the castle is cut a deep foss: the castle consisted of an oblong tower, rounded at the extremity; and its measure within is forty-three feet by twenty-two. Behind that, and joined to it by a wall, are the ruins of a square tower; this lies in the main body of the fortress, whose form, as *Camden* observes, inclines to oval. This had been very considerable; was built with mortar, made of gravel and sea-shells; and was faced with free-stone, squared, and well cut.

I RETURNED towards *Caer Gai;* and, not far from thence, to the village and church of *Llan-uwchllyn.* In the last is the figure of an armed man, in a conic helmet, and mail muffler round his chin and neck; on his breast is a wolf's head, and on his belly another; and in the intervening space, three roses. The first are the arms of *Ririd Flaidd;* the others of *Cynedda Wledig,*([1]) or *The Patriotic,* a *Cumbrian* prince, whose sons (after their father had been defeated by the *Saxons,* in the sixth century) retired, and possessed themselves of these parts of *Wales:* and from *Meirion,* a grandson of his, is said to be given the name

LLAN-
UWCHLLYN.

([1]) *Cynedda Wledig* means simply prince *Cynedda,* or *Cunedda,* as the name is more correctly written: *gwlad* meant in its antient sense dominion, rule, and *gwledig* was a ruler; but now *gwlad* is *rus* and *gwledig* means rustic: at no time did *gwledig* mean patriotic, so far as I can find out. J.R.

of *Meirionedd* to this shire. *Ririd* was lord of
Pen-Llyn, which signifies ths head of the lake,
and forms one of the hundreds of *Meirioneddshire.*
It had also *i*ts castle, which probably was that of
Corndochon. Around the margin of the tomb is a
mut*i*lated *i*nscription, which, as far as I could
discover, runs thus: *Hic jacet Johannes ap* ****
*ap Madoc ap J₁ —·—eth, cujus animæ pr——etur
Deus. Amen. anno Dᵘ* mccc. V. 88.

CLOSE by this village runs *Afon-y-Llan, Afon
Lliw,* or *Amliw,* or *The Colorless.* The last r*i*ses
from two springs, and falls into the former.
Those who chuse to derive the *Dee* from its double
origin, may fix on these: but I met with a third at
the farthest corner of the lake, ar*i*sing from the
ARAN HILL. neighborhood of the lofty *Aran,* to which *Spenser*
gives the honor of forming that celebrated river, I
suppose after running through the lake, unmixed
with the waters. The poet makes the foot of that
m*i*ghty mountain the place of education, of our
renowned prince, *Arthur,* who, on his b*i*rth, being
delivered to a fairy knight, is by him instantly
conveyed to an antient hero,

> To be upbrought in gentle thews and martial might.

IT is evident that *Spenser,* who was deeply read
*i*n all the romance of his romant*i*c days, had heard
the tradition of *Caer Gai,* and its old inhabitant,

Gai, to whom he chuses to give the more classical name of *Timon;* for so prince *Arthur* is made to name his foster-father.

> Unto old *Timon* he me brought bylive,
>> Old *Timon,* who in youthful years had been
>> In warlike feats the expertest man alive,
>> And is the wisest now on earth, I ween:
>> His dwelling is low in valley green,
>> Under the foot of *Rauran* mossie hore,
>> From whence the river *Dee,* as silver clean,
>> His tumbling billows rolls, with gentle rore:
> There all his days he train'd me up in virtuous lore [g].

THIS honored stream, now known by the name of *Afon Twrch,* is a fierce mountain torrent, precipitating itself from the *Aran;* and crosses a road from whence I first begin my journey among the *Alps* of our country, and ascend from hence, then sink into a very deep bottom, called *Cwm Cynllwyd,* bounded on each side by fields of such steepness, as to put the inhabitants to great difficulties in the cultivation[h]. Woods, especially of birch, vary the

[g] *Fairy Queen,* book I. canto ix.

[h] On *June* 20th, 1781, this tract was totally destroyed by the bursting of a cloud. Many other parts of *North Wales* suffered about the same time by similar accidents. The following is an account of this melancholy phænomenon, taken from a newspaper of that period:

"Last *Wednesday* a prodigious quantity of rain fell in the parish of *Llan-uwchlyn,* near *Bala,* accompanied by lightning, which caused the river *Twrch* (whose source is in the noted hill *Bwlch y groes,* and falls into *Llyntegid*) to overflow its banks in such a dreadful torrent, as to sweep away every impediment: the melancholy marks of its

scene. On the right, tower the vast hills of *Aran;*
or rather two heads, arising from one base.

ARRIVE at the foot of *Bwlch y Groes,* or the
pass of *The Cross,* one of the most terrible in

destruction may be traced from *Bwlch y groes* to the lake. Seventeen houses, with the furniture, ten cows, and a vast number of
sheep, were carried away, many fine meadows and corn-fields were
covered with gravel and slime, so as to render the crops for this
season of no value; one meadow in particular was heaped with huge
stones, so as to render it not worthy to be cleared for cultivation;
these stones were tumbled, by the rapidity of the current, several
hundred yards, and are of the following prodigious dimensions,
viz. one 19 feet long, 9 broad, and 6 deep; another $19\frac{1}{2}$ feet by $7\frac{1}{2}$,
and six deep, which was split by the impetuosity of its motion, in
striking upon another; eight other stones, half the above size, were
carried half a mile, and five bridges swept away in that parish.—In
one of the houses a poor woman sick in bed was drowned, the only
person missing here; providentially the inhabitants of *Pandy* were
timely alarmed, the consequence of a few minutes delay would have
proved fatal to the whole village, the houses and fine bridge at that
place being erased, and no remains left. Two young women laying
together in bed, one of them was killed by the lightning, but the cap
of the other only a little scorched."

"Same day at *Ruthin,* the river rose to an amazing height, which
prompted a number of people to go upon the bridge to observe it;
in a few minutes they were surrounded by the flood, and obliged to
remain in that distressing situation all night; *John Bills,* a glazier,
one of the number, leaning over the battlement, it unfortunately
gave way, whereby he was drowned. It is easier to conceive than
express the feelings of his companions thus deplorably circum-
stanced, in full expectation of the bridge being carried away every
moment, and they to share his untimely fate; next morning the
flood was somewhat abated, and the people providentially saved.
At *Penmachno,* thirteen horses, standing in a stable, belonging to two
drovers, seven of them were killed by the lightning; it is somewhat
remarkable, that the seven killed belonged to one of them; the remaining six, owned by the other person, received no injury·
Upon the whole there never was known so general a deluge in these
parts by the oldest inhabitants."

North Wales. The height is gained by going up
an exceedingly steep and narrow zig-zag path: the
pass itself is a dreary heathy flat, on which I suppose the cross stood, to excite the thanksgiving of
travellers, for having so well accomplished their
arduous journey. The descent on the other side
is much greater, and very tedious, into the long and
narrow vale of *Mowddwy.* It is seven or eight Vale of Mowddwy.
miles long; and so contracted as scarcely to admit
a meadow at the bottom. Its boundaries are vast
hills, generally very verdant, and fine sheep-walks;
but one on the left exhibits a horrible front, being
so steep, as to balance between precipice and
slope: it is red and naked, and too steep to admit
of vegetation; and a slide from its summit would
be as fatal as a fall from a perpendicular rock. In
one place on the right, the mountains open, and
furnish a gap to give sight to another picturesque
and strange view, the rugged and wild summit of
Aran Fowddwy, which soars above with tremendous majesty.

THERE is a beauty in this vale, which is not
frequent in others of these mountanous countries.
The inclosures are all divided by excellent quickset
hedges, and run far up the sides of the hills, in
places so steep, that the common traveller would
scarcely find footing. Numbers of little groves
are interspersed; and the hills above them shew a
fine turf to the top, where the bog and heath com-

mence, which give shelter to multitudes of red
grous, and a few[h] black. But their consequences
to these parts are infinitely greater, in being the
beds of fuel to all the inhabitants. The turberies
are placed very remote from their dwellings; and
the turf or peat is gotten with great difficulty.
The roads from the brows of the mountains, in
general, are too steep even for a horse; the men
TURF
SLEDGES. therefore carry up on their backs, a light sledge, fill
it with a very considerable load, and drag it, by
means of a rope placed over their breast, to the
brink of the slope[i]; then go before, and draw it
down, still preceding, and guiding its motions,
which at times have been so violent, as to over-
turn and draw along with it the master, to the
hazard of his life, and not without considerable
bodily hurt.

AFTER riding some time along the bottom of
the vale, pass by the village and church of *Llan y*
ST. TYDECHO. *Mowddwy;* the last is dedicated to *St. Tydecho,*
one of our most capital saints.   His legend[k] is
written in verse, by *Dafydd Llwyd ap Llewelyn ap
Gryffydd,* lord of *Mathafarn;* a person who was

[h] Now extinct. ED.

[i] At this time the turberies lie at a great distance from the brow of
the hill; the natives are therefore obliged to bring a horse by a round-
about way to them, which assists in dragging the turf to the brink of
the slope, where men supply its place.

[k] *Cywydd* TYDECHO SANT yn amser MAELGWYN GWYNEDD: *i.e.* the
poem of *St. Tydecho,* who lived in the time of *Maelgwyn Gwynedd.*

very instrumental in bringing in *Henry* VII. by feeding his countrymen with prophecies, that one of them was to deliver *Wales* from the *English* yoke, by which means thousands of them were induced to rise, under Sir *Rhys ap Thomas*, and several others, and join *Henry*, then earl of *Richmond*, at *Milford*.

THIS illustrious bard informs us, that *Tydecho* had been an abbot in *Armorica*, and came over in the time of king *Arthur;* but after the death of that hero, when the *Saxons* over-ran most of the kingdom, the saint retired, and led here a most austere life, lying on the bare stones, and wearing a shirt of hair: yet he employed his time usefully, was a tiller of the ground, and kept hospitality. *Maelgwyn Gwynedd*, then a youth, took offence at the saint, and seized his oxen; but wild stags were seen the next day, performing their office, and a grey wolf harrowing after them. *Maelgwyn*, enraged at this, brought his milk-white dogs to chase the deer, while he sat on the blue stone, to enjoy the diversion; but when he attempted to rise, he found his breech immoveably fixed to the rock, so that he was obliged to beg pardon of the saint, who, on proper reparation, was so kind as to free him from his awkward pain.

So far legend. That *St. Tydecho* might have

lived, and that *Maelgwyn Gwynedd* did live a
prince of our country, I make no doubt; and that
the former did receive from the prince the priveleges it once enjoyed, of sanctuary for man and
beast, is equally probable: every offender, however
criminal, met with protection here. Legend says,
that it was to endure for a hundred ages; but,
blind to futurity! the reformation was not fore-
seen. This place was also exempted from all
fighting, burning, and killing; nor was it permitted
to affront any of the inhabitants, without making
the most ample reparation.

THE lands of *Tydecho* were also freed from
mortuaries, clames, oppression, and that great
duty, which most places were subject to, the *Gobr
Merched*, the penalty of incontinence; which the
saint, in tenderness to the possible frailty of his
flock, wisely took care to get it exempted from.

ABOUT four or five miles farther, I reached
Dinas y Mowddwy, seated on the plain of an eminence, at the junction of three vales, beneath the
rock *Craig y Ddinas;* whose peat paths I now survey with horror, reflecting on a frolick of my
younger days, in climbing to its summit, to enjoy
the pleasure of darting down again in one of the
peat sledges. The foot of this eminence is watered
by the *Cerris* and the *Dyfi.* The last, which
retains its name till lost in the sea at *Aberdyfi,*

DINAS
MOWDDWY.

rises at the bottom of the rude rock *Craig Llyn Dyfi*, under *Aran Fowddwy*. It abounds with salmon, which are hunted in the night, by an animated, but illicit chace, by spear-men, who are directed to the fish by lighted whisps of straws.

THIS *Mowddwy*, notwithstanding it is dignified with the name of *Dinas*, or city, consists but of one street, strait and broad, with houses ill according with its title; but it still preserves the insignia of power, the stocks, and whipping-post, the *feg-fawr*, or *great fetter*, the mace, and standard measure. It is likewise the capital of an extensive lordship, under the rule of my worthy cousin, *John Mytton*[1] esquire. He derives it from *Wil-* OWNERS. *liam*, or *Wilcocke*, as he is commonly called, fourth son of *Gryffydd ap Gwenwynwyn*, lord of *Powys*. His grand-daughter and sole heir married Sir *Hugh de Burgh*, son of the famous *Hugh*, justiciary of *England*. His son, Sir *John*, left four daughters, married into the houses of *Newport*, *Leighton*, *Lingen*, and *Mytton; Alianor*, the fourth daughter, having given her hand, and this seignory, to *Thomas Mytton*, ancestor of the present lord.

THE powers of this capital over a district, which PRIVELEGES. comprehends this large parish, and seven out of the eight townships of that of *Mallwyd*, are consider-able. The corporation consists of a mayor, alder-

[1] Grandfather to the present owner. ED.

men, recorder, and several burgesses. The mayor
tries criminals; but as the late worthy magistrate,
a very honest smith, told me, that, for some years
past, they have not adventured to whip: the stocks,
or confinement in the *feg-fawr*, or *great-fetter*, is
the utmost severity they have exerted: but then
they retain the exclusive power of licensing ale-
houses in their district, and are likewise justices of
the peace as far as the limits of their little reign.

THE recorder (in absence of the lord) tries
all matters of property, not exceeding forty shillings; and the attornies, whose fees do not exceed
half a crown, are chosen from the lettered part of
the community, or those who can read.

I WAS accommodated with entertainment at the
manor-house, from whence I took a delightful
walk of about two miles, along the vale, on the
banks of the *Dyfi*.   The valley expands, and the
hills sink in height, towards the west.   After passing the *Dyfi*, cross a bridge over the deep and still
water of the *Clywêdog*, black as ink, passing slug-
gishly through a darksome chasm, into open day.

MALLWYD.   REACH *Mallwyd*, remarkable for the situation
of the altar, in the middle of the church; which
Doctor *Davies*, author of the *Welsh* dictionary,
then incumbent, in defiance of the orders of archbishop *Laud*, removed again from its imaginary
superstitious site at the east end.

ONE of the beautiful yew trees in the church-yard, is extremely well worth notice. It is a sort of forest of vast trees, issuing from one stem, forming a most extensive shade, and magnificent appearance. Another reason for planting these trees in church-yards, besides those usually assigned, was a custom in old times, upon *Palm Sunday*, to make this the substitute of the tree, from which that *Sunday* took its name; to bless on that day the boughs; also to burn some of them to ashes; and with those the priest, on the following *Ash-Wednesday*, signed the people on the forehead, saying,

Memento, homo! quod pulvis es, et in pulverem reverteris.

And of the branches, so blessed, it was customary to stick some in the fields, in rogation week, or at the times of processions.

RETURN to *Dinas y Mowddwy*. On the road was informed of the place, not far from hence, where *Lewis Owen*, vice-chamberlain of *North Wales*, and baron of the exchequer of *North Wales*, was cruelly murdered in the year 1555, by a set of banditti, with which this county was over-run. After the wars of the houses of *York* and *Lancaster*, multitudes of felons and outlaws inhabited this country; and established in these parts, for a great length of time, from those unhappy days, a race of profligates, who continued to rob, burn,

and murder, in large bands, in defiance of the
civil power; and would steal and drive whole
herds of cattle, in mid-day, from one county to
another, with the utmost impunity. To put a stop
to their ravages, a commission was granted to *John
Wynn ap Meredydd*, of *Gwedir*, and to *Lewis
Owen*, in order to settle the peace of the country,
and to punish all offenders against its government.
In pursuance of their orders, they raised a body[m]
of stout men, and on a *Christmas-Eve* seized above
four score outlaws and felons, on whom they held
a jail delivery, and punished then according to
their deserts. Among them were the two sons of
a woman, who very earnestly applied to *Owen* for
the pardon of one: he refused; when the mother,
in a rage, told him (baring her neck) *These yellow
breasts have given suck to those, who shall wash
their hands in your blood*. Revenge was determined by the surviving villains. They watched
their opportunity, when he was passing through
these parts to *Montgomeryshire* assizes, to way-
lay him in the thick woods of *Mowddwy*, at a
place now called, from the deed, *Llidiart y Barwn;*
where they had cut down several long trees, to
cross the road, and impede the passage. They
then discharged on him a shower of arrows; one of

---

[m] The origin of sheriff's men in *North Wales* was of a much earlier
date. See *Appendix*, No. IX.

which sticking in his face, he took out, and broke.
After this, they attacked him with bills and javelins,
and left him slain, with above thirty wounds. His
son-in-law, *John Llwyd*, of *Ceiswyn*, defended
him to the last; but his cowardly attendants fled
on the first onset. His death gave peace to the
country; for most rigorous justice ensued; the
whole nest of banditti was extirpated, many suffered by the hand of justice; and the rest fled,
never to return.

THE traditions of the country respecting these
banditti, are still extremely strong. I was told,
that they were so feared, that travellers did not
dare to go the common road to *Shrewsbury*, but
passed over the summits of the mountains, to avoid
their haunts. The inhabitants placed scythes in
the chimneys of their houses, to prevent the felons
coming down to surprise them in the night; some
of which are to be seen to this day. This race
was distinguished by the titles *Gwylliaid y Dugoed*
and *Gwylliaid Cochion Mowddwy*, i. e. *The banditti of the Black Wood*, and *the red-headed Banditti of Mowddwy*.

LEAVE *Dinas*, and take the road towards *Dolgelleu*. Pass by some deserted lead mines, which
as yet have never been worked with success. I may
here mention an earth, which this place is noted for, OCHRE
a bluish ochre, which the shepherds wet, and pound

in a mortar, then form into balls, and use in mark-
ing their sheep. An old proverb of the three
things which *Mowddwy* wishes to send out of the
country, shews their long knowledge of it.

> O Fowddy ddu ni ddaw, dım allan
> A ellir 'i rwystraw,
> Ond tri pheth helaeth hylaw
> *Dyn atgas,* NOD GLAS, *a gwlaw*[n].

ABOUT three miles from *Dinas,* leave on the
left the vast sheep farm of *Pennant-higi:* a deep
bottom, environed on three sides by vast mountains, forming a noble theatre. This whole country abounds ın sheep and cattle; and the wool
is manufactured in all parts into flannel and
stockings[o].

BWLCH OER-
DDRWS.
ASCEND a steep hill, into the pass *Bwlch Oer
ddrws;* and the country beyond suddenly assumes
a new face. Before us is a vast extent of dreary
slope bounded by vast rocky mountains; among
which, *Cader Idris* soars pre-eminent.

THIS pass is noted for being one of the three
places, in which were assembled, six years after
the wars of *Glyndwr,* all the great men of certain
districts, in order to enforce the observation of
justice by their own weight, without any other
legal sanction.

[n] Detested people, blue-marking earth, and rain.
[o] Web, or coarse cloth, now constitutes the principal manufactuıe
of *Meireoneddshire,* which is in a most flourishing state. ED.

This, perhaps, was occasioned by the merciless laws enacted against the *Welsh* by *Henry* IV. At each of these places, they entered into a compact to cause justice to be done for all wrongs inflicted before and after the wars, but not during that turbulent period. Every one was to have his goods, or land, which had been forced from him, restored without law-suit; and any goods detained after this, were to be deemed as stolen; or if his lord sold them, he was fined ten pounds, and the goods, or their value, restored to the owner. If the refractory person was hanged, or died a natural death, the demand continued against the wife, heirs, or executors: but if they or she denied the demand, the plaintiff must procure his compurgators, viz. six persons with him, to swear to the right of his clame; but (like the *English*, in cases of jury) the defendant had a right to challenge one of the six, and another was to be provided in his stead.

After this, follow various regulations for restoring the government of the country in general; and several laws relative to waifs and estrays, vagrants, bail, recovery of debts, manslaughter, thefts, duty of officers, &c. The code concludes with the valuation of several goods and chattels, for which satisfaction was to be made. For example, a horse and mare, on the oath of the owner and two neighbors, were valued at ten shillings; a foal at twenty pence; an ox at a mark;

a cow at ten shillings; the hire of an ox, and the
milk of a cow, were also valued; an ewe was
esteemed at sixteen pence, her wool at four pence,
her milk at two pence, and her lamb at eight
pence.

As a proof of the high value of arms, and that
we had few manufacturers of that kind, a two-
handed sword was valued at ten shillings, a one-
handed at six shillings and eight pence, and a
steel buckler at two shillings and eight pence; but,
what *is* very singular, a bow, which they could
make, was valued at sixteen pence, and an arrow
at sixpence.

No other penalty was annexed to the breach of
these laws, than the forfeiture of the benefit of the
compact, which, in those unsettled times, was probably sufficient, as it left the party unsupported
and friendless.

DESCEND from hence, along very bad stony
DOLGELLEU. roads, to *Dolgelleu;* every entrance to which is
barred by a turnpike, in imitation of other places;
and every approach mended for a short distance°,
by help of the scanty tolls. The town is small,
the streets disposed in a most irregular manner;
but the situation is in a beautiful vale, fertile, well
wooded and embellished with numerous pretty

° The roads, branching in all directions from *Dolgelleu,* are now
excellent. ED.

CADER IDRIS.

seats, and watered by the river *Mynach;* over which, on account of its floods, is a bridge of several arches. The town takes its name from its being placed in a dale abundant in hazels. It has nothing in it remarkable but the church, which, notwithstanding it is pew-less, is a good building. Within is the monument of *Meiric Fychan ap Ynyr Fychan,* of the neighboring house of *Nanneu,* fifth in descent from prince *Cadwgan,* son of *Bleddyn ap Cynfyn,* who resided there, and in whose posterity it continues to this time. He *is* armed in a close mail helmet and neck-guard, sword in hand, and with a short mantle over the rest of his armour.

Cader Idris rises immediately above the town, CADER IDRIS. and is generally the object of the traveller's attention. I skirted the mountain for about two miles, left on the right the small lake of *Llyn Gwernan,* and began the ascent along a narrow steep horse-way, perhaps the highest road in *Britain,* being a common passage even for loaden horses, into *Llanfihangel-y-Pennant,* a vale on the other side. On gaining the brow of the hill, I found it to be a very extensive pasture of coarse grass, mixed with a little bog. The hill slopes from hence upwards: the steeper part, to the highest peak, or the *Pen y Gader,* grows more and more rocky; the approach to the summit extremely so, and covered with huge fragments of discoloured rocks, very rugged, and ce-

mented by an apparently semivitrified matter, which
gives them a very vulcanic look, added to their dis-
joined, adventitious appearance. I met with, on my
ascent, quantities of stone, of the same cellular
kind with the *toadstone* of *Derbyshire*[p], but of a
green color. The day proved so wet and misty,
that I lost the enjoyment of the great view from
the summit. I could only see that the spot I was
on was a rude aggregate of strangely disordered
masses. I could at intervals perceive a stupendous
precipice on one side, where the hill recedes inwards, forming a sort of theatre with a lake at the
bottom; yet very high, in comparison of the base
of the mountain. On the other side, rather nearer,
I saw *Craig Cay*, a great rock, with a lake beneath, lodged in a deep hollow. This is so excellently expressed by the admirable pencil of my
countryman, Mr. *Wilson*, that I shall not attempt
the description.

IN descending from the *Cader*, I kept on the
edge of the greater precipice, till I came near the
Cyfrwy, another peak. The whole space, for a
considerable way, was covered with loose stones,
in the form of a stream, sloping from the precipi-
COLUMNS. tous side. Multitudes of them were columnar,
but not jointed; square, or pentagonal; none erect,

---

[p] The stone here alluded to is probably a coarse species of por-
phyry, rendered cellular by the decomposition of the feltspath. ED.

but lying very disorderly, in all directions. Some
appeared hanging down the face of the precipice;
the ends of others were peeping out at a vast
depth beneath me, which shewed the great thickness of the stream. I wish the day had been
more favorable: but I hope another traveller will
surround the whole, and make a more satisfactory
relation of this mountain than I have been able to
do[p].

OF the heights of this mountain, of *Aran-fow-*   HEIGHT.
ddwy, and of the *Arrenig Fawr*, I am enabled to
give a very exact account, by the assistance of the
ingenious Mr. *Meredith Hughes* of *Bala;* who
assures me that the *Pen y Gader* is nine hundred
and fifty yards higher than the green near *Dolgelley; Aran-fowddwy*, seven hundred and forty
above *Llyn-tegid*; and the *Arrenig*, only twenty
yards short of the *Aran;* that the fall from the
lake to *Dolgelley Green*, is one hundred and eighty
yards; so that the real difference of height between the *Cader* and the *Aran*, is only thirty
yards.

AFTER recovering the fatigue of this journey, I
began another, in order to encircle the vast base of
the mountain. I took the same road as I did

---

[p] Mr. *Aikin*, jun. in his "Tour through *Wales*," appears to have
described, with considerable accuracy, the component parts of *Cader
Idris*, and of the other mountains of the principality. ED.

before; and continued my ride beneath *Tyrrau Mawr*, one of the points of *Cader Idris*, the highest rock I ever rode under. Beyond, on the right, are the two pools called *Llyniau Cregenan;* and not far distant, are some remains of circles of upright stones, with many carns; a vast stone, raised erect on the top of a neighboring rock; and several *meini hirion*, or rude upright columns.

LLYS BRAD-
WEN.

AT some distance beyond these, near the river *Cregennan*, I saw the remains of *Llŷs Bradwen*, the court or palace of *Ednowen*, chief of one of the fifteen tribes of *North Wales*, either in the reign of *Gryffydd ap Cynan*, or soon after. The reliques are about thirty yards square: the entrance about seven feet wide, with a large upright stone on each side, by way of door-case: the walls formed with large stones, uncemented by any mortar: in short, the structure of this palace shews the very low state of architecture in those times: it may be paralleled only by the artless fabrick of a cattle house.

Ednyfed ap Aaron, a descendant of this great man, had the honor of entertaining *Owen Glyndwr*, in one of his sad reverses of fortune; and is said to have concealed him from the pursuit of his enemies, in the parish of *Llan Gelynin*, in a cave, to this day called *Ogof Owen*.

I MUST not lead the reader into a belief, that

every habitation of these early times, was equal in magnificence to the palace of *Ednowen ap Bradwen*. Those of inferior gentry were formed of wattles, like *Indian* wigwams, or *Highland* hovels, without gardens or orchard, and formed for removal from place to place, for the sake of new pasture, or a greater plenty of game. The furniture was correspondent; there were neither tables, nor cloths, nor napkins[o]; but this is less wonderful, since we find, that even so late as the time of *Edward* II. straw was used in the royal apartment[p]. Notwithstanding this, the utmost hospitality was preserved: every house was open, even to the poorest person. When a stranger entered, his arms were taken from him, and laid by; and, after the scriptural custom, water was brought to wash his feet. The fare was simple; the meal did not consist of an elegant variety, but of numbers of things put together in a large dish: the bread was thin oatcakes, such as are common in our mountanous parts at this time. The family waited on the guests, and never touched any thing till they had done, when it took up with what was left. Music, aud the free conversation of the young women, formed the amusements of the time; for jealousy was unknown among us. Bands of young

ANTIENT HOSPITALITY.

---

[o] *Girald. Cambr. Descr. Walliæ*, 888. Sir *Richard Hoare* Ed. vol. ii. p. 293.

[p] *Anderson's Dict. Com.* ii. 112.

men, who knew no profession but that of arms,
often entered the houses, and were welcome guests;
for they were considered as the voluntary defenders of the liberties of their country.   They mixed
with the female part of the family, joined their
voices to the melody of the harp, and consumed
the day with the most animated festivity.   At
length, sunk into repose, not under rich testers, or
on downy beds, but along the sides of the room,
on a thin covering of dried reeds, placed round
the great fire which blazed in the centre, they lay
down promiscuously, covered only by a coarse
home-made cloth, called *Brychan*, or plaid, the
same with the more antient *Bracha;* and kept one
another warm, by lying close together; or, if one
side lost its genial heat, they turned about, and
gave the chilly side to the fire[q].

ANTIENT
MINSTREL-
SIE.

SOME vein of the antient minstrelsie is still to
be met with in these mountanous countries.   Numbers of persons, of both sexes, assemble, and sit
around the harp, singing alternately *pennills*, or
stanzas of antient or modern poetry.   The young
people usually begin the night with dancing, and
when they are tired, sit down, and assume this
species of relaxation.   Oftentimes, like the modern
Improvisatori of *Italy*, they sing extempore verses.
A person conversant in this art, will produce a

[q] *Giraldus*, 888.

pennill apposite to the last which was sung: the subjects produce a great deal of mirth; for they are sometimes jocular, at others satyrical, and often amorous. They will continue singing without intermission, and never repeat the same stanza; for that would occasion the loss of the honor of being held first of the song. Like nightingales, they support the contest throughout the night: *Certant inter se, palamque animosa contentio. Victa morte finit sæpe vitam, spiritu prius deficiente quam cantu*, may almost be added. The audience usually call for the tune; sometimes only a few can sing to it; and in many cases the whole company: but when a party of capital singers assemble, they rarely call for a tune; for it is indifferent to them, what tune the harper plays. Parishes often contend against parishes; and every hill is vocal with the chorus.

CONTINUE the ride, as before, between high mountains in a narrow glen. Quit the narrow pass, and go along a good road, formed on the sides of the hills, with a fine slope from it to the sea, at this time strangely mottled with black and green, varied by the light through the broken clouds. The road now passes between verdant and smooth hills, the great sheep-walks of the country; they are round at their tops, and covered with flocks, which yield the materials for the neighboring manufactures. *F*rom a place called *Allt-*

lwyd, have a very full view of the flat called *Towyn Meireonydd*, a mixture of meadow land and black turbery, watered by the *Dysynni*, which falls into the sea a few miles lower. On one side is

TOWYN.   the village and church of *Tywyn*, or *Towyn*. The rectory is an impropriation in the bishop of *Lichfield:* the vicarage formerly belonged to the nunnery of *Barking*, in *Essex*, now in the patronage of the bishop of *Bangor*. I neglected visiting this place; but believe my trouble would not have been thrown away; for I find, among Mr. *Llwyd's* papers[r], a drawing of the sepulchral effigies of a churchman, another of a warrior, and two rude pillars, one seven feet high, with the figure of the cross, and an inscription on each side, in old characters. Another column, marked likewise with a cross, but inscribed with letters of a different form, is drawn in the same collection, from one in the church-yard of *Llanfihangel y Traethau* in this country.

*F*ROM the place where I made this digression, I descended a steep path through fields; and, crossing the river, dined on a great stone beneath the

CRAIG Y
DERYN.   vast rock *Craig y Deryn*, or *The Rock of Birds*, so called from the numbers of corvorants, rock pigeons, and hawks, which breed on it. At the foot is a prodigious stream of stones, which extends some hundreds of yards from the bottom of the

[r] *Sebright MSS.*

rock, and is formed by the continual lapse of fragments from it. Here the *Towyn* is contracted into a fertile vale, which extends about two miles further. Near its end is a long and high rock, narrow on the top. Here stood the castle of *Teberri*, which extended lengthways over the whole surface of the summit, and was a fortress of great strength and extent. The most complete apartment was thirty-six feet broad, and was cut out of the rock on two sides; for much of it is hollowed. In some parts, the precipices, skirted by a wall, formed the defence. The remaining walls are well built: the stones squared: the mortar composed of shells and gravel, is at present very rotten. The whole of this place is so overgrown with bushes, as to render the survey very difficult. It lies in the parish of *Llanfihangel y Pennant*, and is said to have been once defended by a *Coch o'r Pennant*, or *The Red* of that place.

This probably was the castle *Bere* belonging to our last *Llewelyn*, which was taken not long before the final conquest of *Wales*, by *William de Valence* earl of *Pembroke*[s]. It seems to have been likewise the same which was committed by *Edward* I. to the custody of *Robert Fitzwalter*, who had, at the same time, the liberty of hunting all kinds of wild beasts in this country[t]. It is fit to mention

Teberri Castle.

[s] *Leland's Collect.* i. 178.   [t] *Rotulæ Walliæ*, 99.

this, as there was another strong fortress in *Cardi-ganshire*, of a similar name.

RETURN about half a mile, and ride several
TAL Y LLYN. miles along the pretty vale of *Tal y Llyn;* very narrow, but consisting of fine meadows, bounded by lofty verdant mountains, very steeply sloped. Went by *Llyn y Myngil*, a beautiful lake, about a mile long, which so far fills the valley, as to leave only a narrow road on one side. Its termination is very picturesque; for it contracts gradually into the form of a river, and rushes through a good stone arch into a narrow pass, having on one side the church, on the other a few cottages, mixed with trees. The church, and that of *Llanfihangel y Pennant*, are chapels to *Towyn*[u].

ADJACENT to this valley, at a place called *Llwyn Dôl Ithel*, in the year 1684, was found, in
SINGULAR COFFIN. digging turf, about three yards deep, a coffin, made of deal, about seven feet long, carved and gilt at both ends. Two skeletons, supposed of different sexes, were deposited in it, placed with the head of the one parallel to the feet of the other; the bones were moist and tough, and of an uncommon size; the thigh bones being twenty-seven inches long. Within a yard of the coffin, were found two other skeletons, of the same dimensions with the former, layed on the bare clay: and within two

[u] *Ecton*, 499.

roods of them, a grave, with a skeleton of the usual size. Along the graves and coffin were laid hazel rods,([1]) with the bark on, and so tough, as to be flexible[x]. The high preservation of these rods, and the toughness of the bones, were owing to the bituminous quality of the turbery in which they were deposited. The rods were placed for some superstitious purpose, perhaps to avert the power of witchcraft, a double hazel-nut, in some parts of the Highlands of *Scotland*, being to this day supposed to have that virtue.

A FEW miles beyond *Tal y Llyn* church, the hills almost meet at their basis, and change their aspect. No verdure now is to be seen, but a general appearance of rude and savage nature. The sides are broken into a thousand crags; some spiring and sharp pointed; but the greater part project forward, and impend in such a manner, as to render the apprehension of their fall tremendous. A few bushes grow among them; but the dusky color of them, as well as of the rocks, only serves to add horror to the scene.

([1]) Hazel rods were sometimes placed in graves. A hazel rod with the bark on was found in the grave of Randulph Higden, the author of the "*Polychronicon*," at the recent restoration of Chester Cathedral. And a similar rod was found in another grave on the same occasion. Several theories have been put forward to account for this curious practice, but no satisfactory explanation of it has been given. T.P.

[x] *Llwyd's Itin.* MS. Another instance is related in *Camden*, ii. 793.

ONE of the precipices is called *Pen y Delyn*,
from some resemblance it has to a harp.   Another

LLAM Y LLADRON. is styled *Llam y Lladron*, or *The Thieves Leap*,
from a tradition that thieves were brought there,
and thrown down.   I have no doubt but that such
a punishment might have been inflicted from this
Welsh Tarpeian, by order of an arbitrary lord; but
we formerly very rarely used capital punishments
for any crime; the gallows were occasionally in
use for theft[y], but fines were accepted in almost all
instances, even in cases of murder; which gave
rise to private revenge, and brought on a train of
endless feuds and bloodshed.

ON the left, is the rugged height of *Cader Id-*

LLYN Y TRI GRAIENYN. *ris*([1]).   Pass near a small lake, called *Llyn y tri
Graienyn*, or of *the three grains*; which are three
vast rocks, the ruins of the neighboring mountain,
from whence they had fallen.   These, say the peasants, were three grains which had fallen into the
shoe of the great *Idris*, which he threw out here,
as soon as he felt them hurting his foot.

PASS over *Bwlch Coch*, and after descending a

---

[y] *Leges Walliæ*, 221.

([1]) *Idris* was not only a giant, but an enlightened giant, who studied
astronomy; and as he did not wish anybody to stand in his light, he
chose the top of the highest mountain in Merioneth for observing
the skies.   It is little hard on him that *Cadair Idris* is rendered into
English as Arthur's Seat: who invented this brilliant translation I
know not. J.R.

very bad road[z], again reach *Dolgelley;* from whence
I visited *Nanneu*[a], the antient seat of the antient
family of the *Nanneus,* now of the *Vaughans.* The
way to it is a continual ascent of two miles: so perhaps it is the highest situation of any gentleman's
house in *Britain.* The estate is covered with fine
woods, which clothe all the sides of the dingles for
many miles. On the road side is a venerable oak,
in its last stage of decay, and pierced by age into
the form of a gothic arch; yet its present girth is
twenty-seven feet and a half. The name is very
classical, *Derwen Ceubren yr Ellyll*([1]), the hollow
oak, the haunt of *dæmons.* How often has not warm
fancy seen the fairy tribe revel round its trunk!
or may not the visionary eye have seen the *Ha-
madryad* burst from the bark of its coeval tree?

ABOVE *Nanneu* is a high rock, with the top in-
circled with a dike of loose stones. This had been
a British post, the station, perhaps, of some tyrant,

[z] At present much improved. ED.

[a] *Nanneu* has been rebuilt, in a substantial, yet elegant manner,
by its present respectable owner, Sir *Robert Williames Vaughan* bart.
and the approach to its elevated site facilitated by well constructed
roads. The editor does not wish to make his few notes the vehicle
of panegyric, but it would be unjust to real merit, not to say, that in
the possessor of *Nanneu* are combined, in the highest degree, the
character of an honest and independent member of parliament, with
those most useful qualities which render a RESIDENT COUNTRY GEN-
TLEMAN a blessing to his neighborhood. ED.

([1]) A story relating how *Owen Glyndwr* killed another man, and
threw his body into the hollow of the oak, and how the skeleton was
found in it afterwards, is related in the *Brython,* vol. i. p. 98. T P.

it being called *Moel Orthrwn*, or the hill of oppression.

THE park of *Nanneu* is remarkable for its very
small, but very excellent venison.   I have before
mentioned the ruins of the house of *Howel Sele*,
within this park, and related his unfortunate history[b].

RETURN through *Dolgelley;* and about a mile
beyond, on a rising spot, have a beautiful view of
three vales, finely bounded by hills, embellished
with gentlemen's houses, and watered by the junction of the *Mynach* and the *Maw* or *Mowddach.*
I was diverted from taking the direct road to *Barmouth,* by the great deference I always found reason to pay to the judgment of a gentleman, who, a
few years ago, honored our country with his remarks[c], and has made a particular eulogy on the
cascades of *Glyn-Maw.*   Let me add, that the
consideration of ending this little excursion at the
hospitable house of the late Mr. *John Garnons*, of
Rhiw Goch, was another spur to my design.

LLAN
ELLTYD.

CROSS the bridge of *Llan Elltyd.*   Below are fine
meadows, wretchedly deformed by the necessity of
digging into them for turf, the fuel of the country.
The tide flows within a small distance of this place;
and on the banks I saw a small sloop, ready to be

---

[b] See Appendix, No. VII.

[c] A Gentleman's Tour through *Monmouthshire* and *Wales*, in 1774,
printed for *T. Evans*, 1775.

launched. On the left is the church of *Llan Elltyd:* on the right, in a rich flat, stand the remains of the abbey of *Cymmer.* Part of the church is still to be seen, which shews its antient grandeur. At the east end are three lofty, but very narrow windows, pointed at top; and over them three lesser, mantled in a great and gloomy thicket of ivy. The great hall, and part of the abbot's lodgings, now form a farm-house.

THIS had been an abbey of *Cistercians,* not founded by *Llewelyn ap Jorwerth,* as has been supposed, who only confirmed the donations, as prince of *Wales,* but by the two princes *Meredydd* and *Gryffydd,* the sons of *Cynan* and *Howel,* the sons of *Gryffydd,* about the year 1198. In the charter of *Llewelyn,* in 1209, is mention of their benefactions, of his own, and of the boundaries of the abbey lands[c], which shew it had been founded by other persons. This charter is most ample, over rivers, lakes, and sea; birds, and wild beasts and tame; over all mountains, woods, things moveable and immoveable; and over all things under and over the lands so granted; and gives liberty of digging for metals and hidden treasures: all which was done in presence of *Esau,* then *lord* abbot, and others, religious of the house[d]. At the

[c] *Sebright* MSS.

[d] *Dugdale Monast.* i. 826; who, as well as *Tanner,* confounds this with *Cwmhir* abbey, in *South Wales.*

dissolution, its revenues were valued at fifty-one pounds thirteen shillings and six pence, by *Dug-dale*; at fifty-eight pounds fifteen shillings and four pence, by *Speed*. The only charge on it in 1553, was six pounds thirteen shillings and four pence, paid to *Lewis ap Thomas*, supposed to have been the last abbot[e].

CASTLE.   *Uchtryd ap Edwyn* built a castle here, which was taken and overthrown, about 1116, by *Eneon ap Cadwgan*, and *Gryffydd ap Meredydd ap Bleddyn*[f]; and its site even is not at present known.

CONTINUE my journey on a bank high above the *Maw*. The valley grows soon very contracted; the sides of the hills are finely covered with wood, almost to the top; and the river assumes the form of a torrent, rolling over a rocky channel.

ABOUT five or six miles from *Dolgelley*, at *Dôl y Melynllyn*, I turned out of the road, meeting the furious course of the *Gamlan*, that falls, with short interruptions, from rock to rock, for a very consi-derable space, amidst the woods and bushes, till it reaches a lofty precipice, from whence it tumbles into a black pool, shaded by trees, which gives RHAIADER-DU.   to the cataract the name of *Rhaiader-du*[g], or

e *Willis*, ii. 313.   f *Powel*, 183.

g The cataract is now more generally called "*Dol y Melyn-llyn*." ED.

The Black. A noble birch, placed above, finely finishes this picturesque scene[g]

CROSS *Pont ar Gamlan,* below which the river falls into the *Maw.* Not far from hence, the junction of the *Maw* and *Eden* presents another fine scene. A lofty hill, clothed with woods, ends here, and forms the forks of the rivers, corre spondent to the steeps through which these torrents roll, and exhibits a view like those of the shady wilds of *America.*

BEGIN a considerable ascent, and find on the top some groves of handsome oaks; before me, a naked country. Descend through some steep fields, to another set of wooded dingles, that wind along the bottoms, and join with the former. In various parts, *Cader Idris* appears in full majesty over these sloping forests, and gives a magnificent finishing to the prospect. Soon after my arrival among the woods, another cascade astonished me with its grandeur. *F*rom the situation I was in, it formed a vast fall, bounded on one side by broken ledges of rocks, on the other by a lofty precipice, with trees here and there growing out of its mural front. On the summit of each part, oaks and birch form distinct little groves, and give it a sort of character distinct from our other cataracts.

[g] An elegant cottage has been erected near the fall by *William Maddocks* esq. **ED.**

After the water reaches the bottom of the deep concavity, it rushes into a narrow rocky chasm, of a very great depth, over which is an admirable wooden *Alpine* bridge; and the whole, for a considerable way, awfully canopied by trees. This is called *Pistill Cain*, or the spout of the river *Cain*. At no great distance from it, is another,

PISTILL MAW. nature here being profuse in her beauties of this kind. The *Maw*, for some space, runs along a deep glen, finished by a bare mountain, seen through vistas, formed by the woods on each side. The water tumbles down a series of ledges, of different heights, into a very black and sullen pool, from which it reassumes its violence, and is lost among the far extending woods.

In the nakedness of winter, there is a spot far above, from whence these two cataracts may be seen at once, exhibiting through the trees a piece of scenery, as uncommon as it is grand. After emerging from these romantic depths, I reached a long extent of woodless tract, the vast parish of *Trawsfynnydd*, walled in on all sides by lofty rugged mountains, of various forms

BEDD PORUS. In a farmhouse, not far from this road to *Rhiw Goch,* I visited *Bedd Porus*, or the grave of *Porus*. On a flat stone over *it*, *is* the following inscription, copied somewhat differently by Mr. *Llwyd*, in the *Britannia*[h]:

[h] II. 791.

PORVS
HIC IN TVMVLO IACIT,
HOMO   PIANVS FVIT.

SOME have supposed the P to have been an R, and the words to have been CHRISTIANUS FUIT; but whatsoever the letter in dispute might have been, there certainly never was room between HOMO and the next word, for the letters CHRIS.

NOT far from it, in another field, is a great upright stone, called *Llech Idris*. There is some silly legend about it, concerning the giant *Idris;* but it is no more than one of the monumental columns, so frequent in *Wales*, and in many other parts.

AFTER a short ride, see on a common, for the first time, the noted *Sarn*, or *Llwybr Helen*, the SARN HELEN. causeway or path of *Helen;* a road supposed to have been made through part of *North Wales*, by *Helena,* daughter of *Eudda*, or *Octavius*, and wife to the emperor *Maximus*[1].

THIS road is now entirely covered with turf; but, by the rising of it, is in most parts very visible; beneath are the stones which form it, and extend in all its course, to the breadth of eight yards. There are tumuli near it, in various places, it being very usual for the *Romans* to inter near

[1] *Rowland*, 195.

their highways. Close to the part in question is one, in which were found five urns; the whole materials of this tumulus are composed of burnt earth and stones, with several fragments of bricks, which had been placed around the urns, to keep them from being crushed.

AFTER reposing a night at *Rhiw Goch*, I con-
CASTELL PRYSOR.tinned my journey, a few miles to *Castell Prysor*, a very singular little fort, placed in a pass between the hills, on a natural round rock, appearing, at first sight, like the artificial mounts we had before observed. Around its summit had been the wall, whose remains are visible in several places; and in one is the appearance of a round tower; the facings are very regular, but the work is destitute of mortar. Notwithstanding this, the castelet is probably *Roman;* for multitudes of coins and urns are found about it. The name explains the cause of the want of lime in the walls, *Castell Prysor*([1]) signifying a castle *made in haste*, so that there was not time to prepare the usual cement. Around its base are the foundations of several buildings, which were placed there to enjoy its protection.

FROM hence I took the track towards *Festiniog*, and saw, by the road side, *Llyn Rathllyn*([2]), a small

---

([1]) This is harmless, but not likely to be correct; more probably *prys* has something to do with woods or thickets. J.R.

([2]) This I guess to be *Llyn Strallyn*, where the latter word seems to stand for *Ystrad y llyn*, literally therefore the Lake of the Lake-strand. J.R.

lake, noted for a strange variety of perch, with a hunched back, and with the lower part of the back- bone, near the tail, oddly distorted[k]; in other re- spects, they resemble the common kind, which are equally numerous in this water. The same variety is found at *Fahlun*, in *Sweden*.

NOT far from hence, in the inclosed country, I found a very fine *Roman* camp, most judiciously placed, in a situation over an extensive view of the country, partly level, partly inclining from it, and commanding a number of passes to the lesser posts of this mountanous tract. It is surrounded with a ditch and bank, on the last of which are the ves- tiges of a wall[l]: near one end is a great mount of earth, broken and hollow in the middle, from the removal of the stones which composed the fort; round its base is a deep ditch. This camp is called *Tommen y Mur*, or the mount within the wall. Coins and urns are as frequent about this place as the former. *Sarn Helen* runs into it at one end, and is continued to *Rhyd yr Halen*, in *Festiniog* parish, and by the side of *Fannod Fawr*, and over a farm called *Cae Du*, to *Ffridd y Dduallt*, to the

---

[k] *Br. Zool.* iii. tab. xlviii.

[l] Amongst the ruins of the camp was found an inscription, im- porting, as Mr. *Brand* says, that "thirty-nine feet of the wall was built by the *Century* of *Ardesus*."

Archæologia, vol. xiv. pl. 10, fig. 2. App. p. 276. ED.

upper part of a farm called *Croesor*, at the upper
end of *Cwm Croesor*, and through *Cae Ddafydd*,
in *Nanmor*, and perhaps to *Dinas Emrys*. The
branches are numerous: I cannot entertain a doubt
but that one pointed, by *Castell Dolwyddelan*, to
Caer Hên, or *Conovium;* and that by *Pont Aber
Glas Llyn*, and *y Gymwynas*, or the wôrk *done in
kindness*, may be supposed to have been another,
pointing to *Segontium*. I have before mentioned
a *Ffordd Helen*, among the *Berwyn* hills; and let
me add those recorded by the annotator on *Camden*, in *Llanbadarn Odyn*, in *Cardiganshire;* and
from *Brecknock* to *Neath*, in *Glamorganshire;*
which pass under the name of the same princess[m].

OVAL
INCLOSURE.
CLOSE by the road side, on the common, at a
small distance from the camp, is an oval inclosure,
about thirty-six yards long, and twenty-seven wide
in the middle, surrounded by a high mound of
earth, but without a foss. There were two entrances, one opposite to the other; and near one
end, a part seemed to have been divided off by a
wall, whose foundations still remain.

LLAN
ELLTYDD.
I RETURNED out of the parish of *Trawsfynnydd*,
along the beautiful road of the preceding day, till
I reached *Llan Elltydd*, when I kept on the side
of the hill, above the valley which leads to *Bar
mouth*. The ride is very picturesque; the vale

m *Camden*, ii. 790.

watered by the *Maw* (known here only by the
name of *Afon*, or *The River*) which widens as we
advanced: the sides bounded by hills, chequered
with woods.   I found the little town of *Barmouth*,
seated near the bottom of some high mountains,
and the houses placed on the steep sides, one above
another, in such a manner as to give the upper an
opportunity of seeing down the chimneys of their
next subjacent neighbors.   The town is seated
very near to the sea, at the mouth of the *Maw*, or
Mawddach; and takes its name of *Barmouth*, i. e.
Aber Maw, or *Mawddach*, from that circumstance.
At high water, the tide forms here a bay, about a
mile over, but the entrance hazardous, on account
of the many sand-banks.   This is the port of
Meirioneddshire; but not so much frequented as it
ought to be, because the inhabitants do not attempt
commerce on a large scale, but vend the manufactures through the means of factors, who run
away with much of the advantages which the
natives might enjoy; yet ships now and then come
to fetch the webs, or flannels; and I am informed,
that a few years ago, forty thousand pounds worth
have been exported in a year, and ten thousand
pounds worth of stockings.   Many of the webs
are sold to *Spain*, and from thence sent to *South
America.*

WITHIN a few years were the remains of an
antient tower, in which *Henry* earl of *Richmond*

used to conceal himself, when he came over to consult with his friends about the proposed revolution. It is celebrated in a poem of those times, and compared, in point of strength, with *Reinallt's* tower, near *Mold*[n].

IN a former visit[o] to this place, my curiosity was excited to examine into the truth of a surprizing relation of a woman in the parish of *Cylynin*, who had fasted a most supernatural length of time. I took boat, had a most pleasant voyage up the harbour, charmed with the beauty of the shores, intermixed with woods, verdant pastures, and corn-fields. I landed, and, after a short walk, found, in a farm called *Tyddyn Bach*, the object of my excursion, *Mary Thomas*, who was boarded here, and kept with great humanity and neatness. She was of the age of forty-seven, of a good countenance, very pale, thin, but not so much emaciated as might have been expected, from the strangeness of the circumstances I am going to relate; her eyes weak, her voice low; she *is* deprived of the use of her lower extremities, and quite bed-ridden; her pulse rather strong, her intellects clear and sensible.

ON examining her, she informed me, that at the age of seven, she had some eruptions like the measles, which grew confluent and universal; and she became so sore, that she could not bear the

---

[n] See p. 41 of this volume.
[o] *July* 18th, 1770.

least touch: she received some ease by the application of a sheep's skin, just taken from the animal.
After this she was seized, at spring and fall, with
swellings and inflammations, during which time she
was confined to her bed; but in the intervals could
walk about, and once went to *Holywell*, in hopes
of cure.

WHEN she was about twenty seven years of age,
she was attacked with the same complaint, but in
a more violent manner; and during two years and
a half, remained insensible, and took no manner of
nourishment, notwithstanding her friends forced
open her mouth with a spoon, to get something
down; but the moment the spoon was taken away,
her teeth met, and closed with vast snapping and
violence; during that time, she flung up great
quantities of blood.

SHE well remembers the return of her senses,
and her knowledge of everybody about her. She
thought she had slept but a night, and asked her
mother whether she had given her any thing the
day before, for she found herself very hungry.
Meat was brought to her; but so far from being
able to take anything solid, she could scarcely
swallow a spoonful of thin whey. From this time,
she continued seven years and a half without any
food or liquid, excepting sufficient of the latter to
moisten her lips. At the end of this period, she
again fancied herself hungry, and desired an egg,

of which she got down the quantity of a nut-kernel.
About this time, she requested to receive the sacrament; which she did, by having a crumb of bread
steeped in the wine. She now takes for her daily
subsistence a bit of bread, weighing about two
penny-weights seven grains, and drinks a wine
glass of water; sometimes a spoonful of wine: but
frequently abstains whole days from food and
liquids. She sleeps very indifferently: the ordinary
functions of nature are very small, and very seldom
performed. Her attendant told me, that her disposition of mind was mild; her temper even; that
she was very religious, and very fervent in prayer:
the natural effect of the state of her body, long
unembarrassed with the grossness of food, and a
constant alienation of thought from all worldly
affairs. She at this time (1786) continues in
the same situation, and observes the same regimen[p].

[s] *Mary Thomas* is still (Dec. 1809) living: but for some time, has
taken as much nourishment as could be expected at the advanced
age of eighty-five years, sixty-five of which she has been confined to
her bed. Her intellects are perfectly clear; in 1806, she remembered, and spoke with pleasure of Mr. *Pennant's* visit to *Cylynin*.

A case of similar abstinence now occurs at *Tutbury* in *Staffordshire*, in the person of *Anne Moore*, the particulars of which are given
in the "Medical Journal" for *November*, 1808, by Mr. *Robert Taylor*,
formerly a regular practitioner, and by an anonymous writer, in the
"Medical Observer" for *March*, 1809. The former gentleman says;
"She sickened *Nov.* 4, 1806; and, from that period to *March*, 1807,
took no more than half an ounce of sustenance daily, and that chiefly
of tea. From *April* 14, of the same year, she was confined to her

THIS instance of the influence of disease (for such only can it be called) strange as it is, is not without parallel.

THE first is the case of a lady, a patient of the late doctor *Gower*, of *Chelmsford*, who was confined to her bed for ten years, during which time she had an extreme and constant aversion to all kinds of solid nourishment. She drank a pint of tea daily; and once in three or four days chewed, without swallowing, a few raisins of the sun and blanched almonds, about four or half a dozen of each: she seldom eat oftener than onc ea month, and then only a bit of dry bread, of the size of a nutmeg; but frequently abstained from food for many weeks together. This lady recovered by means of constant medical regimen, so that she could walk two miles, without taking either rest or refreshment.

bed for a continuance. *May* 20, she swallowed some biscuit, which was immediately rejected, with vomiting and blood; and, at the end of *June*, eat some black currants; from that period, she subsisted on small quantities of tea and liquids. *Sept.* 18, 1808, was the fifteenth day on which she had abstained from all nourishment, and the fourteenth month from all solid aliment."

The other writer, among various interesting particulars, states, "that, for twelve months prior to *August*, 1808, she had no discharge of *fæces;* and then, on the 23d of *January*, 1809, she had existed eighteen weeks and five days without tasting even a drop of water!!"

The editor is informed, on the best authority, that *Anne Moore* still continues in the same state of extreme wretchedness, and so emaciated, that on pressure of the abdomen, scarcely any traces of intestines are perceptible. ED.

I REFER the reader to the *Tour* in *Scotland* of
1769[p], for the extraordinary case of *Katherine
Macleod*, of the county of *Ross;* and finally, shall
mention that of *Martha Taylor*, of ————,
near *Bakewell, Derbyshire*, who abstained from
food from *December* 22, 1669, for thirteen months,
and took nothing the whole time, excepting a few
drops of syrup, water and sugar, or the juice of
roasted raisins.   She was also very religious; was
much emaciated; her palms moist; her other eva-
cuations very small[q].

EVANS THE
CONJURER.

I SHALL now mention another singular personage, but less innocent, a native of the same parish
with *Mary Thomas*.   This was a noted astrologer,
and ill-favored knave, *Arise Evans*, a character and
a species of impostor frequent in the reigns of
Elizabeth and *James* I.   His figure is preserved
in the *Antiquarian Repertory*, and answers the
description given of him by his great pupil, *William Lilly*, as having a broad forehead, beetle
brows, thick shoulders, flat nose, full lips, a down
look, black curling stiff hair, and splay foot.   He
was a deep student in the *black art;* and *Lilly*
assures us, that he had most *piercing judgment
naturally upon a figure of theft,* and many other
questions, he ever met withal; was well versed in

[p] Vol. i. p. 186.   Vol. iii. Appendix, N. iv. p. 391.
[q] *Harleian* Miscell. iv. 41. 55. See *London* Magazine, 1762, p. 340,
in which is another instance of long abstinence.

the *nature of spirits;* and had many times used the *circular way of invocating.* He then tells how his friend, *Evans,* by means of the angel *Salmon,* brought to him a deed, which one of his customers had been wronged of, at the same time blowing down part of the house of the person in whose custody it was: and again, how, to satisfy the curiosity of lord *Bothwell* and Sir *Kenelm Digby,* who wanted to see a spirit, he liked to have lost his life, being carried over the *Thames,* and flung down near *Battersea,* by the spirits whom he had vexed at the time of invocation, for want of *making a due fumigation*[r]. These ridiculous impostures were encouraged by the fashionable credulity of the times; and the greatest men were the dupes of these pretenders to occult science. To shew that *Wales* was fertile in geniuses of every kind, we must lay clame to the celebrated doctor *John Dee,* or *Dû,* who was born at *Nant-y-Croes, Radnorshire*[s], and was sought after by the greatest princes in *Europe.* *Ben Jonson,* in his excellent comedy of *The Alchemist,* for a time, gave almost as fatal a blow to the black art, as *Cervantes* did in *Spain* to chivalry; but since avarice and curiosity are passions most difficult of conquest, it rose again

[r] In the life of *Benvenuto Cellini,* is a most ridiculous tale of this nature.

[s] *J. D. Rhys, Cambr. Brit.* Ling. Institut. p. 60.

with fresh vigour, and maintained its ground till the restoration[t].

MR. *Walpole* is in possession of the famous *shew-glass* of doctor *Dee;* it is no more than a piece of canal coal, finely polished like a mirror, and let into the broad end of a racket-shaped frame. This was to be inspected by some confederate, and the fortune of any simple inquirer to be told, from what was pretended to be seen in it. This was different from his *shew-stone* and *holy stone*[u], which was a ball formed of crystal, beautifully and wonderfully polished, in days when the use of iron was unknown. It was to be inspected by a chaste boy, and the *Druid* was to pronounce the fate of the inquirer, from his report. The use of this was continued long after the days of druidism, one being found in the tomb of *Childeric,* king of *France,* who died in 480[x].

ON my return to *Barmouth,* I proceeded for some time along the coast, among shifting sands. Pass near *Cail Wart,* by a stone, now serving as a foot bridge, on which is this inscription: *Hic jacet* CALIXTUS *Monedo Regi.* There is no tradition of the place it was removed from.

[t] See *Lilly's* Life *passim.*

[u] Doctor *Woodward's* method of fossils, i. 30.

[x] See my Tour in *Scotland,* 1769. ed. 3d. p. 115.—I am in possession of three of these curious antiquities, purchased at the duchess of *Portland's* sale, *April* 28, 1786, No. 453 of the Catalogue.

ASCEND from the coast to *Corsygedol*[y], the antient seat of the *Vaughans*, where I was entertained by the late *William Vaughan*, esquire, for some days, in the style of an antient baron. The woods near the house are extensive, but affected by the west-winds in a very surprising manner: the tops are shorn quite even, and the boughs so interwoven, as to form seemingly a close and almost inpenetrable surface.

THERE are few places which abound more in *British* antiquities, than the environs of *Corsygedol*. I first visited *Craig y ddinas*, the summit of a hill, surrounded with a vast heap of stones, the ruins of a wall, which, in many parts, retain a egular and even facing: this, and some others similar, are the first deviations from the rude ramparts of stone, and prior to the improvement of masonry by the use of mortar. Into this is an oblique entrance, with stone facings on both sides; and near it are two ramparts of stones. The whole is on the steep extremity of the hill, near to which is a pass into the country.

ABOUT a mile farther, is *Llyn Bodlyn*, a small lake, beneath a lofty precipice, well stocked with char, which will take a bait, and afford good diversion to the angler. *Llyn Cwm Howel* is another

---

[y] This property now constitutes, by inheritance, part of the vast estates of Sir *Thomas Mostyn* bart. ED.

lake in this neighborhood, noted for a race of trouts (which I have seen) with most deformed heads, thick, flatted, and toad-shaped; and which, probably, might give rise to the fabled accounts of the monstrous species recorded by *Giraldus*.

LLYN
IRDDIN.

AFTER passing by *Llyn Irddin*, a small piece of water, on a plain, arrive amidst a wondrous group of *Druidical* antiquities. On the flat appear two circles. The first is about fifty-six feet in diameter, formed of piles of loose stones, with upright columns, placed at five yards distance from each other, in pairs, so as nearly to divide the circle into four parts. About thirty yards from this, is a lesser, with several upright stones among the smaller, but placed with less regularity. Design, not chance, certainly directed the founders of these circles in the disposition of the columnar stones; but I fear, when I come to speak more fully of them, the cause must remain unaccounted for, by reason of the remoteness of the time, and the mystery of the antient priesthood.

CIRCLES OF
STONES.

HALF a mile south of these, on the side of a hill, are two carnedds, of a most stupendous size, containing an uncommon assemblage of druidical customs, or religion, in form of *Cromlech, Maen Hîr,* and *Cist Vaen.* Both are of an oblong form, and composed of loose stones: the largest is fifty-five feet long, and twelve high, in the mid-

CARNEDDAU
HENGWM.

dle. At the east end is a great *Cromlech*, composed of two sloping stones, one placed over the edge of the other, upon five flat upright stones, seven feet high in one part, and four feet ten in the lowest. About eight yards from this, is the upper stone of a *Cromlech*, lying flat on the carnedd, without the appearance of any other support.

ELEVEN yards farther, is another great heap of stones, and in it a large *Cromlech*, supported by upright stones. It is now converted into a retreat for a shepherd, who has placed stone seats within, and formed a chimney through the loose stones above. In the same carnedd, a little farther on, is another magnificent *Cromlech*, whose incumbent stone is twelve feet by nine; four vast columns, or *maeni hirion*, three now fallen, and a third erect. The columns are from the height of ten feet four, to that of twelve feet eight; and each between four and five feet broad.

NORTH-WEST of these antiquities, on the top of a hill, is a strong post, called *Castell Dinas Cortin*, entrenched around; with an advanced work on one side. This and *Castell Craig y Dinas*, were doubtlessly formed as defences to the sacred ground, the subject of the above description. I may add likewise another object of protection, of the same nature, which I met with on my return to *Corsygedol*, two great *Carnedds*, placed on small eminences, near to each other; and within

CASTELL DINAS COR-TIN.

one, the five square flags of a *Cist vaen,* the top
being destroyed. The place is most remarkable
for the name, *Bryn Cornyn* JAU. The neighbors
of this antiquity are fond of rendering it, *The Hill
of the horns of* JOVE. It more probably was a
place of sacrifice before or after the chace, and

CERNUNNOS. derived its title from the horned diety *Cernunnos,*
who was venerated by the *Gauls,* and applied to
as a protector from the dangers attendant on the
diversion[z]. Both the *Gauls* and *Britons* had one
common religion; so that *Cernunnos* might as rea-
sonably be supposed to have a place here as in
France.

CROMLECHS. THIS neighborhood also abounds with *Cromlechs* of very great size. I measured one, in a
tenement called *Bryn-y-Foel,* which was sixteen
feet four inches long, seven feet four broad, and
twenty inches thick. It lay about two feet above
the ground, supported by small stones, and was
surrounded with a circle of loose stones. Most of
the *Cromlechs* of these parts lie very near to the
ground, and in that respect differ from those of
other places. They lie likewise horizontally, which
shews that their object, whatever it might have
been, was different.

THIS country is in the hundred of *Ardudwy.*
The entrance into it from *Trawsfynnydd* is called

---

[z] Religion de *Gaulois,* ii. *85.

PASS OF DRWS ARDUDWY.

Drws Ardudwy, or the door of *Ardudwy*, formed
by nature through the sterile mountains, which
separate the districts. I was tempted to visit this
noted pass, and found the horror of it far exceeding the most gloomy idea that could be conceived
of it. The sides seemed to have been rent by
some mighty convulsion into a thousand precipices,
forming at their tops rows of shelves, which the
peasants, comparing to the ranges in a dove-cot,
style *Carreg y Clommenod*, or the rock of the
pigeons. The bottom of this passage is covered
with a deluge of stones, which have streamed from
the sides; and along it is a narrow horse-path, on
the slippery rock, formed by the removal of a few
of the fragments, which, in other places, are disposed into the shape of most steep and hazardous
flights of steps: and yet, as if the natural and artificial difficulties of these ways were not sufficient
to terrify invaders, there are, in one place, the
vestiges of a wall, which went across the pass, in
which might have been the door which gave name
to it.

On my return, I visited an ordinary house,
called *Maes y Garnedd*, the birth-place of the
regicide colonel *Jones;* whose insolence to the
neighboring gentry is still spoken of, even to this
day, with much warmth. Actuated by enthusiasm,
he went every length that the congenial *Cromwell*
dictated; and was a brave and successful officer in

a cause, which, after a certain period, was the result of ambition, and the foundation of tyranny.

FROM some of the adjacent heights of this ride,
I had a full view beneath me (it being low water)
of the long range of sand and gravel, which runs
from this coast twenty-two miles into the sea. It
is deservedly called *Sarn Badrig*,([1]) or more properly, *Badrhwyg*, or *Ship-breaking Causeway*, from
the number of ships lost upon it. This shoal is
dry at the ebb of spring-tides, and marked in
storms by horrible breakers. Tradition says, that
all this part of the sea had been a habitable hundred, called *Cantre'r Gwaelod*, or *The Lowland
Hundred*; and that it was overwhelmed by the sea,
about the year 500, in the time of *Gwyddno
Goronhir*.

SARN BADRIG.

A SIMILAR accident happened in some distant
period on the coast of *Essex*. The canons of *St.
Paul* must be possessed of a prebend, before they
can become residentiaries; and the one usually
given is, *The præbenda consumpta per mare*, which
lay on the coast of that county.

FROM *Corsygedol*, I pursued my journey towards
Harlech; but, on the road, was tempted, by my
constant fellow-traveller, the reverend *John Lloyd*,
to make a small deviation to visit a near relation

([1]) The ordinary Welshman still sticks to *Sarn Badrig*, and knows
nothing of *Badrhwyg*, or of a boat of any kind under the name of
bad; that is left to the poets. J.R.

of his, who lived a few miles to our right, in his antient territories of *Cwm Bychan*. We approached it through *Glyn Artro*, a little valley, watered by a river of the same name, and prettily wooded. The view upwards was extremely picturesque, of a conic rock, skirted by a sweet grove; and beyond soared the naked mountains, which bounded the object of our ride.

AFTER passing through the wood, and ascending *Dinas Porchellyn*, we had before us a wild horizon of rocks and rocky mountains. Even these tracts, unfriendly as they seem to vegetation, had once been covered with venerable oaks; and there still remained a few, between eight and nine feet in circumference. We went under their shade, above a rapid torrent, with a delightful view before us of a true wooden *Alpine* bridge, and a small mill; and, a little farther, an antient arch, flung from rock to rock, giving passage over a still and black water, shaded by trees. *F*ord the river again near *Llyn Sarph*, or *The Serpent's Hole*. Wind up a rocky stair-case road, and arrive full in sight of *Cwm Bychan*, embosomed with rocks of magnificent height. After a short ride, high above a lake of the same name, descend, and reach the house of the venerable *Evan Llwyd*, who, with his ancestors, boast of being lords of these rocks, at lest since the year 1100. This, and the fortified pass of *Drws Ardudwy*, were most probably occupied

CWM
BYCHAN.

by the sons of *Cadwgan*, in their contests with the
sons of *Uchtryd ap Edwyn*, whom they at last
expelled the country.

THE following, as it is the true descent of Mr.
Evan Llwyd, and my fellow-traveller, who being
brother's children, are eighteenth in descent from
Bleddyn ap Cynfyn, so it is a genuine copy of the
form of a *British* pedigree;

*Evan ap Edward, ap Richard, ap Edward, ap
Humphrey, ap Edward, ap Dafydd, ap Robert, ap
Howel, ap Dafydd, ap Meirig Llwyd o Nannau,
ap Meirig Vychan, ap Ynyr Vychan, ap Ynyr, ap
Meuric, ap Madog, ap Cadwgan, ap Bleddyn, ap
Cynfyn*, prince of *North Wales* and *Powys*[a].

I WAS introduced to the worthy representative
of this long line, who gave me the most hospitable
reception, and in the style of an antient *Briton*.
He welcomed us with ale and potent beer, to wash
down the *Coch yr Wden*, or hung goat, and the
cheese, compounded of the milk of cow and sheep.
He likewise shewed us the antient family cup,
made of a bull's scrotum, in which large libations
had been made in days of yore. The family lay in
their whole store of winter provisions, being inaccessible a great part of the season, by reason of
snow. Here they have lived for many generations

---

[a] Numbers of respectable families in this country, are of the same
descent.

without bettering or lessening their income; without noisy fame, but without any of its embittering attendants.

OF this house was the valiant *Dai Llwyd*, to whom is said to have been addressed the noted *Welsh* tune, *Ffarwel* DAI LLWYD, on occasion of his going with *Jasper Tudor*[b] and *Owen Lawgoch*, to fight *Risiart Frawdwr*, or *Richard the Traitor*, by which name the *Welsh* stigmatized *Richard* the Third.

THE mansion is a true specimen of an antient seat of a gentleman of *Wales*. The furniture rude: the most remarkable are the *Cistiau Styffylog*, or the oatmeal chests, which held the essential part of the provision.

THE territories dependant on the mansion, extend about four miles each way, and consist of a small tract of meadow, a pretty lake swarming with trout, a little wood, and very much rock; the whole forming a most august scenery. The naked mountains envelope his vale and lake, like an immense theatre. The meadows are divided by a small stream, and are bounded on one side by the lake; on the other, by his woods, which skirt the foot of the rocks, and through which the river runs, and beyond them tumbles from the

[b] There was a person of the same name with *Owen Tudor*, at the battle of *Mortimer's Cross*, and beheaded with him. See *Holinshed*, p. 660.

heights, in a series of cataracts. He keeps his whole territory in his own hands; but distributes his hinds among the *Hafodtys,* or summer-dairy houses, for the conveniency of attending his herds and flocks: he has fixed his heir on another part of his estates. His ambition once led him to attempt draining the lake, in order to extend his landed property: but, alas! he gained only a few acres of rushes and reeds; so wisely bounded his desires, and saved a beautiful piece of water. He found on one side a stratum of fine white earth, about half a yard thick, which I perceived was what mineralogists dignify with the name of *Lac Lunæ,* and *Agaricus Mineralis*[e]. The *Germans* use it as an absorbent in dysenteries and malignant fevers[d]; and it would prove a good manure.

Stools and roots of firs, of vast size, are frequently found near the lake. Mr. *Llwyd* observed one, with the marks of fire on it, which he used to repair the *Tyddyn y Traian,* or jointure-house of his family; an antient customary appendage to most of the *Welsh* houses of any note.

Among the mountains which guard the *Cwm,* is one named *Carreg y Saeth,* on whose verge is a great *Maen Hir,* and *Carnedd. Saeth* signifies an arrow; so probably the antient sportsmen here

[e] A friable variety of chalk or carbonate of lime. Ed.
[d] *Da Costa's* Fossils. i. 83.

took their stand, to watch the passing of the deer, which formerly abounded in these parts. Nor have they long been extinct; a person of the last generation informed my host, that he had seen eighteen at once, grazing in the meadow.

THE *Welsh* had several animals, which were the objects of the chace; such as, *y Carw*, or the stag; *Haid Wenyn*, a swarm of bees; and *y Gleisiad*, or the salmon; *yr Arth*, the bear; *y Dringhedydd*, climbing animals, I suppose wild cats, martins, and squirrels; and *Ceiliog Coed*, or cock of the wood. The last division was, y *Llwynog*, the fox; *Ysgyfarnog*, the hare; and *yr Ywrch*, the roe. Some of the above come very improperly under our idea of hunting, yet were comprehended in the code of laws relative to the diversion, formed, as is supposed, by *Gryffydd ap Cynan*[e].

I SUSPECT also, that the otter was an object of diversion; there being a *Cylch Dyfrgwn*, or an annual payment, by the *Welsh*, for the prince's water dogs[f].

THE three first were *Helfa Gyffredyn*, or the common hunt. The stag, because he was the noblest animal of chace; and because every body, who came by at his death, before he was skinned, might clame a share in him. The next animals

[e] *Lewis's Hist. Wales*, Introd. 56.
[f] Record of *Caernarvon, Harl. MSS.*

ANTIENT HUNTING.

were, *Helfa Gyfarthfa*, or the animals which could be brought to bay, such as the bear, &c. which were hunted with hounds till they ascended a tree. The bird mentioned here, is the cock of the wood, whose nature it is to sit perched on a bough, where it will gaze till it is shot, as it was, in old times, by the bow, or cross-bow.

THE third division was *Helfa Ddolef*, or the shouting chase, because attended by the clamor of the sportsmen; and comprehended the fox, the hare, and the roe. The method of hunting was either with hounds, or grehounds, which they let slip at the animals, holding the dogs in leashes. No one was to slip his grehound when the hounds were in chace, unless he had a hound in the pack, on penalty of having the grehound ham-strung; neither was it allowed to kill any animal of chace on its form, or at rest, on pain of forfeiting his bow and arrow to the lord of the manor. When several gre-hounds, the property of different persons, were slipt at any animal, the person whose dog was nearest the beast, when last in sight, clamed the skin. A bitch was excepted, unless it was proved she was preg-nant by a dog which had before won a skin.

EVERY person who carried a horn, was required to give a scientifical account of the nine objects of chace, or else he was looked on as a pretender, and forfeited his horn. The same penalty attended the *Cynllafan*, or leash; he was never again to wear it round his middle, on pain of forfeiture; but then he was suffered to wear it round his arm.

THE antient *Welsh* held the flesh of the stag, hare, wild boar, and the bear, to be the greatest delicacies among the beasts of chace.

THE prince had his *Pencynydd*, or chief huntsman. He was the tenth officer of the court. He had for his own supper one dish of meat; and after it, three horns of mead, one from the king, another from the queen, and a third from the steward of the houshold. He was never to swear, but by his horn and his leash. He had a third of the fines and heriots of all the other huntsmen; and likewise the same share of the *amobr*, on the marriage of any of their daughters. At a certain time of the year, he was to hunt for the king only: at other seasons, he was permitted to hunt for himself. His horn was that of an ox, of a pound value. He had in winter an ox's hide, to make leashes; in summer, a cow's, to cut into spatter-dashes.

THE king had liberty of hunting wheresoever he pleased; but if a beast was hunted and killed on any gentleman's estate, and not followed and clamed by the huntsmen that night, the owner of the land might convert it to his own use; but was to take good care of the dogs, and preserve the skin.

THE penalty of killing a tame stag of the king's,
was a pound; and a certain fine: if it was a wild
one, if it was killed between a certain day of
November, and the feast of *St. John,* the value was
sixty pence; but the fine for killing it, a hundred
and eighty pence. A stag was also reckoned
equivalent to an ox; a hind to a well-grown cow;
a roe to a goat; a wild sow to a tame sow; a badger
had no value, because in some years it was measled;
wolves and foxes, and other noxious animals, had
no value, because every body was allowed to kill
them; and there was none set upon a hare, for a
very singular reason, because it was believed every
other month to change it's sex[g].

HARLECH.   FROM *Cwm Bychan,* took the road to *Harlech*([1]),
a small and very poor town, remarkable only for
its castle, which is seated on a lofty rock, facing
the *Irish* sea, above an extensive marsh, once occupied by the water.   This fortress was antiently
called *Twr Bronwen,* from *Bronwen,* or *The White-
necked,* sister to *Brân ap Llŷr,* king of *Britain.*
In after-times, it got the name of *Caer Collwyn,*
from *Collwyn ap Tango,* one of the fifteen tribes of
North Wales, and lord of *Efionydd, Ardudwy,* and

----

[g] See *Leges Wallicæ,* xxxix. 256 to 260.

([1]) There is a harmless etymology current of this name which
makes it into *Hardd-lech,* the handsome stone, or rather the handsome slate, which does not exactly suit.   The name is Scandinavian,
and occurs as *Hardlech, Hardelay,* and other forms, I believe. J. R.

HARLECH CASTLE

part of *Llŷn*. His grand-children flourished in the reign of *Gryffydd ap Cynan*. He resided for some time in a square tower in the antient fortress, the remains of which are very apparent; as are those of part of the old walls, which the more modern, in certain places, are seen to rest on.

THE present castle, the work of *Edward* I. is a noble square building, with a round tower at each corner, and one on each side the entrance, with elegant turrets issuing out of the great rounders, like those of his other castles of *Caernarvon* and *Conwy*. It was completed before the year 1283: at lest, I then find, that a hundred pounds was the annual salary of *Hugh de Wlonkeslow*, the constable[h]; but it was afterwards reduced; for it appears that the annual fee was only twenty-six pounds thirteen shillings and four pence, and in some accounts fifty pounds, which was supposed to be for both constable and captain of the town. The whole garrison, at the same time, consisted of twenty soldiers, whose annual pay amounted to a hundred and forty pounds[i]. The present constable[k] is *Evan Lloyd Vaughan* esq; with a salary of fifty pounds a year, payable out of the revenues of *North Wales*. It was impregnable on the side next to the sea: on the other, it was pro-

---

[h] *Ayloffe's Welsh Calendar*, 92.   [i] *Doddridge*, 58.
[k] The office is now held by Sir *Robert Vaughan* bart. ED.

tected by a prodigious foss, cut with vast expence
and trouble in the hard rock.

This place was possessed, in 1468, by *Dafydd
ap Jevan ap Einion*, a strong friend of the house of
Lancaster, and distinguished as much by his valour,
as his goodly personage, and great stature[1]. He
was besieged here by *William Herbert*, earl of
Pembroke, after a march through the heart of our
Alps, attended with incredible difficulties; for in
some parts, the soldiers were obliged to climb; in
others, to precipitate themselves down the rocks[m];
and at length invested a place, till that time
deemed impregnable. *Pembroke* committed the
care of the siege to his brother, Sir *Richard*, a hero
equal in size and prowess to the *British* command
ant. Sir *Richard* sent a summons of surrender;
but *Dafydd* stoutly answered, that he had kept a
castle in *France* so long, that he made all the old

---

[1] *Gwedir Family*, 77.

[m] *Camden*, ii. The road is to this day called *Lle Herbert*.—The
names of the valiant defenders of this fortress were as follow:

Dafydd, ap Jevan, ap Einion.	*Mauris, ap Dafydd, ap Jeffre.*
Gruff. Vychan, ap Jevan, ap Einion.	*Dafydd, ap Einion, ap Jevan Rymus.*
Siankyn, ap Jorwerth, ap Einion.	*Howel, ap Morgan, ap Jorth Goch.*
Gr. ap Jevan, ap Einion.	
Tho. ap Jevan, ap Einion.	*Ednyfed, ap Morgan.*
John Hanmer.	*Thomas, ap Morgan.*
Dafydd, ap Jevan, ap Owen o Bowis.	*John Tudur, Clerck.*
Rhinallt, ap Gryff. ap Bleddyn, of Tower, near Mold.	*Gr.' ap Jevan, ap Jorwerth, senior.*

women in *Wales* talk of him; and that he would keep this so long, that all the old women in *France* should talk of him. *Famine* probably subdued him; he yielded on honorable terms, and *Richard* engaged to save his life, by interceding with his cruel master, *Edward* IV. The king at first refused his request; when *Herbert* told him plainly, that his highness might take his life, instead of that of the *Welsh* captain; or that he would assuredly replace *Dafydd* in the castle, and the king might send whom he pleased to take him out again. This prevailed; but Sir *Richard* received no other reward for his service[u]

Margaret of Anjou, the faithful and spirited queen of the meek *Henry* VI. found in this castle, in 1460, an asylum, after the unfortunate battle of *Northampton.* She first fled to *Coventry,* and from thence retired to this fortress[o]: after a short stay here, she went to *Scotland,* and, collecting her friends in the north of *England,* poured all her vengeance on her great enemy, the duke of *York,* at the battle of *Wakefield.*

THE place more than once changed masters, during the last civil wars. It was well defended by major *Hugh Pennant,* till he was deserted by his men. It was finally taken in *March* 1647, AND IN 1647. by general *Mytton,* when Mr. *William Owen* was

[n] Life of Lord *Herbert,* 7, 8.   [o] *Carte,* ii. 757.

governor, and the whole garrison consisted but of twenty-eight men. It had the honour of surrendering on articles, and of being the last fortress in *North Wales* which held out for the king[p]. It is also said to have been the last in *England* which held out for the house of *Lancaster*.

Edward I. formed the town into a borough, and conferred on it grants of certain lands, and other emoluments.

NEAR this place was found the celebrated piece of antiquity[q], on which the learned have thought TORQUES. fit to bestow the name of *Torques*. It is well described in *Camden*, as a wreathed rod of gold, about four feet long, with three spiral furrows, with sharp intervening ridges running its whole length to the ends, which are plain, truncated, and turn back like pot-hooks. Whether this was purely *Roman*, or whether it might not have been common to both nations, I will not dispute. The use was that of a baldric, to suspend gracefully the quiver of men of rank, which hung behind by means of the hook, and the golden wreath crossed the breast, and passed over the shoulder. *Virgil*, in his beautiful description of the exercises of the *Trojan* youth, expresses the manner in these frequently misconstrued lines:

[p] *Whitelocke*, 242.
[q] In possession of Sir *Roger Mostyn*.

TORQUES.

Cornea bina ferunt præfixo hastilia ferro :
Pars læves humero pharetras; it pectore summo
Flexilis obtorti per collum circulus auri.

Each brandishing aloft a cornel spear.
Some on their backs their burnished quivers borc,
Hanging from wreaths of gold, which shone before[r].

THE *Torch*, or *Torques*, of the *Gauls* and *Britons*, was very different, being a collar of gold, or other metal, worn round the neck. Our heroine *Boadicea* had a great one of that precious metal; and *Virdomarus* wore round his neck another, fastened behind with hooks, which fell off when the conqueror cut off his head.

Illi virgatis jaculanti ex agmine braccis
Torquis ab incisâ decidit unca gula[s].

Manlius acquired the addition of *Torquatus*, from a *Torques* which he won from a *Gaul*, whom he slew in single combat, in sight of the army; and *Publius Cornelius*, after his slaughter of the *Boii*, took, among other spoils, not fewer than four thousand and seventy golden *Torques*[t].

THEY were also in use among the *Romans*, who bestowed them as military rewards; and, as *Pliny* pretends, the golden on the auxiliaries, the silver

[r] A little altered from the translation in *Camden*, ii. 788.
[s] *Propertius*, lib. iv. eleg. x. v. 43.
[t] *Livij*, lib. xxxvi. c. 40.

on the citizens[n]. They probably were made in several ways: I have seen a very beautiful one (I think at present in possession of the reverend Mr. *Prescot*, of *Cambridge*) composed of several links of silver wire, most elegantly twisted together; it was long enough to go twice round the neck, and had clasps, which fastened it on.

THE custom of wearing the *Torques* was continued from the more remote periods of *Britain*, to later times. *Llewelyn*, a lord of *Yale*, was called *Llewelyn aur Dorchog*, *Llewelyn* with the golden torques, on that account; and the common proverb, *Mi a dynna'r dorch a chwi*, I will pluck the *Torques* with you, signifies, to this day, a hard struggle of a person before he would yield a victory.

FROM *Harlech* I ascended a very steep hill, and on my way observed several *maeni hirion*, and circles formed of large common pebble-stones, and of different diameters; sometimes appears circle within circle; in other places, they intersect each other. I should have doubted whether they had not been the foundations of *Cyttiau'r Gwyddelod*, or the cottages of the wood rangers, a sort of temporary hovels, erected for the purpose of hunting, by our remotest ancestors[x], had it not been for their intersections. The learned *Borlase* gives instances of such, in the circles of *Botallek*[y],

CYTTIAU'R GWYDDELOD.

[n] *Plin.* lib. xxxiii. c. 2.   [x] *Mona Antiqua.*
[y] *Antiq. Cornwal* 188. tab. xiv.

which he supposes to have been formed for religious ceremonies; and that one rite might have been performed in one particular circle, and another again in a compartment allotted for it by the superstition of *Druidism.* Clusters of circles were not peculiar to our island: baron *Dahlberg*[z] has given a plate of similar assemblages, near the town of *Wexio,* in *Smaland,* in *Sweden,* which are on a flat, at the foot of a vast sepulchral *tumulus,* with a high column, and great globe of stone on the summit. Some columnar stones, or *maeni hirion,* appear in the ranges of stones composing the circles.

THE *tumulus* is called that of king *Ingo:* but, since the three monarchs of that name were said to have been steady Christians, and to have lived in the eleventh century, I do guess both tumulus and circles are of earlier date, and formed in honor of some pagan potentate; for the northern *Christendoms old*[a], or æra of Christianity, abolished all such customs.

I MUST observe that this place is called *Bon-lef Hir,* or the loud shout or *cry to battle.* Possibly it had been a field of combat, and a chieftain had fallen here, for one of the *maeni hirion* is of a distinguished size.

FROM hence the road is intolerably bad and

[z] *Suecia Antiqua,* &c. tab. 322.   [a] *Wormii Mon. Dan.* 4.

GLYN.

stoney, till I reached *Glyn*, a house of my kinsman, *Robert Godolphin Owen*[b], esq; seated in a
romantic bottom, well wooded.   This had been the
residence of the antient family of the *Wynnes*, from
whom it passed to the *Owens*, by the marriage of
Sir *Robert* with the heiress of the place in the last
century.

LLYN-
TEGWYN.

PASS by the village of *Llan-Tegwyn*, and near
a small lake, filled by that beautiful aquatic, the
Water Lily.   Somewhat farther is *Llyn-Tegwyn*([1])
which well merits the name of *Fair and Lovely*, a
lake about a mile round, whose waters are of a
crystalline clearness; its margin full; its boundaries neat and clean.   The narrow path we rode
on, impends over it, and is cut out of a hill, whose
sides are composed of shivering slate, starting out
at an immense height above, threatening destruction: they were much enlivened by flocks of milk-
white goats, which skipped along the points, and
looked down on us with much unconcern.

FROM one of the heights, a vast *Alpine* prospect
appears in view.   The stupendous mountains of
Caernarvonshire, and those of *Meirioneddshire*,
not much inferior, form a tremendous scenery, and

---

[b] At present the property of his niece, daughter and sole heiress
of the late *Owen Ormsby* esq. ED.

([1]) The name of the saint is now pronounced *Tecwyn*, and speaking
in a more matter of fact way, I fear *Llyn Tecwyn* would have to be
rendered into English as simply Tecwyn's Lake. J. R.

rise divided into a multitude of craggy heads. The last are particularly barren, and appear quite naked, excepting where varied by a mossy verdure, or whitened by the *lichen tartaricus*. The highest summit of *Snowdon*, called *y Wyddfa*, soars preeminent. From thence, the mountains gradually lower, to *Lleyn*, which stretches in view far to the west, and terminates on the point of *Aberdaron*. Descend into a deep glen, cloathed on each side with trees, with the *Felyn-Rhyd*, or *Yellow Ford*, at bottom; notwithstanding its name, a most inky stream; the fine cataract a little above, being most fitly styled *Rhaiadr-du*, or *The Black*. FELYN-RHYD.

AFTER a short ride, reach the village and chapel of *Maen Twrog*, dependent on the church of *Festiniog*. Near one end is a great upright stone, called *Maen Twrog*, from a saint of that name, son of *Cadfan*, and who built the church of *Llandwrog*, and was cotemporary with *St. Bruno*. The place lies in the *Tempe* of this country, the vale of *Tan y Bwlch*, a narrow, but beautiful tract, about three or four miles long, divided by the small river *Dwyryd*, or *The Two Fords*, being formed by the *Cynfael* and another stream, which unite towards the upper ends. The vale is composed of rich meadows; the sides edged with groves; and barren precipitous mountains close this gem, as it were, in a rugged case. Here is a very neat small inn, for the reception of travellers, who ought to TAN Y BWLCH.

think themselves much indebted to a nobleman[c], for the great improvement it received from his munificence.

ABOVE it is a house, embosomed in woods, most charmingly situated on the side of the hill. This seat, from the quick succession of owners by the fatal attachment to the bottle, has occasioned many a moral reflection from the *English* traveller. "A heavy glutinous ale has charms enough to debauch the senses of the whole principality[d];" and, let me add, after a certain stage, the fiery dram is called in, to effect the destruction the former had begun; yet I trust that its charms do not fascinate the senses of the WHOLE principality; but that, after a fair scrutiny, there may be found some corner free from the *Bacchanalian* rout.

THE river hereabouts widens into a good salmon fishery; and, at some distance, falls into an arm of the sea, called *Traeth Bach*, or the little sands.

FALLS OF THE CYNFAEL. RIDE up the vale, and dismounting, meet the course of the *Cynfael*, which tumbles along the bottom of a deep time-worn chasm, sided with sharp and rugged rocks for a very considerable space, darkened by trees that overspread the whole, issuing both from the sides and margin.   Near

[c] The present earl of *Radnor*.

[d] This was a hasty judgment formed by a very amiable traveller, which he had the candour to omit in the second edition of his pleasing tour.

PULPIT HUGH.

Festiniog is one cascade, remarkably fine, consisting of three great falls, the lowest dropping into a deep pool, black, and over-shadowed by far impending rocks. Below, is a magnificent columnar rock, rising out of the torrent, and called *Pulpit Hugh Llwyd Cynfael.* *Hugh* lived in the time of *James* I. was supposed to have been a magician, and from thence to have delivered his nocturnal incantations; a place fit, indeed, for the purpose as the pit of *Acheron.*

ABOUT a mile from the *Cynfael*, is another comfortable inn, which has often received me, after my toilsome expeditions. Opposite to it lies *Cwm Cwmorthin;* a retreat much more sequestered, and much more difficult of access, than even *Cwmbychan.* In my visit to it, I descended through woods, along a steep road, into a very deep, but narrow valley, which I crossed, and began a very hazardous and fatiguing ascent up the rocky front of a lofty mountain: the path narrow and dangerous, and, I believe, very rarely attempted by horses. After the labor of a mile, reached this strange habitation of two farmers, in a hollow surrounded on three parts by the rudest of environs, and containing a pretty lake, and two tenements, which yield only grass; so that, in case the inhabitants have any other wants, they must descend from their *Cwm* to get them supplied. The mountains which inclose it, are the *Moel-wyn yr Hydd,* and the

Moel-wyn Gwyn, and others equally rude. High in the first is the lake *Du-bach*, which affords perch; and another, called *Llyn Trwstyllon;* and opposite to the last, a third, called *Llyn Conglog;* all of which, after hard rains, form noble cataracts down the fronts of the hills. We preferred another way out of this singular place, and wound up a narrow path at the farthest end, on part of *Moelwyn yr Hydd*, in order to descend through *Cwm Croesor;* being then desirous of getting by the nearest road to *Pont Aber Glâs Llyn*. But in our descent we met with such narrowness of path, such short turnings, and horrible precipices, that our poor beasts, with much reason, trembled in every limb; and, in fact, had a wonderful escape in getting safe to the bottom. The traveller who chuses to follow our steps, will find a narrow grassy bottom in *Cwm Croesor*, with a few tenements: he will pass through a pretty wood, and soon after find himself on the high road from *Tan y Bwlch* to *Caernarvon*.

In this journey, I went from *Festiniog* on a less hazardous way. Not two miles from thence, on the road from *Trawsfynnyd* to *Yspytty*, I fell again into *Fford Helen*, which is here quite bare, and exhibits the rude stones with which it was made.

BEDDAU GWYR ARDUDWY. Near it, at *Rhyd yr Halen*, on the right, are the remains of *Beddau Gwŷr Ardudwy*, or the graves of the men of *Ardudwy*. These graves

are about six feet long, marked at each end by
two upright stones; but most of the stones are now
removed. There are yet to be seen several circles
of stones, the largest about fifty-two feet in diameter; a vast carnedd, with two upright stones
placed on one part, as if to mark the entrance to
the cell, which it probably incloses; and near it a
lesser heap, and a small circle; all of which had
been surrounded with a larger circle, now incom-
plete, by the application of the materials to the
making of walls. The tradition relating to these
monuments is classical; nearly parallel with the
rape of the *Sabines*. The men of *Ardudwy*, to
populate their country, made an inroad into the
vale of *Clwyd*, and layed violent hands on the
fair ladies of the land: they carried them in safety
to this place, where they were overtaken by the
warriors of the vale: a fierce battle ensued, and
the men of *Ardudwy* were all slain; but the ravish-
ers had some how or other so gained the hearts of
their fair prey, that, on their defeat, the ladies,
rather than return home, rushed into an adjacent
water, called, from the event, *Llyn y Morwynion*,
or the *Maidens' Lake*, and there perished. That
this has been the scene of a bloody conflict, there
is a probability: the graves and carnedds prove it;
and the circles evince, that it was in the time when
the ceremonies of druidism existed.

FROM hence I descended the long and tedious

steep of *Bwlch Carreg y Frân*, into the narrow
vale of *Penmachno;* and after ascending another
hill, turn to the right, into the black and moory

mountains, to visit *Llyn Conwy*, the source of the
noted river of that name.   It is a very large piece
of water, most dismally situated among rock and
bog, and the sides very irregularly indented.   It is
placed the highest of any large piece of water I
have met with in these parts.   In it are three
islands, one of which is the haunt of the black-
back Gulls, during the breeding season.   They are
so exceedingly fierce in the defence of their young,
that I knew of a man who was nearly drowned, in
an attempt to swim to their nests, being so violently
beaten by the old birds, that he thought he escaped
well, with the dreadful bruises he received on all
the upper part of his body.   The water issues out
of the end of the lake, in form of a little rill; but
in the course of a few miles, before it reaches
Llanrwst, becomes a most considerable river, by
the addition of the various mountain streams.

DESCEND for two or three miles, and reach the

village of *Yspytty Jevan*, or the hospital of *St.
John* of *Jerusalem;* so styled from its having
formed, in the then inhospitable country, an asylum and guard for travellers, under the protection
of the knights, who held the manor, and made its
precincts a sanctuary.   After the abolition of the
order, this privelege became the bane of the neigh-

borhood; for the place, thus exempted from all jurisdiction, was converted into a den of thieves and murderers, who ravaged the country far and wide with impunity, till the reign of *Henry* VII., when they were extirpated by the bravery and prudence of *Meredydd ap Evan*.

AFTER a very long interval, another charity succeeded, in the alms-houses for six poor men, founded in 1600, by captain *Richard Vaughan*, a poor knight of *Windsor*, and descended from the neighboring house of *Pant Glâs*.

IN the church are three alabaster figures. The first is the valiant *Rhys Fawr ap Meredydd*, of the house of *Plâs Yolyn;* to whom, at the battle of *Bosworth, Henry* VII. entrusted the standard of *England*, after the bearer, Sir *William Brandon*, was slain by *Richard:* a proper respect to the *Welsh*, who so highly favored the *Lancastrian* cause. The next is an ecclesiastic, his son, *Robert ap Rhys*, cross-bearer and chaplain to cardinal *Wolsey:* and the third *Lowry*, the wife of the great *Rhys*. I may add, that he left several sons, from whom were descended many families, particularly those of *Rhiwlas, Pant Glâs, Giler*, and *Voelas*.

TOMBS.

FROM *Yspytty* I made an excursion to *Voelas*, about two miles distant, remarkable for a great column, with an inscription in memory of *Llewelyn*, prince of *Wales*, who was slain in the year 1021.

VOELAS.

Here is likewise a vast artificial mount, the site of a *Welsh* castelet, destroyed by *Llewelyn* the Great[e]. Mr. *Llwyd* confesses the inscription to be very obscure. It is part in *Latin*, part in *Welsh*. The last line says, *Levelinus optimus princeps hic humatus;* which, if meant of any of the actual princes of *Wales*, must intend *Llewelyn ap Sitsyllt;* he being the only one of the three of the name of *Llewelyn*, of whose place of interment we are ignorant[f].

Turn back, and again reach the river *Conwy.* Enter

CAERNARVONSHIRE,

Rhaiadr y Graig Lwyd. And, after a short ride, arrive at its celebrated falls, not very far from its junction with the *Machno.* The prospect is very extraordinary, from the neighborhood of a fulling mill, where the channel of the rivers form a triangle of deep and doleful chasms, worn by the water through the live rock. Not far below begins the cataract, the most tremendous I ever saw, and whose roaring gives sufficient notice of its vicinity. The rocks which bound it are of a vast height, and approach very near to each other, but want the pleasing *ac-*

[e] See the Poem addressed to him by *Llywarch Brydydd y Moch*, in *Evans's* Coll. *Awdl* vii.

[f] *Camden,* ii. 816.

FALLS OF THE CONWY.

compagnement of trees, attendant on most of our cascades. One fall is of a very great height; and beneath that, full in view, is a succession of four lesser. The descent is steep and dangerous, and not to be attempted but by those who have strength of body, and steadiness of head. When at the bottom, I found myself environed with naked precipices, faced with angular columnar rocks, pointing in a sloping direction towards the river, adding to the strangeness of the scenery.

DESCEND a steep hill, and arrive in *Nant Conwy*, or the vale of *Conwy*, after passing over *Pont-ar-Leder;* beneath which, the river *Lleder* hastens to join that which gave name to the valley. Observe, in the course of the *Conwy*, a deep, wide, and still water, called *Llyn yr Afangc*, or *The Beavers Pool*, from being, in old times, the haunt BEAVERS. of those animals. Our ancestors also called them, with great propriety, *Llost-Lydan*, or the broad-tailed animal. Their skin was in such esteem, as to be valued at a hundred and twenty pence; while that of the martin took no more than twenty-four pence; an ermine, twelve; an otter, wolf, or fox, only twelve[g]. They seem to have been the chief finery and luxury of the days of *Hoel Dda*.

THE vale gradually expands from this end, and extends about twenty miles, terminating at the

[g] *Leges Walliæ*, 260, 261.

town of *Conwy*. It soon widens to about a mile
in breadth, and improves in beauty, especially in
the neighborhood of *Llanrwst*, where it is divided
into the most beautiful meadows. The sides of
the hills are finely cultivated: on the western, the
vast mountains of *Snowdon* rise in a majestic
range: the eastern consists of low and broken hills,
chequered with rich pasturage, corn-fields, and
groves. The river meanders through the whole,
and, before it reaches *Llanrwst*, is of a considerable size.

BETTWS
WYRION.
VISIT the church of *Bettws Wyrion Iddon*, or
the bead-house of the grandchildren of *Iddon*.
Within is the figure of *Gruffydd ap Dafydd Goch*,
son to *Dafydd Goch*, natural son of *Dafydd*,
brother to the last prince of *Wales*. He is in armour, recumbent, with this inscription: *Hic jacet
Grufud ap Davyd Goch, agnus* DEI *misere mei*.

PONT Y PAIR.
A LITTLE farther, pass by *Pont y Pair*, a most
singular bridge, flung over the *Llugwy*, consisting
of five arches, placed on the rude rocks, which
form most durable piers. These rocks are precipitous, and in high floods exhibit to the passen-
ger most awful cataracts below the bridge. The
scenery beyond, of rocky mountains, fringed with
woods, is very striking.

This bridge was built from the following circumstance: one *Howel*, a mason from *Penllyn*,

having occasion, about the year 1468, to attend the *Meirioneddshire* assizes, then held at *Conwy*, had his passage over the *Lleder* obstructed by floods. This determined him to remove to the spot, where he built a bridge, at his own expence, and received no other gratuity than what resulted from the spontaneous generosity of passengers. He afterwards moved to the *Llugwy*, and began that of *Pont y Pair*, but died before he completed his work[h].

I soon left the bridge, and after a deep ascent, arrive at *Dolwyddelan* castle, seated in a rocky valley, sprinkled over with stunted trees, and watered by the *Lleder*. The boundaries are rude and barren mountains; and, among others, the great bending mountain *Siabod*, often conspicuous from most distant places.

The castle is placed on a high rock, precipitous on one side, and insulated: it consists of two square towers: one forty feet by twenty five; the other thirty one by twenty. Each had formerly three floors. The materials of this fortress are the shattery stone of the country; yet well squared, the masonry good, and the mortar hard. The castle-yard lay between the towers.

DOLWYDDE-
LAN CASTLE.

[h] *Llwyd's Itin.* MS. i. The same authority says, that near this place is a great Cromlech, called *Cromlech Hwva*, so named from one *Hwca ap Kyfnerth*, at *Rhyddon*, who concealed himself under it, when the earl of *Pembroke* desolated these parts.

THIS had been founded by some of our princes;
but we are ignorant of its origin. There were
very few castles in *North Wales,* before its conquest by the *English.* They were needless; for
nature created, in our rocks and mountains, fortifications (until our fatal divisions) quite impregnable. Had there been occasion for artificial retreats, the wealth of our country could readily
have supplied the means of erecting them. We
had the balance of trade in our favor. This prevented our princes from ever making use of their
third prerogative, that of coining[i]. Our herds
and flocks were the frequent resource of the *English,* and brought into *Wales* large sums, which
we too frequently were obliged to pay, as purchasers of disgraceful peace. For other purposes
money was unnecessary, since, by our laws, every
subject was bound to assist in building the royal
castles, excepting the husbandmen belonging to
the king[k].

Jorwerth Drwndwn made this place his residence; and here is said to have been born his son,
Llewelyn the Great[l], who began his reign in the
time of *Richard* I. If *Dolinchalan* castle is, as I
suppose, the same with this, *Gryffydd ap Tudor,*
in the reign of *Edward* I. had, as constable, an

---

[i] Tertium est, jus leges condendi, et MONETAM PERCUTIENDI. *Wotton's Leges Wallicæ,* 71.
   [k] *Leges Wallicæ,* 71.   [l] *Gwedir Fam.* 7.

annual salary of forty marks, payed at the exchequer at *Caernarvon*, at two different payments.

Meredydd ap Jevan, an ancestor of the *Wynns* of *Gwedir*, in the reign of *Henry* VII. purchased the lease of this castle, and the inclosures belonging to it, from the executors of Sir *Ralph Berkenet*; it having been excepted among the places granted by *Richard* III. and resumed by his successor[m]. Before that time, *Hoel, ap Evan, ap Rhys Gethin*, a noted outlaw, resided here. As soon as it came into the possession of *Meredydd*, he removed his residence from *Efionedd*, a hundred in the county, to this castle; giving this excellent reason: "I had " rather fight with outlaws and thieves, than with " my own blood and kindred: If I live in mine own " house in *Efionedd*, I must either kill my own " kinsmen, or be killed by them!" The feuds among the gentry in *Efionedd*, occasioned perpetual murders; and *Nant-Conwy* was filled with banditti.

THIS gentleman soon reformed the country: he established colonies of the *most tall and able men* he could procure; till at last they amounted to seven score tall bowmen, every one arrayed in a " jacket or armolet coate, a good steele cap, a " short sword and dagger, together with his bow

---

[m] *Gwedir Family*, 137; a publication we are indebted for, to my respected friend, the honorable DAINES BARRINGTON.

" and arrowes; many of them alsoe had horses and
" chasing slaves, which were ready to answer the
" crie on all occasions[n]."

PENAMNAEN. HE founded the strong house of *Penamnaen*, a
mile distant from the castle. He removed the
church, which before lay in a thicket, to a more
open place, by way of security; for he never dared
to quit this house, without leaving in it a strong
guard; and another of twenty tall archers to attend
him, whenever he went to church; besides a watch-
man, on a rock called *Carreg y Big*, to give notice
of the approach of the banditti. He ended his useful life in 1525, and left behind him twenty-three
legitimate, and three natural children.

THE church, once an impropriation of the abby
of *Bedd Kelert*, is very small; and has in it a monument, commemorating such of the family who were
buried here.

IN my return to *Pont y Pair*, digressed a little
up the river *Llugwy*, to see a noted cascade, called
RHAIADR Y *Rhaiadr y Wenol*, or *The Water-fall of the Swal-*
WENOL. *low*[1]. The river runs along a strait stony channel,

---

[n] *Gwedir* family.

[1] This is now well known as the Swallow Falls, but I believe the
rendering is wrong, as *gwennol* is not only a swallow, but the angle
in the swallow's tail-feathers, and a narrow triangular piece cut out
of a sheep's ear, for instance, as a mark, is called a *gwennol* by the
shepherds. The reference in the case of the fall, is to the rock which
divides the water into two sheets, so that the name was meant to be
more descriptive than would seem from the English rendering of it. J.R.

for a considerable way, amidst narrow meadows, bounded by majestic *Alpine* scenery; then falls into an amazing hollow. The bottom is difficult of access; but when arrived at, exhibits a wonder-ful scene of mountain and precipice, shaded with trees, which fringe the top, and start even from the fissures of the sides.

CROSS *Pont y Pair*, and go beneath a very lofty rock, cloathed with wood, called *Carreg y Gwalch,* or *The Rock of the Falcon.* Here was the retreat of a famous partizan of the house of *Lancaster*, called *Dafydd ap Shenkin*, who lurked in a cave, still named, from him, *Ogo Dafydd ap Shenkin.* The noblest oaks in all *Wales* grew on this rock, within memory of man. I remember the stools of several, which proved that they were equal to any which flourish in the deepest soil; yet these rocks are totally destitute of earth for a considerable way, so that the nutriment which the oaks received, must have been derived from the deep penetration of the roots, through the fissures of the stones, into some nutritive matter.

CARREG Y GWALCH.

THE antient house of *Gwedir* stands near the foot of this rock. It is built round a greater and lesser court. Over the gate-way is the date, 1555, with I. W. *John Wynn ap Meredydd,* grandfather to the famous Sir *John,* author of the memoirs of the family. This shews 1553, the supposed time

GWEDIR.

of the death of the former, to be a mistake. The
place takes its name from *Gwaed-dir*([1]), the bloody
land, from the battles fought here by *Llywarch
Hên*[o], about the year 610; or perhaps from the
cruel battle in 952, between the sons of *Hoel*, and
the princes *Jevaf* and *Iago*[p]; and a third may be
added, between *Gryffydd ap Cynan*, and *Trahaern
ap Cradog*, equally bloody[q]. The supposition that
it was derived from its being the first house in
Wales which had *glass windows* is not well founded,
those conveniences having been known long before.
Sir *John Wynn* himself even mentions a date of
1512, on a window at *Dolwyddelan*, which is long
before the building of *Gwedir*. But the following
lines of a poet, who flourished some centuries
before, is still a stronger proof of the antiquity of
glass in our country:

> Trwy ffenestri *Gwydir* yd ym gwelent[r]
> They see me through the glass windows.

ON a rock, high above the *Lower Gwedir*, stood
another, called *The Upper*, seemingly built for the
enjoyment of the beautiful view it commands of
the rich meadows watered by the *Conwy*, and their
elegant boundaries. It was a sort of *Diæta*, or

([1]) The name is pronounced *Gwydir*, and I fear we must still regard the meaning of it as uncertain. J.R.
   [o] See his works.   [p] *Powel* 60.   [q] *Vide* his Life.
   [r] See the poems of *Cynddelw Brydydd Mawr*, who flourished about
the year 1250.

summer-house, erected by Sir *John Wynn,* in 1604,
who had a classical taste. The walls were covered
with inscriptions; and the situation well deserved
the panegyric bestowed on it in the following
Welsh lines, placed over the entrance:

> Bryn *Gwedir* gwelir goleu adeilad
> Uwch dolydd a chaurau
> Bryn gwych adail yn ail ne;
> Bron wen Henllys brenhinlle.

" A conspicuous edifice on *Gwedir* hill, towering over the adjacent
" land; a well-chosen situation, a second paradise, a fair bank, a
" palace of royalty[s]."

THIS has been of late demolished; but the family
chapel, which stands near the site of the old house,
is still preserved, and service performed in it every
Sunday evening. Among various papers belonging to *Gwedir,* communicated to me by my friend,
Paul Panton esq; is a curious one, drawn up by
old Sir *John Wynn,* prescribing the rules to his
chaplain; an odd mixture of insolence and piety[t].
The inventory of his wardrobe, drawn up in his
own hand, is also worth preservation, as it shews
not only the complete dress of a man of rank in
those days, but the great œconomy of the times,
among people of fashion, when their wardrobe
was bestowed by will, and passed from generation
to generation[u].

[s] *Hist. Gwedir Fam.* xii.

[t] Appendix, No. X.   [u] The same, No. XI.

SIR *John* was sent to *London* in 1574, to study
the law; was a man of abilities, and particularly
attentive to the antiquities of his country and
family.   His consequence gained him the notice
of the court; for he was made a baronet in *June*
1611.

THIS place continued in the family till the year
1678, when it passed into that of the late duke of
Ancaster, by the marriage of *Mary*, daughter and
heiress of Sir *Richard Wynn*, with *Robert* marquis of *Lindsey;* and is now possessed by Sir
Peter Burrel[x], knight, in right of his wife *Pris-
cilla*, baroness *Willoughby*, eldest sister to *Robert*,
late duke of *Ancaster*.

LLANRWST
BRIDGE.
FROM hence to *Llanrwst* is a pretty walk, mostly
by the side of the river.   The town lies in *Denbighshire*, on the opposite bank to *Gwedir*.   The approach is over the bridge, the boasted plan of *Inigo*

INIGO JONES.
Jones.   It consists of three arches; the middle
fifty-nine feet wide: two are extremely beautiful,
and mark the hand of the architect: the third differs greatly, having been rebuilt in 1703, by a very
inferior genius.   I wish I could do more honor to
my country, and suppose *Inigo* to have been a
native of this neighborhood: but he seems to
have been by birth a *Londoner*, the son of a cloth-

[x] Created Baron *Gwydir* in 1796.   ED.

worker[y], who, in all probability, was of this part of *Wales;* our clame, however, to the son is supported by the universal tradition of the country. The turn of his countenance, and the violence of his passions[z], at lest legitimate no distant descent. He was patronised by the earl of *Arundel,* and *William* earl of *Pembroke;* and by one or other sent into *Italy.* His real christian name was *Ynyr,* which he there changed into *Inigo,* or *Ignatius.* Thus, *John Cooper,* master of tho *Viol de Gamba* to *Charles* I. after he had been in *Italy,* assumed the name of *Giovani Coperario*[a]. It is vain to give the life of a man, which has been so amply written by one of the ablest pens in the fine arts. Let it suffice to say, that the first Sir *Richard Wynn* procured from *Jones* the plan of this bridge, of which he was founder, in 1636; determined to do his country all possible honor, by the beauty of the design, invented by an architect to which *Wales* had at least a near relation[b].

THERE is one circumstance attending this great genius, which deserves mention, as it bears some relation to the country from whence he may have derived his origin. When he was employed to

[y] Mr. WALPOLE's Anecd. Painting, ii. 142.

[z] His print, tab. at p. 142. Anecd. and his Life, *passim.*

[a] *Hawkin's* Hist. Music, iv. 55.

[b] Among all the family papers, there is not the least mention of *Inigo,* which must have been the case, had he been an *eleve* of the *Wynns,* as has been popularly asserted.

furnish rare devices, and paint the scenery for the
masques of the festive year 1619, he selected the
Creigie'r eira, or a scene in *Snowdonia,* for the
masque FOR THE HONOR OF WALES. He did it
with such success, as to excite the envy of the
poet, *Ben Jonson;* for the scenes were more admired than the entertainment, which might very
well be: but *Jonson* was so offended, as to give
vent to his spleen in a copy of verses, as imbecil as
they were rancorous and ill-founded[c].

THE river here makes a handsome appearance,
extending in a direct line far above the bridge, and
often enlivened with the coracles, the *vitilia na-
vigia* of the antient *Britons,* busied in taking salmon; and in the months of *February* and *March,*
numbers of smelt. The tide does not flow nearer
than *Llyn y Graig,* a mile and half below the
bridge, where, in spring tides, boats of twelve tons
may come.

TOWN OF
LLANRWST,
AND CHURCH. THE town of *Llanrwst* is small, and ill built;
and has nothing remarkable, except the church,
which is dedicated to *St. Rystyd,* or *Restitutus*([1]),
archbishop of *London* in 361, present at the council of *Arles* in 353. The ground on which it is
built, is said to have been given by *Rhun,* the son

---

[c] *Ben Jonson's* Works, vi. 294.

([1]) The name involved in *Llanrwst* was *Grwst* or *Gwrwst,* the exact
equivalent of the Goidelic Fergus. J.R.

of *Nefydd Hardd*, to expiate the foul murder of prince *Idwal*, a son of *Owen Gwynedd*, slain by order of his foster-father, *Nefydd*, to whom he had been intrusted[d]. Some curious carving, said to have been brought from the neighboring abby, graces the inside. The *Gwedir* chapel, founded in 1633, by the above-mentioned Sir *Richard Wynn*, from a design of *Inigo*, would be another ornament, if not so shamefully neglected. On the wall is a ruinous marble monument[e], elegantly ornamented with trophies: it was meant to commemorate the ancestors of the family; but soon promises to tumble into a heap of undistinguishable rubbish.

TRAMPLED under feet, are several brass plates[f], admirably engraven with the heads of several of the family, who rest beneath. Among them is that of Sir *John Wynn*, compiler of the memoirs, who died in 1626. The country people have a tradition, that he was a great oppressor; and accordingly have sent his perturbed spirit to reside in the neighboring cataract of *Rhaiadr y Wenol*. The head of his wife, *Sidney*[g], daughter of Sir

BRASSES AND TOMBS.

[d] XV Tribes, of which *Nefydd* was one.
[e] Appendix, No. XII.
[f] Since the publication of this work, some attention has been paid to these venerable remains; the brass plates have been removed, and judiciously fixed in the walls of the chapel. ED.
[g] Died in 1639.

William Gerard, chancellor of *Ireland,* is elegantly
engraven on a plate near him: that of their daughter, *Mary,* wife of Sir *Roger Mostyn,* on another.
These were the work of *Sylvanus Crue.* But a
half-length of dame *Sarah Wynn*[h], daughter of Sir
Thomas Middleton, of *Chirk castle,* and wife to Sir
Richard Wynn, by *William Vaughan,* is by far
the most beautiful piece of engraving I ever saw:
yet neither the name of this, nor of the foregoing
artist, is on the records of the fine arts. Her
husband was a gentleman of distinguished merit,
groom of the bed-chamber to *Charles* I. when
prince of *Wales,* and one of his attendants in the
wild expedition into *Spain,* in 1623. He left
behind him an excellent account of the journey,
which was published by Mr. *Hearne.* He died
the 19th of *July* 1649, and was interred distant
from his country, in the church of *Wimbledon.* A
fine head of him, by *Jansen,* is preserved at *Wynn-
Stay;* and the charming print from it, by that ini-
mitable artist, Mr. *Bartolozzi,* lays me under very
great obligations to Sir *Watkin Williams Wynn,*
to whose spontaneous munificence I am indebted
for so considerable an ornament to my book[i].

A VERY plain stone records the death of his
eldest brother, Sir *John Wynn* knight, who died
at *Lucca,* on his travels, in 1614, and was buried

---

[h] Died in 1671.   [i] Journey to *Snowdon,* Pl. iv. ED.

there, in the parish of *St. John*.   I have seen numbers of his letters, which shew him to have been a very observant man; some of them may, in the Appendix[k], prove an amusement to the reader.

ONE other tomb, of far greater antiquity than the others, remains to be mentioned; that of *Howel Coytmor*, whose figure, armed, is represented in stone.   He was grandson of the knight at *Bettws;* owned *Gwedir*, which was sold by one of his posterity to the family of the *Wynns*.

IN this church is preserved the stone coffin of *Llewelyn the Great*, with the sides curiously cut into quatre-foils.   That prince was interred in *Conwy* abby; but at the dissolution, the coffin was removed to this place.

I MADE from *Llanrwst* two excursions; one to visit *Maynan Abby*, translated hither in 1289, from *Conwy*, by permission of pope *Nicholas*[l], as he says, at the request of *Edward* I. and the monks.   The king bestowed on them the township of *Maynan*, in lieu of *Conwy*, and confirmed to them all the revenues and privileges they before enjoyed, together with various immunities from taxes, tolls, and duties[m]; and besides, gave them the patronage of their antient church at *Conwy*[n]

MAYNAN
ABBY.

[k] No. XIII.   [l] *Rymer*, ii. 427.
[m] *Dugdale Mon.* i. 921.   *Stevens's Transl.* 106.
[n] *Rotulæ Walliæ*, 92.

The revenues of this house, at the dissolution, were, according to *Dugdale*, one hundred and sixty-two pounds fifteen shillings; to *Speed*, one hundred and seventy-nine pounds ten shillings and tenpence. The last abbot was *Richard Kyffyn*[o], who had a pension of twenty pounds a year. The abby was granted, in the fifth of queen *Elizabeth*, to *Elizeus Wynne;* and it is still[p] possessed by his descendant, lady *Wynne*, widow of the late Sir *John Wynne*, of *Glynllivon*. A large old house[q], built from the materials of the abby, still remains.

I RETURNED through *Llanrwst*, and about two miles beyond, high over the *Conwy*, visit the village

of *Trefriw*, where numbers of small vessels are built, and sent down the river at spring tides. It is said that *Llewelyn the Great* had near this place a palace; and, as a proof, several hewn stones have been found, in ploughing a field called *Gardd y Neuodd*. The church of *Trefriw* was originally built by *Llewelyn*, for the ease of his princess, who before was obliged to go on foot to *Llanrhychwyn*, a long walk among the mountains[r].

FROM hence I went back as far as *Gwedir*, and ascended a very steep hill, leaving the park be-

[o] *Willis* calls him *Richard ap Rhys.*

[p] At present (1809) it belongs to Lord *Newborough*, grandson to Sir *John Wynne*, of *Glynllivon*. ED.

[q] This house has recently been enlarged and improved. ED.

[r] *Sebright MS.*

longing to the house on the left. Go over an
open space, called *Bwlch yr Haiarn,* full of turberies, the providential fuel of the country. Some
lead-mines have been discovered in these parts,
but none of any consequence. The *Gale,* or bog GALE, OR
BOG MYR-
TLE.
myrtle, abounds here, and perfumes the air with its
spicy smell. It is a northern plant, but does not
extend far. It is found in *Lapland, Norway,* and
Sweden, and in several parts of the *Alpine* regions
of *Great Britain.* It is called *Bwrli,* or the eme
tic plant; and *Gwyrddling,* or green plant. Our
countrymen use it as a yellow dye. They lay
branches of it upon and under their beds, to keep
off fleas and moths; and also give it in powder or
infusion, and apply it to the abdomen as a vermi-
fuge. It is besides sometimes used as a *succeda-
neum* for hops.

THE *Sorbus aucuparia*[s], or mountain ash, is frequent in these parts. The poorer sort of people
make a drink, called *diodgriafol,* by infusing the berries in water. In former times, a superstitious use
was made of the wood: a piece, made in form of a
cross, was carried in the pocket, as an infallible
preservative against all sorts of fascinations.

AFTER gaining the summit, visit, to the right,
Llyn Geirionnydd, a small lake, noted for having
had near it the habitation of the celebrated *Taliesin,* TALIESIN.

---

[s] Pyrus aucuparia. *Smith, Fl. Br.* p. 533. ED.

who flourished about the year 560, in the time of
Gwyddno Garanhir, a petty prince of *Cantre'r
Gwaelod*. The history of our famous bard begins
like that of *Moses;* for he was found exposed on
the water, wrapped in a leathern bag, in a wear
which had been granted to *Elphin*, son of *Gwyddno*, for his support. The young prince, reduced by
his extravagance, burst into tears, at finding, as he
imagined, so unprofitable a booty. He took pity
on the infant, and caused proper care to be taken
of him. After this, *Elphin* prospered: and *Taliesin,*
when he grew up, addressed to him the following
moral ode, styled *Dyhuddiant* ELPHIN, or ELPHIN's
Consolation; supposed to have been addressed to
the prince by the infant bard, on the night he was
found. I take the liberty of using the beautiful
translation, with which a fair countrywoman of
mine hath lately favored the world[t].

ELPHIN deg taw ath wylo
Na chabled, &c[u].

I.

ELPHIN! fair as roseate morn,
Cease, O lovely youth! to mourn;
Mortals never should presume
To dispute their Maker's doom.
Feeble race! too blind to scan
What th' Almighty deigns for man;

---

[t] Printed in M.DCC.LXXX. 4to. and sold by *Dodsley* and *Elmsly*.
[u] See Mr. *Evan Evans's* Collection, 150.

Humble hope be still thy guide,
Steady faith thy only pride,
Then despair will fade away,
Like demons at th' approach of day,
CUNLLO's prayers acceptance gain,
Goodness never sues in vain;
He, who formed the sky, is just,
In him alone, O ELPHIN! trust.
See glist'ning spoils in shoals appear,
Fate smiles this hour on *Gwyddno*'s wear.

II.

ELPHIN fair! the clouds dispell
That on thy lovely visage dwell!
Wipe, ah! wipe the pearly tear,
Nor let thy manly bosom fear;
What good can melancholy give?
'Tis bondage in her train to live.
Pungent sorrows doubts proclaim,
Ill suit those doubts a Christian's name;
Thy great Creator's wonders trace
His love divine to mortal race,
Then doubt, and fear, and pain will fly,
And hope beam radiant in thine eye.
Behold me, least of human kind,
Yet Heav'n illumes my soaring mind.
Lo! from the yawning deep I came,
Friend to thy lineage and thy fame,
To point thee out the paths of truth,
To guard from hidden rocks thy youth;
From seas, from mountains, far and wide,
God will the good and virtuous guide.

III.

ELPHIN fair! with virtue blest,
Let not that virtue idly rest;
If rous'd, 'twill yield thee sure relief,
And banish far unmanly grief:
Think on that Pow'r, whose arm can save,
Who e'en can snatch thee from the grave;

He bade my harp for thee be strung,
Prophetic lays he taught my tongue.
Though like a slender reed I grow,
Toss'd by the billows to and fro,
Yet still, by Him inspir'd, my song
The weak can raise, confound the strong:
Am not I better, ELPHIN, say,
Than thousands of thy scaly prey[x]?

IV.

ELPHIN! fair as roseate morn,
Cease, O lovely youth! to mourn.
Weak on my leathern couch I lie,
Yet heavenly lore I can descry;
Gifts divine my tongue inspire,
My bosom glows celestial fire;
Mark! how it mounts! my lips disclose
The certain fate of ELPHIN'S foes.
Fix thy hopes on Him alone,
Who is th' eternal Three in One;
There thy ardent vows be given,
Prayer acceptance meets from Heav'n·
Then thou shalt adverse fate defy,
And ELPHIN glorious live and die.

GLYN LLUGWY. FROM this lake I descended a great steep, into *Glyn Llugwy*, a bottom watered by the *Llugwy*, fertile in grass, and varied by small groves of young oaks; very unlike the great woods which cloathed this place, *Dyffryn Mymbyr, Llanberis*, and other parts of *Snowdon*, in the time of *Leland*[y]. Go through a narrow pass, high above a raging torrent, falling in broken cascades from rock to rock.

[x] In the original, SALMONS.　　　[y] *Itin.* v. 45.

SNOWDON FROM CAPEL CURIG.

At a small distance from hence, enter *Dyffryn Mymbyr*, a valley in which woods, and even trees, disappear. The small church of *Capel Curig*, and a few scattered houses, give a little life to this dreary tract. *Snowdon* and all his sons, *Crib Goch, Crib y Distill, Lliwedd yr Aran*, and many others, here burst at once in full view, and make this far the finest approach to our boasted *Alps*. The boundaries of this vale are, on one side, the base of the crooked mountain, *Moel Siabod;* on the other, that of the *Glyder Bach* and several other hills of lesser note. The bottom is meadowy; at this time enlivened with the busy work of hay harvest, and filled with drags, horses, and even men and women, loaden with hay. The middle is varied with two small lakes[z], along whose sides we rode; and at some distance beyond them, near *Pont y Gwryd*, quitted our horses, to visit the summit of the *Glyder*, noted for the report, the editor of *Camden* had made, of the singular disposition of the rocks. We directed our servants to go on to *Llanberis*, with our steeds. The ascent was extremely long, steep, and laborious, wet and slippery; and almost the whole way covered with

[z] Above the lower of these lakes, amongst this scene of grandeur and desolation, a large and commodious inn was erected by the late Lord P*enrhyn*. It forms an intermediate stage betwen *Bangor* and *Kenioge*. The view of "*Snowdon* and all his sons," from the terrace at the back of the house, is peculiarly striking. ED.

loose fragments of rocks, beneath which was a
continual roar of waters, seeking their way to the
bottom.

GLYDER
BACH. OUR pains were fully repaid on attaining the
summit. The area was covered with groupes of
stones, of vast size, from ten to thirty feet long,
lying in all directions: most of them were of a columnar form, often piled on one another: in other
places, half erect, sloping down, and supported by
others, which lie without any order at their bases.
The tops are frequently crowned in the strangest
manner with other stones, lying on them horizontally. One was about twenty-five feet long, and
six broad: I climbed up, and on stamping with
my foot, felt a strong tremulous motion from end
to end. Another eleven feet long, and six in circumference in the thinnest part, was poised so
nicely on the point of a rock, that, to appearance,
the touch of a child would overset it. A third
enormous mass had the property of a rocking
stone.

I SHOULD consider this mountain to have been
a sort of wreck of nature, formed and flung up by
some mighty internal convulsion, which has given
these vast groupes of stones fortuitously such a
strange disposition; for had they been settled strata,
bared of their earth by a long series of rains, they
would have retained a regular appearance, as we
observe in all other beds of similar matter.

TREVAEN & PART OF LLYN OGWEN.

One side of this mountain is formed into a gap, *herissée,* I may call it, with sharp rocks, pointing upwards, one above the other, to a great height. In the midst of a vale far below, rises the singular mountain *Trevaen,*([1]) assuming on this side a pyra- TREVAEN. midal form, naked, and very rugged. A precipice, from the summit of which I surveyed the strange scene, forbad my approach to examine the nature of its composition.

FROM *Glyder Bach* I passed over a plain, above half a mile broad, called *Y Waun Oer, The Chilly Mountainous Flat.* Observe from the edge in a tremendous hollow, *Llyn y Bwchllwyd,* or *The Lake of the Grey Goat;* and in the bottom of the valley, near the foot of the *Trevaen, Llyn Ogwen,* noted for its fine trout.

FROM *Waen Oer* we made a most hazardous descent to *Cwm Bwchllwyd,* and from thence to *Llyn Ogwen.* The way from that place into the valley, or rather chasm, of *Nant Francon,* is called *The Ben-glog,* the most dreadful horse path[a] in BEN-GLOG. *Wales,* worked in the rudest manner into steps, for a great length. On one side, in a deep hollow, formed under fallen rocks, was once the hiding place of *Rŷs Goch o'r Eryri,* or *Rhys the Red* of

(¹) It is called *Tryfan.* J.R.

[a] Converted by the enterprizing spirit of the late Lord *Penrhyn* into an excellent road, forming the most frequented thoroughfare to *Ireland.* ED.

Snowdon; a mountain bard, patronised by *Robert ap Meredydd,* a partizan of *Glyndwr,* an outlawed chieftain, of whose fortunes he partook. I do assure the traveller, who delights in wild nature, that a visit to it up *Nant Francon*[b], from *Bangor,* will not be repented. The waters of five lakes dart down the precipice of the middle of the *Ben-glog,* and form the torrent of the *Ogwen,* which falls into the sea a few miles lower. This bottom is surrounded with mountains of a stupendous height, mostly precipitous; the tops of many edged with pointed rocks. I have, from the depth beneath, seen the shepherds skipping from peak to peak; but the point of contact was so small, that from this distance they seemed to my uplifted eyes like beings of another order floating in the air.

THE *Trevaen,* from this bottom, makes also a very singular appearance, resembling a human face, reclined backward. Forehead, nose, lips, and chin, are very apparent; and you may add, without any great strain of fancy, the beard of an antient inhabitant, an arch-druid.

CWM IDWAL.   BEGIN another hard ascent to *Cwm Idwal,* in-famous for the murder of a young prince of that

[b] Exclusive of the interest arising from the grandeur of the scenery, the traveller has now the opportunity of being gratified in the course of his excursion with a sight of *Ogwen Bank,* the slate quarries, the well constructed railways, and the great and various improvements effected by the late Lord *Penrhyn* in the previously desolate tract of *Nant Francon.* ED.

name, son of *Owen Gwynedd*, by *Dunawt*, son of *Nefydd Hardd*, one of the fifteen tribes of *North Wales*, to whom *Owen* had entrusted the youth, to be fostered, according to the custom of the country. It was a fit place to inspire murderous thoughts, environed with horrible precipices, shading a lake, lodged in its bottom. The shepherds fable, that it is the haunt of *Dæmons;* and that no bird dare fly over its damned water, fatal as that of *Avernus*.

> Quam super haud ullæ poterant impunè volantes
> Tendere iter pennis.

NEAR this place is a quarry, noted for excellent hones, of which quantities are sent annually to London.

A NEW and greater toil is to be undergone in the ascent from *Cwm Idwal*, to the heights I had left. The way lies beneath that vast precipice, *Castell y Geifr*, or *The Castle of the Goats*. In some distant age, the ruins of a rocky mountain formed a road by a mighty lapse. A stream of stones, each of monstrous size, points towards the *Cwm;* and are to be clambered over by those only, who possess a degree of bodily activity, as well as strength of head to bear the sight of the dreadful hollows frequent beneath them.

OBSERVE, on the right, a stupendous *roche fendue*, or split rock, called *Twll-Du*, and *The Devil's Kitchen*. It is a horrible gap, in the TWLL-DU.

centre of a great black precipice, extending in
length about a hundred and fifty yards; in depth,
about a hundred; and only six wide; perpendicu-
larly open to the surface of the mountain.   On
surmounting all my difficulties, and taking a little
breath, I ventured to look down this dreadful aper-
ture, and found its horrors far from being lessened
in my exalted situation; for to it were added the
waters of *Llyn y Cwm*, impetuously rushing through
its bottom.

KLOGWYN
DU.

Reach the *Glyder Fawr*, and pass by the edge
of *Klogwyn Du Ymhen y Glyder*, as dreadful a
precipice as any in *Snowdonia*, hanging over the
dire waters of *Llyn Idwal*.   Its neighborhood is of
great note among botanists for rare plants, among
which may be reckoned the *Saxifraga nivalis, Bulbocodium,*[a] and the *Lichen islandicus*.   The last[b] is
of singular use to the *Icelanders*.   A decoction of
the fresh leaves in water serves them in the spring
as a powerful cathartic; and yet, when dried, changes its quality, and, if grinded to powder, is a
common food, either made unto bread, or boiled
with milk, or water.   *Haller* and *Scopoli* also men-

---

[a] The BULBOCODIUM of *Ray*, Syn. 274, the ANTHERICUM *serotinum*
of later writers, which the reverend author of a Tour of "Botanical
Researches," misled by a name, has converted into the BULBOCODIUM
vernum; a plant he pretends to have discovered on the *Glyder*, but
which certainly was never found in a wild state either in *Wales* or
England.   ED.

[b] *Lightfoot's Fl. Scotica,* ii. 83.

tion its use, at their time, in *Vienna*, in coughs and consumptions, made into broth, or gruel.[c]

THE prospect from this mountain is very noble. *Snowdon* is seen to great advantage; the deep vale of *Llanberis* and its lakes, *Nant Francon*, and a variety of other singular views. The plain which forms the top is strangely covered with loose stones like the beach of the sea; in many places crossing one another in all directions, and entirely naked. Numerous groupes of stones are placed almost erect, sharp pointed, and in sheafs: all are weather-beaten, time-eaten, and honey-combed, and of a venerable grey-color. The elements seem to have warred against this mountain: rains have washed, lightnings torn, the very earth deserted it, and the winds made it the constant object of their fury. The shepherds make it the residence of storms, and style a part of it *Carnedd y Gwynt*, or *The Eminence of Tempests*.

GLYDER FAWR.

THIS mountain is connected to the lesser *Glyder* by the *Waun Oer*: the traveller therefore has his choice of ways to these wondrous mountains; but the most preferable for ease, is the road I descended into the vale of *Llanberis*. In my way, pass close by a rugged brow of a hill, which I think is *Rhyw y Glyder*, recorded by LLWYD and RAY,

[c] It has since been introduced into the *British* Pharmacopeia. *Woodville* Med. Bot. p. 566, tab. 203. ED.

for its variety of plants.   From thence descend by
Oleu Fawr.

LLYN Y CWN.   SOON after, visit the small lake, called *Llyn y
Cwn,* noted for the tale of *Giraldus*[a], who informs
us, that in his days the three kinds of fish it yielded,
trouts, perch, and eels, were monocular, every
one wanting the left eye.   At present there is not
a fish in it to disprove the relation.   To make
amends the botanists will find in it the *Lobelia
dortmanna, Subularia aquatica,* and *Isoetis lacus-
tris;* and not far from it the *Juncus triglumis,*
common to this, and some of the *Highland* mountains.   The *Hieracium alpinum, Rubus saxatilis,
Solidago cambrica,* and other rare plants, are to be
met with.   In the course of this part of the descent, leave on the right *Llider*([1]) *Fawr* and *Llider
Fach,* two great mountains, part of the boundaries
of *Nant-Beris;* and arrive in that vale by *Caunant
yr Esgar*([2]), or *The Dingle of the Enemy.*

NANT-BERIS.   THIS is a very picturesque vale, bounded by the
base of *Snowdon, Cefn Cwm Gafr,* the two *Glyders,*
and two *Lliders,* each of them first-rate mountains.
It is strait, and of nearly an equal breadth, filled

[a] Sir *Richard Hoare's* Ed. vol. ii. p. 131.

([1]) *Llider* is not to be heard, but only *Y Lidir,* which may be for
some such a name as *Elidir,* meaning Elidir's Mountain. J.R.

([2]) The explanation is much too serious: the word is *esgair,* which
means the spur of a mountain, or a low ridge connected with higher
ground. J.R.

NANTBERIS WITH THE GLYDER & CRIB GOCH.

by some meadows and two magnificent lakes, which communicate to each other by means of a river. The venerable oaks, spoken of by *Leland*, are no more. Avarice, or dissipation, and its constant follower, poverty, have despoiled much of our principality of its leafy beauties. Among the numberless errors of this performance, I fear the word IS cloathed with trees, must be supplied by the traveller, with WAS. But this shadeless tract is still worthy his attention. A road, once a succession of rude and stony stairs, made with much labor, ran on one side, high above the lake, and was often cut out of the rock. This is, I am informed now, changed into a road, which too much facilitates the approach, and lessens its propriety, and its agreement with the wild environs.

ON a lofty rock, above one of the lakes, stand the remains of *Castell Dolbadern*, consisting of a round tower, and a few fragments of walls. CASTELL DOLBADERN. It was constructed with the thin laminated stones of the country, cemented with very strong mortar, without shells. The inner diameter of the tower is only twenty-six feet. This seems to have been built to defend the pass into the interior parts of *Snowdonia;* it was likewise used as a state prison. The founder was evidently a *Welsh* prince. I am informed that it was *Padarn Beisrydd*([1]) son of *Idwal.*

IN this valley are two groupes of wretched houses. The farthest is near the end of the upper lake, with its church, dedicated to *St. Peris,* who was, we are told, a cardinal. Here is to be seen the well of the saint, inclosed with a wall. The sybil of the place attends, and divines your fortune by the appearance or non-appearance of a little fish, which lurks in some of its holes.

FROM hence I took a ride above the lakes, to their lower extremity. The upper is the lest, but much the most beautiful piece of water. It is said to be in places a hundred and forty yards deep; to have abounded with char, before they were reduced by the streams flowing from the copper mines, which had been worked on the sides of the hills. The lower lake is about a mile and a half long, narrows gradually into the form of a river, called the *Rythell*([2]), and flows in a diffused channel to *Caernarvon,* where it assumes the name of *Seiont.*

MARGARET
UCH EVAN.   NEAR this end of the lake lives a celebrated personage, whom I was disappointed in not finding at home. This is *Margaret uch Evan,* of *Penllyn,*

([1]) *Padarn Beisrydd* (more correctly *Beisrudd,*) was the grand-father of *Cunedda,* and much too early for this. J.R.

([2]) The name of this river is now *Rhythallt.* J.R.

the last specimen of the strength and spirit of the antient *British* fair. She is at this time[c] about ninety years of age. This extraordinary female was the greatest hunter, shooter, and fisher, of her time. She kept a dozen at lest of dogs, terriers, grehounds, and spaniels, all excellent in their kinds. She killed more foxes in one year, than all the confederate hunts do in ten: rowed stoutly, and was queen of the lake: fiddled excellently, and knew all our old music: did not neglect the mechanic arts, for she was a very good joiner: and, at the age of seventy, was the best wrestler in the country, and few young men dared to try a fall with her. Some years ago, she had a maid of congenial qualities; but death, that mighty hunter, at last earthed this faithful companion of her's. *Margaret* was also blacksmith, shoe-maker, boat-builder, and maker of harps. She shoed her own horses, made her own shoes, and built her own boats, while she was under contract to convey the copper ore down the lakes. I must not forget, that all the neighboring bards payed their addresses to *Margaret*, and celebrated her exploits in pure *British* verse. At length she gave her hand to the most effeminate of her admirers, as if predetermined to maintain the superiority which nature had bestowed on her.

[c] 1786.

ABOUT half a mile farther, I visited the remains
of *Llys Dinorddwig*([1]), a house said to have been
one of the palaces of prince *Llewelyn ap Gryffydd:*
the walls high and strong; the hall twenty-four
yards long; and before the house is a deep ditch
over which had probably been a draw-bridge.   Not

very far from hence is a spot, called *Rhyw'r Cyrn,*
or *The Brow of the Horns;* where, according to
old usage, an officer stood and blew his horn, to
give notice to the houshold of the approach of
their master, or to summon the vassals to assemble
on all occasions of emergency.

THIS is part of the woodless flat, between the
mountains and the *Menai.*   Its want of strength
is supplied by several posts, fortified in the *British*
manner.   *Dinas Dinorddwig*, about half a mile
south-east of the church of *Llandeniolen*[*], is the
chief.   The area is very large, surrounded with an
agger of small stones, backed by another of very
large ones, then succeeds a deep ditch, a rampart
of earth, a second vast ditch, and a third rampart:
within the area is a circle of stones, the post probably of the commander in chief.

([1]) This is now always pronounced *Dinorwig*, and it would be interesting to know what authority there is for the longer form given
by *Pennant*, as it would seem to connect the name with the *Ordovices:* it is right to add that it is printed *Dinorddwig* in Johnson's
Diary of a Journey in North Wales in 1774. J.R.

[*] In the church-yard is an yew tree, twenty-seven feet in girth.

To the east is a strong chalybeate water, formerly in much repute. It is called *Ffynon Cegin Arthur*, or *The Water of Arthur's Kitchen*, and is the source of *Aber Cegin*, which falls into the sea between *Bangor* and *Penrhyn*.

In our way from hence, we passed by another post, called *Pen y Gaer;* and soon after, by a smaller, called *Bryn y Castrelau*, surrounded with a single wall; and on an eminence on the other side of the *Rythell*, is another, named *Caer Cwm y Glo*, or *Caer Carreg-y-Fran*, from which had been (as we were informed) a paved way to *Llys Dinorddwig*. I may here add, that after the death of *Llewelyn, Edward* I. bestowed that palace on Sir *Gryffydd Llwyd*, the same gentleman who first brought him the news of the birth of his son *Edward* of *Caernarvon*.

Return by the same road, and, after refreshing myself with a night's rest at Mr. *Close's*, agent to the mines in *Llanberis*, early in the morning began our ascent to the highest peak of *Snowdon*, under the guidance of *Hugh Shone*, whom I beg leave to recommend as a most able conductor. Keep upon the side of the lake, for a considerable way; then turn to the left, and see, not far from the road, *Ceunant Mawr*, a noble cataract, precipitating over two vast rocks into two most horrible chasms. Near this place were found several beads; some of glass, and one of jet.

CEUNANT MAWR.

THE beads and a remarkable shell, that were found in the same place, are in the possession of the Reverend *John Llwyd* of *Caerwys.* The beads are known in *Caernarvonshire,* &c. by the name of *Glain Neidr,* and are worn as amulets against the chin-cough, &c.

ASCEND, above *Cwm Brwynog,* a very deep bottom, fertile in *Gwair y Rhosydd,* which is composed chiefly of different kinds of rushes, particularly *Juncus squarrosus,* the moss rush, *Scirpus cœspitosus,* the heath club rush, *Schœnus nigricans,* the black bog rush, and *carices,* intermixed with a few kinds of grass. The hay which the lower meadows produce, is very different in quality, being remarkable fine and soft; and consists in great part of the fine bent grass[g], *Agrostis capillaris.* As

GRASSES. we are on the subject of grasses, it may be pleasing to observe, how wonderfully some of them change their appearance as they ascend the higher hills; the turfy hair grass, *Aira cœspitosa,* sheep's fescue grass, *Festuca ovina,* Alpine meadow grass, *Poa Alpina,* and some others, which in the low countries, where they enjoy the due influence of the sun, and length of summer, to ripen their seeds, are propagated in the usual manner of grasses; but as they reach a more exalted situation, where they want a continuance of summer, and the necessary power of the

[g] *Hudson Fl. Ang.* ed. 1ma. *Agrostis vulgaris Smith. Fl. Br.* ED.

sun, to perfect their seeds, they become viviparous; that is, the rudiment of the *germen* vegetates, and shoots into blade in the cup, from whence falling, it readily takes root, and grows; a kind and providential dispensation, for the advantage of those colder climates, which are less favorable to vegetation!

THIS mountanous tract scarcely yields any corn. Its produce is cattle and sheep, which, during summer, keep very high in the mountains, followed by their owners, with their families, who reside in that season in *Hafodtai,* or summer dairy-houses, as the farmers in the *Swiss alps* do in their *Sennes.* These houses consist of a long low room, with a hole at one end, to let out the smoke from the fire, which is made beneath. Their furniture is very simple: stones are the substitutes of stools; and the beds are of hay, ranged along the sides. They manufacture their own cloaths; and dye their cloths with *Cenn du y Cerrig,* or *Lichen omphaloides;* and another *Cenn,* the *Lichen parietinus;* native dyes, collected from the rocks. During summer, the men pass their time either in harvest work, or in tending their herds: the women in milking, or making butter and cheese. For their own use, they milk both ewes and goats, and make cheese of the milk, for their own consumption. The diet of these mountaneers is very plain, consisting of butter, cheese, and oat-bread, or *Bara*

SUMMER DWELLINGS.

Ceirch: they drink whey: not but they have a reserve of a few bottles of very strong beer, by way of cordial, in illness. They are people of good understanding, wary and circumspect; usually tall, thin, and of strong constitutions, from their way of living. Towards ~~winter~~, they descend to their *Hên Dref,* or *old dwelling,* where they lead, during that season, a vacant life.

In the course of our ascent, saw on the left, above the *Cwm, Moel y Cynghorion,*([1]) or *The Hill of Council.* Pass through *Bwlch y Maes-cwm,* and skirt the side of *Snowdon,* till we reach *Bwlch y Cwm Brwynog,* where the ascent becomes very difficult on account of its vast steepness. People here usually quit their horses. We began a toilsome march, clambering among the rocks. On the left were the precipices over *Cwm Brwynog,* with *Llyn du yr Arddwy*([1]) at their foot. On our right were those over the small lakes *Llyn Glâs, Llyn-y-Nadroedd,* and *Llyn Goch.*([1]) The last is the highest on this side of the mountain; and, on whose margins, we were told, that, in fairy days, those diminutive gentry kept their revels. This space between precipice and precipice, formed a short, and no very agreeable isthmus, till we reach-

THE HIGH LAKES.

([1]) These names are now respectively *Moel Gynghorion, Llyn du'r Arddu* and *Llyn Coch. Pennant's Llyn Goch* has the mutation which one frequently meets out of its place in his rendering of Welsh names. J.R.

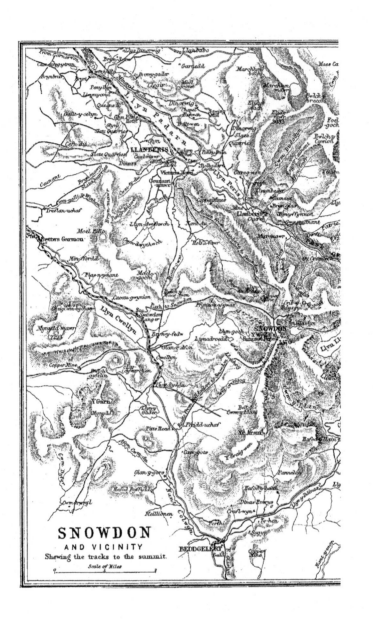

SNOWDON
AND VICINITY
Shewing the tracks to the summit.
Scale of Miles

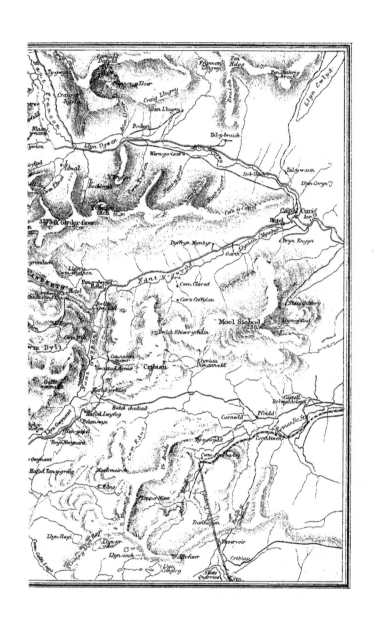

ed a verdant expanse, which gave us some respite, before we labored up another series of broken crags: after these, is a second smooth tract, which reaches almost to the summit, which by way of pre-eminence, is styled Y WYDDFA, or *The Conspicuous*.(1) It rises almost to a point, or, at best, there is but room for a circular wall of loose stones, within which travellers usually take their repast.

TOP OF SNOWDON.

THE mountain from hence seems propped by four vast buttresses; between which are four deep *Cwms*, or hollows: each, excepting one, has one or more lakes, lodged in its distant bottom. The nearest was *Ffynnon lâs*, or *The Green Well*, lying immediately below us. One of the company had the curiosity to descend a very bad way to a jutting rock, that impended over the monstrous precipice; and he seemed like *Mercury* ready to take his flight from the summit of *Atlas*. The waters of *Ffynnon lâs*, from this height, appeared black and unfathomable, and the edges quite green. From thence is a succession of bottoms, surrounded by lofty and rugged hills, the greatest part of whose sides are perfectly mural, and form the most magnificent amphitheatre in nature. The *Wyddfa* is on one side; *Crib y Distill*, with its serrated tops, on another; *Crib Goch*, a ridge of fiery redness,

FFYNNON LAS.

(1) This interpretation is very pretty, but the meaning is more probably to be sought in the word *gwŷdd*, wood, which would connect the name with the mountain as a Royal Forest. J.R.

appears beneath the preceding; and opposite to it
is the boundary called the *Lliwedd.* Another
very singular support to this mountain is *Y
Clawdd Goch,* rising into a sharp ridge, so narrow,
as not to afford breadth even for a path.

THE view from this exalted situation is unboun-
ded.   In a former tour[h], I saw from it the county
of *Chester,* the high hills of *Yorkshire,* part of the
north of *England, Scotland,* and *Ireland:* a plain
view of the *Isle of Man;* and that of *Anglesey* lay
extended like a map beneath me, with every rill
visible.   I took much pains to see this prospect to
advantage: sat up at a farm on the west till about
twelve, and walked up the whole way.   The night
was remarkably fine and starry: towards morn, the
stars faded away, and left a short interval of darkness, which was soon dispersed by the dawn of
day.   The body of the sun appeared most distinct,
with the rotundity of the moon, before it rose high
enough to render its beam too brilliant for our
sight.   The sea which bounded the western part
was gilt by its rays, first in slender streaks, at length
glowing with redness.   The prospect was disclosed
like the gradual drawing up of a curtain in a theatre.   We saw more and more, till the heat became so powerful, as to attract the mists from the
various lakes, which in a slight degree obscured
the prospect.   The shadow of the mountain was

---

[h] *August 25th, Old Stile.*

flung many miles, and shewed its bicapitated form; the *Wyddfa* making one, *Crib y Distill* the other head. I counted this time between twenty and thirty lakes, either in this county or *Meirionedd-shire*. The day proved so excessively hot, that my journey cost me the skin of the lower part of my face, before I reached the resting-place, after the fatigue of the morning.

On this day[1], the sky was obscured very soon after I got up. A vast mist enveloped the whole circuit of the mountain. The prospect down was horrible. It gave an idea of numbers of abysses, concealed by a thick smoke, furiously circulating around us. Very often a gust of wind formed an opening in the clouds, which gave a fine and distinct vista of lake and valley. Sometimes they opened only in one place; at others, in many at once, exhibiting a most strange and perplexing sight of water, fields, rocks, or chasms, in fifty different places. They then closed at once, and left us involved in darkness; in a small time they would separate again, and fly in wild eddies round the middle of the mountains, and expose, in parts, both tops and bases clear to our view. We descended from this various scene with great reluctance; but before we reached our horses, a thunder-storm overtook us. Its rolling among the mountains was inexpressibly awful: the rain un-

[1] *August 15th, New Stile.*

commonly heavy.   We remounted our horses, and
gained the bottom with great hazard.   The little
rills, which on our ascent trickled along the gullies
on the sides of the mountain, were now swelled
into torrents; and we and our steeds passed with
the utmost risque of being swept away by these
sudden waters.   At length we arrived safe, yet
sufficiently wet and weary, to our former quarters.

It is very seldom that the traveller gets a proper day to ascend *Snowdon;* for often, when it
appears clear, it becomes suddenly and unexpect-
ATTRACTION
OF CLOUDS. edly enveloped in mist, by its attraction of clouds,
which just before seemed remote and at great
heights.   At times, I have observed them lower to
half their height, and notwithstanding they have
been dispersed to the right and to the left, yet
they have met from both sides, and united to in-
volve the summit in one great obscurity.

RIVERS.   THE quantity of water which flows from the
lakes of *Snowdonia,* is very considerable; so much
that I doubt not but collectively they would exceed the waters of the *Thames,* before it meets the
flux of the ocean.

HEIGHT.   THE reports of the height of this noted hill have
been very differently given.   A Mr. *Caswell,* who
was employed by Mr. *Adams,* in 1682, in a survey
of *Wales,* measured it by instruments made by the

directions of Mr. *Flamstead*[k]; and asserts its height
to be twelve hundred and forty yards: but for the
honor of our mountain I am sorry to say, that I
must give greater credit to the experiments made
of late years, which have sunk it to one thousand
one hundred and eighty-nine yards and one foot,
reckoning from the quay at *Caernarvon* to the
highest peak.

THE stone that composes this, and indeed the
greatest part of *Snowdonia*, is excessively hard.
Large coarse crystals are often found in the
fissures, and very frequently cubic *pyritæ*, the
usual attendants on *Alpine* tracts. These are also
frequented by the rock ouzel, a mountain bird,
and some of the lakes are stocked with *char* and
gwyniads, *Alpine* fish. The antient inhabitant,
the goat, decreases daily in value, since the de-
cline of orthodoxal wigs, to which its snowy hair
universally contributed. Still large flocks are kept
for the dairy, and milked with great regularity.

BOTANY is not within my province. I shall
therefore say nothing more of the plants, than that
those species which LINNÆUS so very expressively
styles *Ethereæ*, are entirely confined to the higher
parts of the mountains; and notwithstanding the
seeds must be blown downwards, they never vege-

BOTANY.

---

[k] *Wren's Parentalia*, i. 253. I suppose *Caswell* was employed by
Mr. *Adams*, author of the *Index Villaris*.

tate in the lower parts, which are deserted by certain plants, natives of a higher tract of the same
hill.

THE animals of these regions are chiefly foxes.
Stags were found here in the days of *Leland,* in
such numbers, as to destroy the little corn which
the farmers attempted to sow: but they were ex-
A ROYAL   tirpated before the year 1626[1]. *Snowdon* being a
FOREST.   royal forest, warrants were issued for the killing of
the deer.   I have seen one from the duke of *Suf-*
folk, dated *April* the 30th, 1552, and another[m], in
the first year of queen *Elizabeth,* signed by *Robert*
Tounesend; and a third, in 1561, by *Henry Sidney*[n].
The second was addressed to the master of the
game, ranger and keeper of the queen's highness
forrest of SNOWDON, in the county of *Caernarvon.*
The last extended the forest into the counties of
Meirionedd and *Anglesey,* with the view of gratifying the rapacity of the favorite *Dudley,* earl of
Leicester, who had by letters patent been appointed
chief ranger.   In consequence, he tyrannised over
these counties with great insolence.   A set of in-
formers immediately acquainted him, that most of
the freeholders' estates might be brought within the
boundaries.   Commissioners were appointed to en-
quire into the encroachments and concealments of
lands within the forest.   Juries were empannelled;

[1] *Gwedir* MSS.   [m] Appendix, No. XIV.   [n] Ib.

but their returns were rejected by the commissioners, as unfavourable to the earl's designs. The
jurors performed an honest part, and found a verdict for the country. *Leland,* no longer before
than the reign of *Henry* VIII. had gone over this
tract, as he did most of *England,* under the royal
commission; and yet reports, that all *Cregery, i. e.
Snowdon,* is in *Caernarvonshire,* and no part in
Meirioneddshire; though, says he, that shire be
montanius[n].

A NEW commission was then directed to Sir
Richard Bulkeley, of *Baron Hill, Anglesey,* Sir
William Herbert, and others; this, by the firmness
of Sir *Richard,* was likewise soon superseded; but,
in 1578, another was appointed, dependent on the
favorite. A packed jury was directed to appear
at *Beaumaris,* who went on the same day to view
the marsh of *Malltraeth,* ten miles distant; and
found that marsh to be in the forest of *Snowdon,*
notwithstanding it was in another county, and
divided from the forest by an arm of the sea; because the commissioners had told them, that they
had met with an indictment in the exchequer of
Caernarvon (which they had the year before broke
open and ransacked), by which they had discovered
that a stag had been roused in the forest of *Snowdon,* in *Caernarvonshire,* was pursued to the banks
of the *Menai;* that it swam over that branch of

[n] *Itin.* v. 43.

the sea, and was killed at *Malltraeth* INFRA *fores-
tam nostram de Snowdon.* The jury appeared in
the earl's livery, blue, with ragged staves on the
sleeves; and were ever after branded with the title
of the *black jury, who sold their country.*

SIR *Richard Bulkeley,* not the least daunted
with this decision, continued steady in his opposition to the tyrant; and laid before the queen the
odiousness of the proceedings, and the grievances
her loyal subjects, the *Welsh,* labored under, by
the commission, insomuch, that, in 1579, her
highness was pleased, by proclamation at *Westminster,* to recall it. *Leicester,* disappointed in
his views, pursued Sir *Richard* with the utmost
inveteracy: he even accused him of a concern in
Babington's conspiracy. "BEFORE GOD," says
the queen, "we will be sworn upon the evange-
" lists, he never intended us any harm;" and so ran
to the bible, and kissed it, saying, "We shall not
" commit him: we have brought him up from a
" boy°."

SACRED.   *Snowdon* was held as sacred by the antient *Britons,* as *Parnassus* was by the *Greeks,* and *Ida* by
the *Cretans.* It is still said, that whosoever slept
upon *Snowdon,* would wake inspired, as much as
if he had taken a nap on the hill of *Apollo.* The
Britons, in very early times, worshipped mountains

° From the communication of *Paul Panton* esq.

and rivers[p]; but that does not appear from the triambics quoted by our able antiquary, Mr. *Row-lands*[q]; for the words *Eiry Mynydd* are applicable, not to this mountain in particular, but to all which are covered with snow. There are multitudes of these triambics, each ending with a moral reflection, the work of *Llywarch Hên;* of· which the following may serve as an example:

> Eiry mynydd, gwancus ɟâr;
> Gochwiban gwynt ar dalar;
> YN YR ING, GORAU YW'R CAR[r].

> While the hill is clad with snow,
> Fowls for food scream out below,
> Fierce the winds on plough-lands blow·
> WHEN DEEP GRIEF AFFECTS YOUR MIND,
> BALMY CURE FROM KIN YOU'LL FIND.

THE *Welsh* had always the strongest attachment to the tract of *Snowdon.* It was, say they, the appertenance of the principality of *Wales*, which the prince and his predecessors held since the time of *Brute. Edward* I. was told by the inhabitants of *Snowdon*, in the treaty he held with our countrymen, in the year 1281, that even should their prince be inclined to gratify the king, in yielding him possession, they would not do homage to strangers, of whose tongue, manners, and laws, they were ignorant[s]. Our princes had, in addition

---

[p] *Gildas.*   [q] *Rowlands*, 253.
[r] Mr. *Rhys Jones's* Coll. of *Welsh* Poems, p. 13.   [s] *Powel*, 369.

to their title, that of LORD OF SNOWDON. They had five hardy barons within the tract, who held of them. Such was the importance of this strong region, that when *Llewelyn* was at the last extremity, he refused to yield it to *Edward*, and rejected that monarch's proposal of a thousand a year, and some honorable county in *England*, well ·knowing that his principality must terminate with the cession.

FAIR HELD THERE.

No sooner had *Edward* effected his conquest, than he held a triumphal fair upon this our chief of mountains; and adjourned to finish the joy of his victory, by solemn tournaments on the plains of *Nefyn*.

NAME.

I SHALL take my leave of *Snowdonia* with some remarks on the name, and the weather. The first is a literal translation[t] of the antient appellation, *Creigiau'r Eira*(¹), *The Snowy mountains*, from the frequency of snow upon them. *Niphates*, in *Armenia*, and *Imaus*, in *Tartary*, derive their name from the same circumstance. Some have supposed it to be taken from *Creigiau'r Eryri*, or *The Eagle Rocks;* but that bird appears very seldom among them. The other circumstance is constant: not

---

[t] By the *Saxons* first into SNAWDUNE. *Sax. Chr*. 203.

(¹) This would seem to be a translation of *Snowdon* back into Welsh, the latter itself being an old mistranslation into English of *Eryri*, the eagle country: the mistake would in the first instance have been occasioned by the similarity between *eiry*, snow, and *eryr* eagle. J.R.

that it is to be imagined that they are covered with snow in some part or other the whole year, as has been idly fabled; there being frequently whole weeks, even in winter, in which they are totally free.

THE earliest appearance of snow, is commonly between the middle of *October*, and the beginning of *November:* the falls which happen then, are usually washed away with the rains, and the hills remain clear till *Christmas.* Between that time and the end of *January,* the greatest falls happen; which are succeeded by others, about the latter end of *April,* or beginning of *May,* which remain in certain places till the middle of *June,* in which month it has been seen of the depth of some feet. It has even happened, that the greatest fall has been in *April,* or beginning of *May;* and that never fails happening, when the preceding winter has had the smallest falls. But the fable of *Giraldus,* concerning the continuance of snow the whole year, is totally to be exploded.

NEAR the end of *Nant-beris,* pass beneath *Glyder Fawr,* and observe the strata of a columnar form, high above our heads. At times, vast fragments of this tremendous rock tumble down, the ruins are scattered about the base, and exhibit awful specimens of the frequent lapses. One is styled the *Cromlech,* for having accidentally fallen on other stones, it remains lifted from the earth, with a hollow beneath, resembling one of those *Druidical* antiquities. The length of the incumbent stone is sixty feet: the breadth forty-six: the thickness sixteen. The hollow is said once to have been occupied by an old woman([1]); but now serves for a sheep pen.

THE ascent from hence is either over loose stones, or solid stair-case, and is exceedingly steep. It is a singular road, lying in a stupendous chasm, bounded for above a mile by nearly equidistant precipices, of prodigious height; those of the *Glyders* being on one side, and on the other those of *Snowdon*.

GORPHWYS-FA.

REFRESH ourselves on a spot called *Gorphwysfa*, or *The Resting-place*. At a small distance from which is *Bwlch y Gwyddyl*, or *The Pass of the Irishmen;* from whence is a singular view of *Dyffryn Mymbyr*, the chasm we had left; and far below us, the picturesque vale of *Nant Gwynan*, the scene of many a bloody skirmish in the time of *Edward* IV. between *William* earl of *Pembroke*, and the *Welsh Lancastrians*, under *Jevan ap Robert*.

CWM DYLI.

DESCEND a very steep road, into that part called *Cwm Dyli;* where we quitted our horses, and began a most toilsome journey to visit the hidden vales lodged in the bosom of the mountains.

[1] This refers to the fabulous cannibal *Cynrig Bwt :* see note p. 213. J.R.

We began with clambering up the rugged face of a rock, broken into a multitude of short precipices, and divided in the middle by a cataract, the discharge of the waters from the *Alpine* lakes. After about a quarter of a mile's labor, we reached *Cwm Dyli*, a flat tract of hay ground, watered by a river, and filled with hay-makers; the farmer and his family being resident here in his *Havodty*, for the summer season. After dining with them on curds and whey, we kept along the river's side, and found opposed to us another front, rugged as the former, and attended with a cataract. This was surmounted with equal difficulty. We found, on arriving at the top, an hollow, a mile in length, filled with *Llyn Llydaw*, a fine lake, winding beneath the rocks, and vastly indented by rocky projections, here and there jutting into it. In it was one little island, the haunt of black-backed Gulls, which breed here, and, alarmed by such unexpected visitants, broke the silence of this sequestered place by their deep screams. We continued our walk, ascending along a narrow path above the lake, as far as the extremity; then descending, reached the opposite side, in order to encounter a third descent, as arduous as the preceding. This brought us into the horrible *crater*, immediately beneath the great precipice of the *Wyddfa*, in which is lodged *Ffynnon Lâs*[u]. Its

LLYN LLYDAW.

FFYNNON LAS.

[u] About two hundred yards above the lake are some copper mines,

situation is the most dreadful, surrounded by more
than three parts of a circle, with the most horrible
precipices of the *Wyddfa, Crib y Distill,* and *Crib
Goch,* with the vast mural steeps of *Lliwedd,* con
tinued over the other lake and *Cwm Dyli.*   In
the *Lliwedd* was a strange break, called *Bwlch y
Saethau,* or *The Pass of the Arrows;* probably a
station for hunters, to watch the wanderings of
the deer.

THE margins of *Ffynnon Lâs* here appeared to
be shallow and gravelly. The waters had a green-
ish cast; but what is very singular, the rocks re-
flected into them seemed varied with stripes of
the richest colors, like the most beautiful lute
strings; and changed almost to infinity.

WHEAT-EAR.   HERE we observed the *Wheat-ear,* a small and
seemingly tender bird; and which is almost the
only small one, or indeed the only one, except the
Rock Ouzel, or *Mwyalchen y Graig,* that frequents
these heights: the reason is evidently the want of
food.

WE descended from this dreary scene, on the
other side of the hill, above *Llyn Llydaw,* having
CRIB GOCH. the tremendous red precipices of *Crib Goch* high
above us, rising into a mere ridge, serrated, or
rather *herissée,* its whole length.   The face of

belonging to Sir *Robert Williams* bt. the produce of which is carried
in bags on the backs of men, nearly a mile, over one of the highest
ridges of *Snowdon,* till it reaches a road accessibie to sledges. ED.

PLATE XXV.

many of the rocks were marked with large veins of coarse white crystal; and others, especially *Crib Goch*, were varied with the deep green of the dwarf *Alpine* juniper. On attaining the tops of the hills, above the lower end of the lake, we descended to the *Gorphwysfa*, where we found our horses, and returned once more into *Nant-Gwynan*.

THIS is the most beautiful vale in *Snowdonia*, varied with woods, lakes, river, and meadows, besides the most august boundaries: being guarded on each side by vast mountains, such as *Crib Du*, or part of *Mynydd Nanmor*, the *Lliwedd*, *Yr Aran*, *Dduallt*, and *Wenallt*, extending about five miles to the church of *Bedd Kelert*. On the left, we passed by *Hafod Lwyfog*, the seat of the late *Meyric Meredydd* esq; surrounded with large woods. A little farther is the pretty lake *Llyn Gwynan*, about three quarters of a mile long, and near it are the ruins of a chapel of the same name. It had been a chapel of ease to the church of *Bedd Kelert*, and was supported by a stipend of five pounds a year from the estate of *Gwedir*. It is said to have been founded by *John Williams*, grandson of *John Coetmor*, *ap Meredydd*, *ap Jevan*, *ap Robert*, of *Ceselgyfarch* and *Gwedir*, goldsmith in *London;* the same who is reported to have furnished *Michael Drayton* with *Leland*'s papers.

NEAR the end of the lake, the valley[x] grows so contracted, as to form only a narrow streight; but almost instantly opens again into a fine expanse, chiefly filled with the beautiful *Llyn Dinas.* Beyond that, is a tract of meads, chequered with woods, and watered by the river created by the various lakes; but retaining the name of *Afon Glâs-Lyn,* from the lofty *Ffynnon-Lâs,* from which it originates.

AT the bottom rises a vast rock, insulated, and cloathed with wood; the famous *Dinas Emris,* from early times celebrated in *British* story; for here

Prophetic *Merlin* sate, when to the *British* king
The changes long to come, auspiciously he told.

DINAS
EMRIS.

ITS LEGEND.   WHEN *Vortigern* found himself unable to contest with the treacherous *Saxons,* whom he had, in the year 449, invited into *Britain,* he determined, by the advice of his magicians, on building an impregnable fortress in *Snowdon.* He collected the materials, which all disappeared in one night. The prince, astonished at this, convened again his wise men. They assured him, his building would never stand, unless it was sprinkled with the blood

---

[x] An excellent carriage road has recently been opened, which passes through this valley, and forms a communication between *Capel Curig* and *Bedd Kelert,* presenting a succession of scenery the most desolate, the sublimest, and the most romantic. ED.

LLYN DINAS & MOEL HEBOG.

of a child born without the help of a father. The
realm was ransacked: at length one of his emissa-
ries overheard some boys at play reproach another,
and call him an unbegotten knave. The child and
his mother were brought before the king. She con-
fessed he was the offspring of an *Incubus;* a species of being, now unhappily out of all credit.
The boy, whose name was *Merlin,* was ordered to
be sacrificed; but on confounding all the magicians
with his questions, and explaining the cause of the
miscarriage, got his liberty[y], and

> to that mighty king, which rashly undertook
> A strong walled tower to rear, those earthly spirits that shook
> The great foundation still, in dragon's horrid shape,
> That dreaming wizard told, making the mountain gape
> With his most powerful charms, to view those caverns deep;
> And from the top of *Brith,* so high and wondrous steep,
> Where *Dinas Emris* stood, shew'd where the serpents fought,
> The WHITE that tore the RED: from whence the prophet wrought
> The *Britons* sad decay, then shortly to ensue[z].

THIS is is the poetical translation of the legend.
Merlin, or *Merddin Emris,* or *Ambrosius,* was in   MERLIN.
fact the son of a noble *Roman,* of the same name.
His mother, a *Vestal,* to save her life and honor[a],
invented the fable of his father, which was swallowed by the credulity of the times. *Merlin* was
an able mathematician and astronomer, and deeply
read in all the learning of his age. The vulgar,

---

[y] *Nennius,* c. xl. xlii. xliii.   [z] *Draiton's Polyolb.* SONG x.
[a] *Powel's* Notes on *Giraldi Itin. Cambriæ,* lib. 1. c. x.

as usual, ascribed all he did to art magic; and his discovery that *Vortigern* had begun to found his castle on a morass, was immediately said to have been attended with most portentous circumstances. Numbers of prophecies were attributed to him; the repetition of which is said to have been forbidden by the council of *Trent*.

THREE sides of this famous rock are precipitous. On the top is a large area; on the accessible part of which are two great ramparts of stone; and within is the ruin of a stone building, ten yards long: the walls are built without mortar, but strong. Since it is certain that *Vortigern*, after his misfortunes, retired to the *Snowdon* hills, and died not very remote from them, it is possible he might have selected this for his strong-hold, as it is admirably adapted for that purpose, and nearly fills the streight of the valley, and *Merlin Ambrosius* might have given to it the name of *Emris*. A place close by styled *Cell y Dewiniaid*, or *The Cell of the* DIVINERS, allusive to the magicians of *Vortigern*'s court, is another circumstance which favors the history of this celebrated supposed prophet.

BEDD
KELERT.

FROM hence is a pleasant, but short ride, near the river, to the village of *Bedd Kelert*, seated in a beautiful tract of meadows, at the junction of three vales, near the conflux of the *Glâs Lyn* and the *Colwyn*, which flows through *Nant Colwyn*, a

vale that leads to *Caernarvon.* Its situation was
the fittest in the word to inspire religious medi-
tation, amidst lofty mountains, wood, and mur-
muring streams. The church is small, yet the
loftiest in *Snowdonia.* The east window consists
of three narrow slips. The roof is neat; and there
yet remains some very pretty fret-work. A side
chapel is supported by two neat pillars, and
gothic arches. I could discover no tombs, nor
any thing worth transcribing, but the following
epitaph:

> Infra jacet corpus *Evani Lloyd,* de
> *Hafod Lwyfog,* Armigeri, qui
> Inhumatus fuit paterno et avito
> Tumulo, sexto die Idus *Maiæ.*
> A. D. 1678. Annos Natus 72.

THIS church had been conventual, belonging
to a priory of *Augustines,* dedicated to *St. Mary.* PRIORY.
There is reason to suppose they might have been
of that class which was called *Gilbertines,* and
consisted of both men and women, who lived under the same roof, but strictly separated from each
other by a wall; as I discovered a piece of ground
near the church, called *Dôl y Lleian,* or *The Meadow of the Nun.*

BEDD KELERT had been the most antient foundation in all the country, excepting *Bardsey.*
Tanner ascribes it to our last prince; but it must
have been long before his days, there being a
recital of a charter for certain lands bestowed on

it by *Llewelyn the Great*[b], who began his reign in
1194. It was favoured in the same manner by
others of the succeeding princes. *Dafydd ap
Llewelyn* bestowed on it some lands in *Pennant
Gwernogan*, belonging to *Tudor ap Madoc*, to
which the prince had no right. This occasioned a
suit between the sons of *Tudor*, and *Philip*, prior
of the house, before *William de Grandison* and *R.
de Stanedon*, at *Caernarvon*, when a verdict was
given against the convent[c]. The prior had for his
support the grange of *Llecheidior* and part of a
mill, the grange of *Fentidilt* and village of *Gwe-
helyn*, the grange of *Tre'rbeirdd*, one plough land,
and a certain share of the bees. The estimation
which these insects were held in by the antient
Britons, on account of their producing the necta-
reous *Medd*, was so great, that they considered
them as created in PARADISE; that when they
quitted it on the fall of man, they were blessed by
God himself; and therefore no mass ought to be
celebrated, but by the light of their wax[d].

THE prior had besides, an allowance of fifty
cows and twenty-two sheep. The expenses of the
house must have been large. It lay on the great
road from *England* and *West Wales* into *North
Wales*, and from *Ireland* and *North Wales* into
England. In order to enable this place to keep

[b] *Rymer*, ii. 316.   [c] *Sebright MSS.*   [d] *Leges Walliæ*, 254.

its usual hospitality, after it had suffered, in 1283, by a casual fire, *Edward* I. most munificently repaired all the damages: and bishop *Anian*, about the year 1286, for the encouragement of other benefactors, remitted to all such who were truly repentant of their sins, forty days of any penance inflicted on them[e].

In 1535, it was bestowed, by *Henry* VIII. on the abbey of *Chertsey*, in *Surry;* and in 1537, it was given with the last, as an appertenance to that of *Bisham*, in *Berkshire*[f]. On the dissolution, the king gave to the family of the *Bodvels*, all the lands in *Caernarvonshire* which belonged to this priory; and all those in *Anglesey*, to that of the *Prydderchs*, excepting the township of *Tre'rbeirdd*[g]. The revenues of *Bedd Kelert* were valued by *Dugdale* at seventy pounds, three shillings and eight pence; by *Speed*, at sixty-nine pounds three shillings and eight pence. *Edward Conway* is mentioned as last prior. There are not the least reliques of the house. In my possession is a drawing of the seal of the priory, dated 1531; on it is the figure of the virgin and child: but no part of the legend except BETHKELE.

In order to complete the mountain ramble, as far as was in my power, I made an excursion from this village up a narrow vale. Ascended a steep

---

Rymer, ii. 317.   [f] *Dugdale Monast.* iii. 21.   [g] *Rowland's MSS.*

Cattle

road, amidst a thin hanging wood; and saw from
the road multitudes of black cattle, coming down
from all parts, on their way from a neighboring
fair. The vale expands, and is watered by the
Colwyn, which flows from a small lake we passed
LLYN CADER. by, called *Llyn Cader*. Left on the right another
ascent to the *Wyddfa*, where its base extends to a
considerable breadth, and is far less steep than
that on the side of *Nant-Beris*. We soon reached
the pretty lake of *Cawellyn*, noted for its Char.
Above the lake stood the house of *Cae uwch Llyn*,
or *The Field above the Lake*, from distant times
the residence of the *Quellyns* (a family now extinct) who derived their name from the place.
The mountains hereabouts approach near to each
other. On the left, *Mynydd Mawr* forms a striking feature: its top is smooth, but its front is formed into a most immense precipice, retiring inwards
in a semicircular shape. *Moel Eilio*, is another
mountain of a stupendous bulk, most regularly
rounded, and of a beautiful verdure. At *Bettws
Garmon*, a village with a church dedicated to *St.
Germanus*, the scene changes into a range of beautiful meadows, watered by a rapid stream.

I HERE turn my back on the humble flats, and
resume my former road, till I had passed *Cawellyn*.
Not far beyond that lake, I turned to the right, to
LLYN Y DY- visit *Llyn y Dywarchen*, or *the Lake of the Sod*,
WARCHEN. long since celebrated by the hyperbolical pen of

Giraldus[h], for its *insula erratica*, its *wandering island*, as he calls it. That little lake is seated in the middle of a turbery; and at this time actually exhibited the phænomenon recorded by our romantic historian. It had on it a floating island, of an irregular shape, and about nine yards long. It appeared to be only a piece of the turbery, undermined by the water, torn off, and kept together by the close entangling of the roots, which form that species of ground. It frequently is set in motion by the wind; often joins its native banks; and, as *Giraldus* says, cattle are frequently surprized on it, and by another gale carried a short voyage from the shore.

CONTINUE our journey to *Drws y Coed*, or *The Door of the Wood*, a pass towards *Clynnog*. It is bounded by vast mountains: on one side by *Tal Mignedd;* on the other, by a great clift of *Mynydd Mawr*. Some years ago here were considerable adventures for copper, of the pyritous kind: and in the rocks were sometimes found some very thin *laminæ* of the native metal. I was tempted here to exceed a little the limits of my *Alpine* tour; for now the mountains descend fast from their majestic heights, growing less and less as they approach the *Irish* sea. My motive was to obtain a sight of two fine lakes, called *Llynnieu Nanlle,* which form two handsome expanses, with a very

DRWS Y COED

LLYNNIEU NANLLE.

[h] *Itin. Cambr.* lib. ii. c. ix. p. 871.

small distance between each. From hence is a noble view of the *Wyddfa,* which terminates the view through the vista of *Drws y Coed.* It is from this spot that Mr. WILSON has favored us with a view, as magnificent as it is faithful. Few are sensible of this; for few visit the spot.

NEAR these lakes *Edward* I. in the summer of 1284, resided for some days; and from hence issued out more than one of his edicts. I find some dated *July* the 17th and the 20th. Others are dated in the same year, from *Bangor, Caernarvon, Mold,* and *Hope.* One from *Caernarvon*[i] is dated as late as the 22d of *October;* which shews what attention he paid to the establishment of government in his new dominions. The place he resided at here, was called *Bala deu Lyn,* or the place where a river discharges itself from two lakes; but at present all memory is lost of the situation of the town, the traces of which might perhaps be still discovered by diligent search.

I RETURNED by the same road; and again reach *Bedd Kelert,* where I made a coarse lodging[k]. The evening was so fine, that we were irresistibly PONT ABER- tempted not to defer till morning our visit to *Pont* GLAS LYN. *Aberglas Lyn,* a short walk from hence. The

[i] *Sebright MSS. Rymer,* ii. 276 to 289.

[k] The traveller will now find a small, but very comfortable inn at *Bedd Kelert.* The improvement of the houses of accommodation throughout *North Wales* has of late years been very considerable. ED.

first part is along the narrow vale; but in a very
little time the mountains approach so close, as to
leave only room for the furious river to roll over
its stony bed; above which is a narrow road[1],
formed with incredible labor, impending over the
water. The way seems to have been first cut out
of the rock, and then covered with great stones, as
usual in several of our narrow passes. The scenery is the most magnificent that can be imagined.
The mountains rise to very uncommon height, and
oppose to us nothing but a broken series of precipices, one above the other, as high as the eye can
reach. Here is very little appearance of vegetation; yet in spots there is enough to tempt the
poor goat to its destruction; for it will sometimes
leap down to an alluring tuft of verdure, where,
without possibility of return, it must remain to
perish after it has finished the dear-bought repast.

THE bridge terminates the pass; and consists of
a single arch, flung over a deep chasm, from rock
to rock. Above is a considerable cataract, where
the traveller at times may have much amusement,
in observing the salmon, in great numbers, make
their efforts to surmount the wear. Near the
place is a salmon fishery. Here had been a royal
wear in the reign of *Henry* IV. which was then
rented by *Robert ap Meredydd*. It probably be-

[1] At present enlarged to a competent width. ED.

longed in old times to our natural princes; for it seems to have been a most valuable privilege. We have seen before, that young *Elphin* was endowed with one by his royal father; and the effect of his disappointment in missing his usual revenues, by finding (which, I dare say, was in those days a very rare instance) an empty wear. Salmon was the most useful and esteemed fish among the *Welsh:* it was reckoned among the game; and, if I remember right, is the only species which was preserved by law.

OPPOSITE to *Bedd Kelert* is *Moel Hedog.* In a bog, not far from that mountain, was found, in CURIOUS SHIELD. 1784, a most curious brass shield, which Mr. *Williams* of *Llanidan*, favored me with a sight of. Its diameter was two feet two inches; the weight four pounds. In the centre was a plain umbo, projecting above two inches. The surface of the shield was marked with twenty-seven smooth concentric elevated circles; and between each a depressed space, of the same breadth with the elevated parts, marked by a single row of smooth studs. The whole shield was flat, and very limber. I cannot attribute this to the *Welsh*, who seemed to despise every species of defensive armour.

ON my return to *Bedd Kelert*, a stone by the road side was pointed out to me, by the name of RHYS GOCH. the chair of *Rhys Goch O'ryri*, the famous mountain bard, cotemporary with *Owen Glyndwr.* He was of the house of *Hafod Garregog*, at the entrance into *Traeth Mawr*, from whence he used to walk, and sitting on this stone, compose his poems. Among others, is a satire on a fox, for killing his favorite peacock. He died about the year 1420, and was interred in the holy ground at *Bedd Kelert*, after escaping the vengeance of the *English*, for inspiring our countrymen with the love of liberty, and animating them, by his compositions, into a long and gallant resistance to the galling yoke.

FROM *Bedd Kelert* I returned to *Pont Abergla lyn;* and soon reached *Traeth Mawr*, a large extent of sands, between the counties of *Caernarvon* and *Meirionedd*, of most dangerous passage to strangers, by reason of the tides which flow here with great rapidity. This forms the bottom of the vast bay of *Cardigan*. In the year 1625, Sir *John Wynn*, of *Gwedir*, conceived the great design of gaming this tract, and a lesser, called *Traeth Bychan*, from the sea, by an embankment[m]. He

[m] This bold design is now attempting to be carried into effect by *William Madocks* esq. who, in 1807, obtained a grant from the crown, confirmed by act of parliament, vesting in him and his heirs, all the sands of the *Traeth Mawr* between *Pont Aberglaslyn* and the point of *Gêst.*— To secure this tract, consisting of about three thousand five hundred acres, from the inroads of the sea, a vast dike is forming, which is to extend sixteen hundred yards in length from the shore of *Caernarvonshire* to that of *Meirionedd;* one thousand yards were nearly completed in *August* 1809. This embankment,

implored the assistance of his illustrious countryman, Sir *Hugh Myddleton.*   Sir *John's* letter,
and Sir *Hugh's* reply, will be the best account I
can give of the affair; which never was carried into
execution, as I imagine, for want of money.   Sir
John's is as follows:

which is to be twelve yards in breadth at the top, and proportion-
ally wide at its base, is composed of rock and soil brought in small
waggons on railways from the land at each extremity. It was soon
discovered that these materials sunk into the sand, or were removed
by the action of the tides. To obviate the difficulty, a strong and
thick species of matting was invented, made of the rushes which
cover the adjacent marsh; this, secured by stakes driven into the
sand, constitutes a solid foundation. The great body of water,
which flows from an extensive range of the mountains of *Snowdonia,*
is to be discharged by means of five floodgates, each fifteen feet in
height.—The piers to which they are attached, are calculated to
support a bridge, and in their side towards the river are grooves to
admit drop floodgates, for the purpose of warping or irrigating the
recovered lands.—A road, connecting the two counties is to be carried along the eastern side of the embankment, which will not only
prove a most useful means of communication, but prevent the frequent loss of lives occasioned by the dangerous passage of the *Traeth
Mawr.* Mr. *Madocks* has already, by a previous embankment, recovered from the sea nineteen hundred acres of land at the foot of the
vale of *Penmorfa.*   On a portion of this tract, formerly occupied by
the waves at high-water, he has founded the town of *Tre-madoc,*
which consists principally of a square, on one side of which is an
handsome market house.   At a small distance he has built an
extremely neat gothic church, which he proposes to endow. His
charming place of residence, *Tan yr allt,* seated on a rock, high above
the town, amidst flourishing plantations, marks his taste, as the gi-
gantic works below do his bold and enterprizing spirit. May he meet
the success he so amply merits in an undertaking which combines so
much energy, contrivance, and well-applied patriotism! ED.

" Right worthie Sir, my good cousin, and one of
" the great honors of the nation,

" I UNDERSTAND of a greate work that you have
" performed in the *Isle of Wight*, in gaininge too
" thousand acres from the sea.   I may saie to you
" what the *Jewes* said to *Christ*—We have heard
" of thy greate workes done abroade, doe some-
" what in thine own countrey.

" THERE are too washes in *Meirionethshire*,
" whereon some parte of my being lieth, called
" *Traeth Mawr* and *Traeth Bychan*, of a great
" extent of land, and entering into the sea by one
" issue, which is not a mile broad at full sea, and
" verie shallow.   The fresh currents that run into
" the sea are both vehement and greate, and carie
" with them much sand; besides the southerly
" winde usually bloweth fulle to the havens mouth,
" carrieth with it so much sand, that it hath over-
" whelmed a great quantitie of the ground ad-
" jacent.   There, and also in the borderinge
" countreys, abundance of wood, brush, and other
" materialls fit to make mounds, to be had at a
" verie cheape rate, and easilie brought to the
" place; which I hear they doe in *Lincolnshire*, to
" expell the sea.   My skill is little, and my expe-
" rience none at all in such matters, yet I ever had
" a desire to further my country in such actions as
" might be for their profit, and leave a remem-

" brance of my endeavors; but hindred with other
" matters, I have only wished well, and done no-
" thinge.   Now being it pleased God to bring you
" into this country, I am to desire you to take a ride,
" the place not being above a daies journey from
" you; and if you do see the thing fit to be under-
" taken, I am content to adventure a brace of hun-
" dred pounds to joyne with you in the worke.

" I HAVE leade ore on my grounds great store,
" and other minerals near my house; if it please
" you to come hither, beinge not above too daies
" journey from you, you shall be most kindly well-
" come—it may be you shall find here that will tend
" to your commoditie and mine.   If I did knowe
" the day certaine when you would come to view
" *Traeth Mawr*, my son *Owen Wynn* shall attend
" you there, and conduct you thence to my house.
" Concluding me verie kindly to you, doe rest,

" Your loving cousin and friend,

" Gwydir,
" 1st *September*, 1625.   " J. WYNN."

" To the honored Sir *Hugh*
" *Myddleton*, Knt. Bart."

" Honorable Sir,
" I HAVE received your kind letter.   Few are
" the things done by me, for which I give God the
" glory.   It may please you to understand my first
" undertaking of publick works was amongst my
" owne, within less than a myle of the place where

" I hadd my first beinge, 24 or 25 years since, in
" seekinge of coales for the town of *Denbigh.*

TOUCHING the drowned lands near your ly-
" vinge, there are manye things considerable
" therein. Iff to be gayned, which will hardlie be
" performed without great stones, which was plen-
" tifull at the *Weight,* as well as wood; and great
" sums of money to be spent, not hundreds but
" thousands—and first of all his Majesty's interest
" must be got. As for myself, I am grown into
" years, and full of busines here at the mynes, the
" river at *London,* and other places—my weeklie
" charge being above £.200; which maketh me
" verie unwillinge to undertake anie other worke;
" and the least of theis, whether the drowned lands
" or mynes, requireth a whole man, with a large
" purse. Noble Sir, my desire is great to see you,
" which should draw me a farr longer waie; yet
" such are my occasions at this tyme here, for the
" settlinge of this great worke, that I can hardlie
" be spared one howre in a daie. My wieff being
" also here, I cannot leave her in a strange place.
" Yet my love to publique works, and desire to
" see you (if God permit) maie another tyme
" drawe me into those parts. Soe with my heartie
" comendations I comitt you and all your good
" desires to God,

" Your assured loving couzin to command,
" Lodge,   "HUGH MYDDELTON."
" *Sept.* 2d, 1625.

THE view from the middle of the sands towards *Snowdonia*, is most extravagantly wild. Mountain rises above mountain, exposing the most savage and barren aspect imaginable, naked, precipitous, and craggy. The *Cyfnicht*(1) soars into a picturesque rocky cone, and *Y Wyddfa* rises in the back ground pre-eminent among its companions.

ON quitting the sands, arrive in a tract of meadows, sprinkled with insulated rocks rising in various places and embosomed with woods, rocks, and precipices. On the road observed some poor iron ore, and groups of coarse crystals, the reliques of an unprofitable mine adventure. The small PENMORFA. town of *Penmorfa* lies at the head of these meadows. The church is dedicated to *St. Beuno*, and annexed to it is the chapel of *Dolbenmaen*. Here was interred that valiant knight Sir *John Owen*. Besides his monument, is another small one to Sir *William Morris* of *Clenenney*, who died *August* 11th, 1622.

IN former times this neigborhood abounded with gentry. It lies in the hundred of *Efionydd*, in remote days possessed by two clans; one, descended from *Owen Gwynedd*, Prince of *Wales*, consisted of four houses, *Cessail Gyfarch, Ystym-*

---

(1) The pronunciation is at present *Cnicht*: the combination *cht* is not very Welsh, and mostly occurs in borrowed words, such as *dracht* from the English draught. *Siabod* is equally suspicious: the full name I am told is or was *Moel Llys-Abod*. J.R.

cegid, Clenenney, Brynkir, Glasfryn or *Cwm-strallyn;* the other was derived from *Collwyn ap Tangno,* and consisted of the houses of *Whilog, Bron y Foel, Berkin, Gwynfryn, Tal Hên Bont* (now *Plas Hên*), and *Pennardd*[o]. My curiosity once led me to make a tour of a few miles from hence to visit these antient mansions. In the days I allude to, the feuds among the gentry filled the land with blood. The history of our country, during that period, is the history of revenge, perfidy, and slaughter. This consideration induced *Meredydd ap Jevan,* ancestor of the *Wynns* of *Gwedir*[p], to quit this his paternal country.

THERE was not a house in the hundred but had its dreadful tale. They would quarrel, if it was but for 'the mastery of the country, and the first *good morrow*[q]!' *John Owen ap John ap Meredydd* and *Howel ap Madoc Fychan* fell out for no other reason. *Howel* and his people fought valiantly. When he fell, his mother placed her hand on his head, to prevent the fatal blow, and had half of her hand and three of her fingers cut off by some of her nearest kindred. An attempt was made to kill *Howel ap Rhys* in his own house, by the sons of *John ap Meredydd,* for no other

[o] *Gwedir* family, in Mr. *Barrington's Miscell.* 8vo. 143.

[p] For the reason given by him on the occasion, the reader is referred to p. 295 of this volume.

[q] Hist. *Gwedir* family.

reason but that their servants had quarrelled about
a fishery. They set fire to the mansion with
great bundles of straw. The besieged, terrified
with the flames, sheltered themselves under forms
and benches; while *Rhys*, the old hero, stood
sword in hand, reproaching his men with coward-
ice, and telling them *he had often seen a greater
smoke in that hall on a Christmas even.* These
flagitious deeds seldom met with any other punish
ment than what resulted from private revenge; and
too often composition was made for the most
horrible murders. There was a *Gwerth*, or *price of
blood*, from the slaughter of a king, to the cutting
off of one of his subject's little fingers.

ANTIQUITIES. SEVERAL antiquities are scattered over this
part of the county. Near *Dolbenmaen* is a large
mount, on which might have been, as Mr. *Rowland*
conjectures, a watch tower. Near *Ystym Cegid*
are three *Cromlechs* joining to each other, possibly
memorials of three chieftain slain on the spot.
And near *Clenenney*, on *Bwlch Craigwen*, is a
fine druidical circle, consisting at present of thirty-
eight stones; at a mile's distance, and within sight
of this, above *Penmorfa*, is another. Before I
returned, I visited *Brynkir*, in my memory inhabited by a family of the same name. It lies beneath the great mountain *Hedog*, which divides
this country from the vale of *Bedd Kelert*. From

hence the land gradually lowers to the extremity of the county.

DURING my stay at *Penmorfa*, I was desired to observe *Dick Bach*, a diminutive person, who casually called there. He was servant to a neighboring gentleman, about the age of thirty, and only three feet eleven inches high. He was pointed out to me only for the sake of describing his sister *Mary Bach o Cwmmain*, or little *Mary of Cwmmain*: a well proportioned fairy, of the height of three feet four. Her virtues are superior to her size: she brews, bakes, pickles; in short, does every thing that the best housekeeper can do. Their parents live in these parts, have many children of the common stature of man; but nature chose to sport in the formation of this little pair.

IN the winter of 1694, this neighborhood was remarkable for an amazing and noxious phænome- non. A *mephites*, or pestilential vapour, resem- bling a weak blue flame, arose, during a fortnight or three weeks, out of a marshy sandy tract, called *Morfa Bychan*[r], and crossed over a channel of eight miles to *Harlech*. It set fire on that side to sixteen ricks of hay and two barns, one filled with hay, the other with corn. It infected the grass in such a manner, that numbers of cattle, horses, sheep and goats, died; yet men went into the

---

[r] *Camden*, ii. 788. *Ph. Trans.* No. 208. *Lowthorp's Abridg.* ii. 183.

midst of it with impunity.   It was easily dispelled;
any great noise, such as the sounding of horns, the
discharging of guns, or the like, at once repelled it.
It moved only by night; and appeared at times,
but less frequently, the following summer; after
which this phænomenon ceased.   It may possibly
have arisen, as the editor of *Camden* conjectures,
from a local casualty, such as the fall of a flight of
locusts in that spot, as really was the case in the
sea near *Aberdaron;* which growing corrupt, might,
by the blowing of the wind for a certain period
from one point, direct the pest to a particular spot,
while other places less remote might, for the same
reason, have escaped the dreadful effects.   *Mouf-
fet* gives an account of a plague in *Lombardy,*
about the year 591, which arose from the fall
of a cloud of locusts, which corrupted the air
to such a degree, that eighty thousand men and
cattle perished[s].

WRECK OF
BIRDS.

    I CONTINUED my journey along the shore which
is for the most part flat, except where some small
headlands jut into it.   On this coast the Reverend
Hugh Davies, of *Beaumaris,* was witness to a very
uncommon wreck of sea-fowl, which happened in
1776.   He saw the beach for miles together,
covered with dead birds, especially those kinds
which annually visit the rocks in summer; such
as Puffins, Razor-bills, Guillemots, and Kitti-

[s] *Theatre of Insects,* Engl. ed. 986.

wakes; of the last there were many thousands. Numbers also of Tarrocks. Of birds which retire to distant countries to breed, were Gannets, Wild-geese, Barnacles, Brent-geese, Scoters, and Tufted-ducks. The frost, from *January* 6th to *February* the 2d, had been in that winter uncommonly severe: a storm had probably overtaken both the migrants and the re-migrants, and occasioned this havock; and the birds, which are perpetually resident with us, underwent the same fate, unable to resist the freezing gale.

PASSED by *Stymllyn*, the seat of —— *Wynne*[t], esq; and soon reach *Crickaeth*, a poor borough CRICKAETH. town, contributory to *Caernarvon*. Its castle is seated on a pretty round hill, jutting far into the sea, and the isthmus crossed, by way of defence, by two deep ditches; on each side of the entrance is a great round tower. The court is of an irregular form, and has the remains of a square tower; beyond is another court, and in it, on the verge of the rock, are two others, also square. It is probable that all the towers were originally square, for the insides of the two round towers are of that form. They have so much the appearance of the architecture of *Dolwyddelan* castle, that I entertain no doubt but that this fortress was founded by a *Welsh* prince, and that its supposed founder *Edward* I. did no more than case the towers, which

[t] Now of *Humphrey Jones*, esq. ED.

at present are the two rounders. After the Conquest, *Edward* appointed *William de Leybourn* to
be constable, with a salary of a hundred pounds a
year; for which he was to maintain a garrison of
thirty stout men (ten of whom were to be crossbow men) one chaplain, one surgeon, one carpenter, and one mason[u].

SIR HOWEL
Y FWYALL.

OUR boasted countryman, Sir *Howel y Fwyall*,
was constable of this castle; a hero descended from
Collwyn ap Tangno. He attended the Black
Prince to the battle of *Poitiers,* and, as we say,
was the person who took the *French* king prisoner;
but history bestows that honour on *Denis de More-
beque,* a knight of *Artois*[x]. Perhaps we must
wave that particular glory; but he undoubtedly
behaved on that occasion with distinguished valour:
for the Black Prince not only bestowed on him the
constableship of this castle, which he afterwards
made his residence, but knighted him, and, in
perpetual memorial of his good services, ordered
that from thenceforth a mess of meat should be
served up before the pole-axe with which he performed such great feats; for that reason he bore it
in his coat of arms, and was styled Sir *Howel y
Fwyall,* or of the *Ax:* after the mess had appeared
before the knight, it was carried down and bestowed on the poor. Eight yeomen attendants

Sebright MSS.
[x] *Froissart,* tom. i. ch. clxiiii. p. 195. *Johnes Froissart,* i. p. 439.

were constituted to guard the mess, and had eight
pence a day constant wages, at the king's charge;
and these, under the name of yeomen of the crown,
were continued on the establishment till the reign
of Queen *Elizabeth.* Some do not scruple to say,
that the yeomen of the crown were grafted upon
this stock. After the death of Sir *Howel,* the
mess was carried as before, and bestowed on the
poor, for the sake of his soul; and probably as low
as the period above mentioned[y].

EIGHT miles farther is *Pwllheli.* In my way
cross over a pretty stream, on a bridge of three
arches, at *Llan Ystyndwy,* a church and village in
a pretty wooded bottom. A little farther inland
is *Plâs Hên,* a seat of *Evan Lloyd Vaughan* esq[z]; PLAS HEN.
by marriage of an heiress of the name of *Vaughan,*
a descendant of *Collwyn ap Tangno;* she afterwards married *William Lloyd,* a younger son of
Bod-Idris. This *William Lloyd* was sheriff in
1648, and was killed in a skirmish near *Bangor,*
by Sir *John Owen*[a]. Cross the little river *Arch,*
at *Aber-arch,* or the port of the coffin, near a
church dedicated to St. *Cwrda.* After another
mile's ride reach *Pwllheli,* the best town in this PWLLHELI.
country, and the magazine of goods which supplies

[y] See *XV Tribes of North Wales;* and *Hist. Gwedir Family* in Mr.
Barrington's Miscell.; and *Hist. Gwedir,* octavo, 143.
[z] Now of Sir *Thomas Mostyn* bart. in right of his mother. ED.
[a] Vide MS. in *Mostyn* library.

all this tract. It lies close on the shore, and has
a tolerable harbour for vessels of about sixty tons.
The entrance is by a high rock called the *Gimlet*,
a mile from land, to which it is joined by a range
of sand-hills. This place was made a free borough
by the Black Prince, by charter, dated the 12th
year of his principality, at *Caernarvon*, in compli-
ment to *Nigel de Loryng* or *Lohareyn*, one of the
gentlemen of his bedchamber, on whom he had
bestowed *Pwllheli* and *Nefyn*, in consideration of
his great service in *Gascony*, and particularly at
the battle of *Poitiers*. He entitles him to *Servitiis
quorumcunque tenentium tam liberorum quam nati-
vorum;* by which it may be presumed that he did
not include the *Welsh* in the privileges. What
those were I do not learn; but they were the same
which the burgesses of *Rosfair* in *Anglesey* enjoyed: and for them *Pwllheli* was to pay to *Nigel*
fourteen pounds a year, and *Nefyn* thirty-two.
This borough and *Nefyn* he freely bestowed on
him, with all its appertenances, together with four
librates of land, towards the repair of his manors;
and for all these he was only to pay an acknowlegement of a rose, in lieu of all services. If
he died without issue, the whole was to revert to
the crown. *Edward* III. afterwards confirmed
these grants at *Sandwich*.

FROM hence I took a ride about five miles in-
CARN
MADRYN. land to *Carn Madryn*, a lofty rocky insulated hill,

noted for having been a strong hold of the sons of
Owen Gwynedd, Roderick and *Malgwyn,* to whom
this part of the country belonged. The bottom,
sides, and top, are filled with cells, oblong, oval,
or circular, once thatched, or covered from the
inclemency of the weather: many of them are
pretty entire. The chieftains resided on the top;
the people of the country, with their cattle, in
times of invasion, occupied the sides and bottom.
The whole summit was surrounded with a wall,
still visible in many places. From the summit is
an extensive view of the country, with the bay of
Caernarvon on one side, and that of *Cardigan* on
the other. *Sarn Badrig*[b] is seen extending from
Meirioneddshire its dangerous length, nearly parallel to the shore of *Llyn. South Wales* may
be seen plainly, and in clear weather *Ireland;* and
in front the whole tract of *Snowdonia* exhibits a
most magnificent and stupendous barrier.

At the foot of this hill is *Madryn,* formerly the
seat of a family of that name. It was sold by the
Madryns, and devised by the purchaser to his
nephew ——— *Bodvel* esq. who, dying without
children, it became the property of his sister, by
whom it was bequeathed to *William Lewis* esq. of
Llysdulas, in *Anglesey,* whose eldest niece brought
it in marriage to *Love Parry* esq. of *Wern Fawr.*

[b] See page 266 of this volume.

FROM *Pwllheli* I continued my journey near the shore to *Llan Badrog,* along the sides of that noble bay the *Tudwal's* road, sheltered by two islands named from St. *Tudwal;* sacred to whom was a small chapel on the greater. Its present inhabitants are sheep, rabbits, and, in the season, puffins.

PENRHYN DU.

IN the promontory *Penrhyn Du,* one of the points of this bay, have been considerable adventurers for lead ore; and of late years attempts have been made to drain the mines, by means of a fire engine: but the expences proved superior to the profits. A little beyond this is another bay, called *Hell's Mouth,* dreaded by mariners, being the *Scylla* to the *Charybdis* of *Sarn Badrig,* whose extremity lies nearly opposite.

ABER-DARON.

IN a small time I reached *Aber-daron,* a poor village, at the very end of *Caernarvonshire,* seated on a sandy bay, beneath some high and sandy cliffs. The mouth of the bay is guarded by two little islands, called *Ynys Gwylan,* a security to the small craft of the inhabitants, who are all fisher men. It takes its name from the small rivulet the *Daron,* which empties itself here.

IN the church are two ailes, supported by four very handsome pillars. This, being the place where devotees usually took boat for *Bardseye* island, was greatly resorted to. It was dedicated to St. *Hywyn,* a saint of that island; was a sanctuary[c], and also much frequented by pilgrims. *Leland* says, it was called *Llan Engas Brenin, Fanum Niniani Reguli*[d]. *Ninian* was a saint, son of a *Cumbrian* prince, and whom legend might have sent here to found the church.

FROM this port I once took boat for *Bardseye* island, which lies about three leagues to the west. The mariners seemed tinctured with the piety of the place; for they had not rowed far, before they made a full stop, pulled off their hats, and offered up a short prayer. After doubling a headland, the island appeared full in view: we passed under the lofty mountain which forms one side. After doubling the farther end, we put into a little sandy creek, bounded by low rocks, as is the whole level part. On landing, I found all this tract a very fertile plain, and well cultivated, and productive of every thing which the main land affords. The abbot's house is a large stone building, inhabited by several of the natives: not far from it is a singular chapel, or oratory, being a long arched edifice, with an insulated stone altar near the east end. In this place one of the inhabitants reads prayers: all other offices are performed at *Aber-daron.*

THE island is about two miles in circumference, contains a few inhabitants, and is rented from Lord

[c] *Powel,* 176.   [d] *Itin.* v. 51. *Ninian* died in 432.

VOL. II.   Z

Newborough. It was granted by *Edward* VI. to his uncle Sir *Thomas Seymour,* and after his death to *John* earl of *Warwick*[*]. The late Sir *John Wynn* purchased it from the reverend Dr. *Wilson* of *Newark.*

THE island, whose spiritual concerns are at present under the care of a single rustic, once afforded, during life, an asylum to 20,000 saints; and after death, graves to as many of their bodies: well therefore might it be called *Insula Sanctorum, The Isle of Saints.* With Dr. *Fuller,* I must observe, that "it would be more facile to find graves "in *Bardseye* for so many saints, than saints for "so many graves[t]." But to approach the truth;

ST. DUBRI-
TIUS.

let it be said, that *Dubritius,* archbishop of *Caerleon,* almost worn out with age, resigning his see to St. *David,* retired here, and according to the best account, died in 612; he was interred on the spot, but in after times his body was removed to *Llandaff.* The slaughter of the monks of *Bangor,* about the year 607, is supposed to have contributed to the population of this island; for not only the brethren who escaped, but numbers of other pious *Britons,* fled hither to avoid the rage of the *Saxons.*

CONVENT.

THE time in which the religious house was founded, is very uncertain; it probably was before the retreat of *Dubritius;* for something of that kind must have occasioned him to give the prefer-

* *Tanner,* 703.   [t] *Worthies of Wales,* 29.

ence to this place. It seems likely to have been a
seat of the *Culdees*, or *Colidei*, the first religious
recluses of *Great Britain;* who sought islands and
desert places in which they might in security worship the true GOD. It was certainly resorted to
in very early times; for our accounts say, that it
flourished as a convent in the days of *Cadwan*,
king of *Britain*ᵍ, coeval with *Dubritius*. It was
an abbey dedicated to St. *Mary*. I find among
the *Sebright* MSS. mention of a petition from the
abbot to *Edward* II. in which he sets forth the
injuries he had received from the sheriff of *Caernarvon*, who had extorted from him 68*s*. and 6*d*.
contrary to his deed of feoffment: on which the
king directed *Roger de Mortimer*, justiciary of
Wales, to make enquiry into the matter; who reported, that the abbot held his lands in the county
of *Caernarvon* in *puram et perpetuam elemosynam*,
without any service or secular acknowlegement;
and further, that *Dafydd*, lord of *Llyn*, and brother to the last Prince of *Wales*, had exacted the
same sum; as did his *Pencynydd*, or master of his
dogs, possibly under pretence of maintaining them.
The king therefore, by his special favor, and by
advice of his council, does for ever remit the said
sum, and all arrears; and directs that no one in
future, either on his account, or that of his heirs,
ever should molest the convent.

ᵍ *Rowland*, 137.

THE house underwent the common fate of
others at the dissolution. Its revenues were, as
Dugdale says, 46*l.* 1*s.* 4*d.;* according to *Speed,*
58*l.* 6*s.* 2*d.* In the year 1553, only 1*l.* 6*s.* 8*d.*
remained in charge to the surviving religious of
this place.

THE *British* name of the island is *Ynys Enlli,*
or the Island in the Current, from the fierce current which rages particularly between it and the
main land. The *Saxons* named it *Bardseye,* probably from the bards who retired here, preferring
solitude to the company of invading foreigners.

THERE are great plenty of fish round the island,
and abundance of lobsters: the spiny lobster, *Br.*
Zool. iv. N°. 22. is more frequent here than in
most other places.

We re-embarked from the rocks on the opposite
side of the island to that on which we landed.
Rowed through the rapid current called the *Race*
of Bardsey, between the island and the great
promontory *Braich y Pwll,* the *Canganum Pro-*
montorium of *Ptolemy:* part of it is called, from
certain yellow stones, *Maen Melyn;* the rest is a
vast precipice, black and tremendous. After landing at *Aber-daron,* I rid to its summit, and found
CAPEL FAIR. the ruins of a small church, called *Capel Fair,* the
Chapel of our Lady; and I was informed, that at
the foot of the promontory, below high-water mark,
was a fountain of fresh water, to which devotees

were wont to descend by a circuitous and most hazardous path, to get, at the recess of the tide, a
mouthful of the spring; which, if they carried up
safe to the summit, their wish, whatsoever it was,
was to be surely fulfilled.   This was under the protection of our Lady, and called *Ffynnon Fair*.   The
chapel was placed here to give the seamen opportunity of invoking the tutelar saint for protection
through this dangerous sound, and I dare say, in
old times the walls were covered with votive tables.
Not far from hence I passed by the ruins of *Capel
Anhelog*, or, the Chapel without Endowment.

AFTER going through a fertile bottom, ascend a
lofty mountain impending over the sea, called *Uwch
Mynydd;* on which were several circular hollows,
edged with stone, the temporary habitations of per
haps some invader.   Descend, and pass by a large
and antient house, called *Bethelem*.

NOT far from thence, about a quarter of a mile
from the shore, rises a high rock called *Maen y*   MAEN Y
Mellt, or, The Stone of Lightning.   Ride by *Cefn-*   MELLT.
amlwch, the seat of *John Griffith*[h] esq; and soon
after to *Brynodol*, that of *Hugh Griffith* esq;
where I met with a most hospitable reception for
two nights.   From hence I visited the neighboring
shore, which is low and rocky, opening into fre-

---

[h] *Cefn-amlwch* is now the property of Mrs. *Wynne*, of *Voelas;*
Brynodol of *John Griffith* esq. ED.

quent little creeks, useful to the fishermen, who find in them, during the herring-fishery, a safe retreat from storms. Among these are, *Porth Towyn, Porth Colman, Porth Gwylan,* and *Porth Ysgadan.* Near the last, about thirty years ago, a rock, which towered a great height out of the sea, was suddenly missed, after a horrible night of thunder and lightning, supposed to have been struck down by the resistless bolt. I observed that the fields about *Porth Gwylan* were covered with[1] *sampier y ddafad,* or sheep's samphire, which sheep and cattle eagerly feed on, and grow very fat. I was pleased here with the fine blossom of thrift glowing over numbers of the pastures.

LLYN or *Lleyn* is a very extensive hundred: in general flat, but interspersed with most character-istic hills or rocks, rising insulated in several parts· none makes so conspicuous a figure as *Carn Ma-dryn* and *Carn Boduon.* The houses of the com-mon people are very mean; made with clay, thatch-ed, and destitute of chimnies. Notwithstanding the laudable example of the gentry, the country is in an unimproved state, neglected for the sake of the herring-fishery. The chief produce is oats, barley, and black cattle. I was informed that above three thousand are annually sold out of these parts. Much oats, barley, butter and cheese,

---

[1] SALICORNIA *herbacea. Sm. Fl. Br.* p. 2. ED.

are exported. The land is excellent for grazing, being watered by a thousand little rills. It is destitute of trees, except about the houses of the gentry.

THE herrings, about the year 1771, were taken HERRINGS. here in vast abundance, from *Porth Ysgadan,* or the *Port of Herrings,* to *Bardseye* island. The capture amounted usually to the value of about four thousand pounds. They were sometimes salted on shore; at other times bought from the fishers by the *Irish* wherries at sea, and carried to be cured in *Dublin.* These desultory fish, about the period mentioned, appeared in *July* and went away in *October;* in earlier times they came in *September* and went away in *November. Dories* are often taken here. The fishermen were wont to fling them away, on account of their ugly appearance: nor was this luxury known to the gentry, till one of their servants, who was acquainted with the fish, informed them of its being an inhabitant of these seas. The *Atherine, Br. Zool.* iii. N° 157, is taken near *Pwllheli*; and a small lobster is often found burrowing in the sand; but differs from the common kind only in its place of residence, and in size. The traps for lobsters are made with packthread, like thief-nets, and baited with pieces of the *lesser spotted shark, Br. Zool.* iii. N° 47. The fishers remark, that the sexes of these voracious fish consort, at times, apart; for at certain

periods they take only males, at others only females.

THE churches in this country are of very antient foundation.   Some cause or other prevented
me from seeing several old inscriptions; a few of
which I have since picked up.   In the church of
Llangynodol is said to be this; *Hic jacet* GWEN
HOEDL, a holy lady, who lived in very early times.
DERVORI *hic jacet*, is another inscription, on a
stone now placed over a door of *Penprys* stable,
in *Llannor* parish[i]; and at *Capel Yverach*, in
Aber-daron parish, is another[k].   They are cut on
very rude stones, and were certainly the work of
the early times of Christianity.

BRYNODOL.   BRYNODOL, being situated on the side of a hill,
commands a vast view of a flat woodless tract, the
sea, and a noble mass of mountains.   The *Eifl*
hills, *Boduon*, and the vast *Carn Madryn*, rise in
the fore ground; and beyond these soars all *Snowdonia,* from those alps which surround the *Wyddfa,*
to the most remote in the county of *Meirionedd.*

ON quitting *Brynodol* I descended into an ex-
PORTH YN   tensive flat; reached *Porth yn Llŷn*[l], a fine safe and
LLYN.
sandy bay, guarded on the west by a narrow head-

---

[i] *Sebright MSS.*   [k] The same.
[l] In the year 1806, an act was passed for erecting a pier and other
works at *Porth yn Llyn*, and incorporating a company with power to
raise money and collect rates.   Application was subsequently made
to parliament for pecuniary aid towards carrying the plan into effect,
which was refused. ED.

land, jutting far into the sea. On part of it are the remains of very strong entrenchments; probably an out post of the *Romans:* who, as I shall have occasion to mention, had another between this place and *Caernarvon.*

SEPARATED from this bay by a small headland, is that of *Nefyn;* and near it a small town of the same name, a contributory borough of *Caernarvon.* This place had been bestowed on *Nigel de Lohareyn* by the Black Prince, in the 12th year of his principality, and made a free borough: was allowed a guild mercatory, with every privilege attendant on other free boroughs, and all the liberties and customs granted heretofore to that of *Newborough* in *Anglesey.* He also gave it a grant of two fairs annually, and a market on a Sunday, to which the inhabitants of that part of the *Commot y Llyn,* then called *Dinthlayn*(¹), were obliged to resort.

HERE *Edward* I., in 1284, held his triumph on the conquest of *Wales;* and, perhaps to conciliate the affections of his new subjects, in imitation of

NEFYN.

(¹) *Dinthlayn* means of course *Dinllayn,* which is now pronounced *Din Llaen,* and I suspect that Pennant's *Porth yn Llŷn* has been slightly mended from *Porth Din Llaen,* since it is now always called either *Porth din Llaen* or *Port Din Llaen.* There would thus seem to have been two words, Lleyn, *lagin-i,* and Llaen, *lagin-a;* we have a cognate word in *Leinster,* which, stripped of its Scandinavian ending, was in old Irish, *Lagin,* from *Lagin,* a spear. The map-makers who insist on writing *Llaen* as *Lleyn,* because the Port is in Lleyn, are not likely to allow the natives a voice in the matter. J.R.

our hero *Arthur, held a round table, and celebrated
it with dance and tournament*[m].

> Where throngs of knights, and barons bold
> In weeds of peace high triumphs hold,
> With store of ladies, whose bright eyes
> Reign influence, and judge the prize
> Of wit or arms, while both contend
> To win her grace, whom all commend.

The concourse was prodigious; for not only the
chief nobility of *England,* but numbers from foreign
parts, graced the festival with their presence.

THE custom is very antient; for it may be traced
even higher than the days of *Arthur.* We may
allow that he held his round table on account of
one of his victories; and that he had four-and-
twenty knights who sate at the festive board;
which might have been designedly made of a circular form, in order to destroy all dispute about
pre-eminence of seat. But the *Gauls* also sate at
their round tables, and every knight had at his
back a squire with his armour, in waiting[n]. This
gallant assembly was held for many ages after.
Besides this held at *Nefyn,* another was presented by earl *Mortimer* at *Kenilworth,* where the
knights performed their martial exercises, and the
ladies danced in silken mantles[o].

[m] Ad rotundam tabulam juxta *Snowdon* præconizatam in choreis
et hastiludiis ad invicem colludentibus. *Annal. Waverleins.* in *Gale,*
ii. 239.

[n] *Athenæus,* lib. iv.   [o] *Dugdale's Warwickshire,* i. 247.

THE first, I apprehend to have been performed in those circular *areæ*, which we still meet with in some parts of *England*, surrounded with a high mound, a ditch in the inside, and two entrances one opposite to the other, for the knights to enter at and make their onset. One of these I have seen by *Penrith*, which bears the name of *Arthur*'s round table[p]; others which are far larger, I found on *Thornborough* heath, in *Yorkshire;* of which I may in future[q] give some account.

ASCEND from *Nefyn* for a considerable way up the side of the high hill; and after a short ride on level ground quit our horses, in order to visit *Nant y Gwytherin*, or *Vortigern's Valley*, the immense hollow, to which *Vortigern* is reported to have fled from the rage of his subjects, and where it was said that he and his castle were consumed with lightning. *Nennius*[r] places the scene near *Teivi*, in *Caermarthenshire;* but I believe that the historian not only mistakes the spot, but even the manner of his death. His life had been profligate; the monks therefore were determined that he should not die the common death of all men, and accordingly made him perish with signal marks of the vengeance of Heaven. Fancy cannot frame a place more fit for a retreat from the knowlege of mankind, or better calculated to inspire confidence of security from any

VORTIGERN'S VALLEY.

[p] Tour in *Scotland*, 1769, 3d ed. p. 275.
[q] Tour to *Harrowgate*, p. 48. ED.   [r] *Hist. Br.* c. xlviii.

pursuit.   Embosomed in a lofty mountain, on two
sides bounded by stony steeps, on which no vege-
tables appear but the blasted heath and stunted
gorse; the third side exhibits a most tremendous
front of black precipice, with the loftiest peak of
the mountain *Eifl* soaring above; and the only
opening to this secluded spot is towards the sea,
a northern aspect! where that chilling wind exerts
all its fury, and half freezes, during winter, the few
inhabitants.   The glen is tenanted by three families, who raise oats, and keep a few cattle, sheep,
and goats; but seem to have great difficulty in getting their little produce to market.

JUST above the sea is a high and verdant mount,
natural; but the top and sides worked by art; the
first flatted; the sides marked with eight prominent
ribs from top to bottom.   On this might have
been the residence of the unfortunate prince; of
which, time has destroyed every other vestige.
Till the beginning of the last century, a tumulus,
of stone within, and externally covered with turf,
was to be seen here; it was known by the name of
Bedd Gwrtheyrn: tradition having regularly delivered down the report of this having been the place
of his interment.   The inhabitants of the parish,
perhaps instigated by their then minister, Mr.
Hugh Roberts, a person of curiosity, dug into the
carn, and found in it a stone coffin, containing the

bones o a tall man[s]. This gives a degree of cre-
dibility to the tradition, especially as no other
bones were found near the carn; nor were there any
other *tumuli* on the spot: which affords a proof at
lest of respect to the rank of the person, and that
the place was deserted after the death of the royal
fugitive, about the year 465.

AFTER emerging out of this chearless bottom,
I found fresh and amazing matter of speculations.
I got into a *bwlch*, or hollow, between two summits
of the *Eifl* mountains; a range that makes a most   THE EIFL
distinguished figure, with the sugar-loaf points,   HILLS.
from various and distant parts of the country: they
range obliquely, and separate *Lleyn* from the
hundred of *Arfon*, and jut into the sea near *Vorti-*
gern's Valley.

ACROSS this hollow, from one summit of the
Eifl to the other, extends an immense rampart of
stones, or perhaps the ruins of a wall, which effec-
tually blocked up the pass. On the *Eifl* is the
most perfect and magnificent, as well as the most
artfully constructed *British* post I ever beheld.
It is called *Tre'r Caeri*, or, the *Town of the for-* TRE'R CAERI.
tresses.([1]) This, which was the accessible side, is

[s] *Kennet's Paroch. Antiq. Hist. Allchester*, 698.

([1]) This explanation is the usual one; but it will not stand examination, for the place is called, not *Tre'r Caeri*, but *Tre'r Ceiri*, or *Tre
Ceiri* which is pronounced differently, and means in the Carnarvon-
shire dialect the Town of the Giants,—*ceiri* being a plural of *cawr*,
giant, in that county. J.R.

defended by three walls; the lowest is very imperfect, the next tolerably entire, and has in it the
grand entrance.   This wall in one part points upwards towards the third wall, which runs round
the edges of the top of the hill: the second wall
unites with the first, which runs into a point, re-
verts, and joins the highest, in a place where the
hill becomes inaccesssible.   The facings on the two
upper walls are very entire, especially that of the
uppermost.   They are lofty, and exhibit from
below a grand and extensive front.   The space
on the top is an irregular area; part is steep, part
flat: in most parts covered with heath, giving shelter to a few red grouse.   The whole is almost
filled with cells.   To be seen to advantage, the
station should be taken from the summit, about
which the cells are very distinct, and disposed with
much art.   About the middle is a square place
fenced with stones; a sort of *prætorium*, surrounded
with two rows of cells: numbers are also scattered
about the plain, and others again are contiguous
to the wall along the inside.

THE cells are mostly perfect; of various forms;
round, oval, oblong, square.   Some of the round
were fifteen feet in diameter; of the oblong, thirty
feet in length, with long entrances regularly faced
with stone.   All of them, when inhabited, were
well protected from the weather by roofs of thatch
or sod.

THE upper wall was in many places fifteen feet high on the outside, and often sixteen feet broad. It consisted of two parallel and contiguous parts, one higher than the other, serving as a parapet to the lower, which seemed to have had its walk, like that on the walls of *Chester*. There was in one place a cell in the thickness of the wall, or perhaps a sally-port, in part stopped by the falling-in of the stones.

I WAS determined to trace every species of fortress of this nature which lay in the neighborhood. On descending from *Tre'r Caeri* to the south, I very soon ascended *Moel Garn Guwch*, a hill of conic form, on the summit of which is a prodigious heap of stones, seemingly a shapeless ruin; but from the appearance of certain facings of a central cell still remaining, it seems to have been a large tower, and an outpost to the preceding place. These ruins are called by the country people *Arffedoged y Gowres,* or, the apron-full of stones flung *down by the Giantess.*

GARN GUWCH.

I MUST remark, that from the *Eifl* I saw several other lesser eminences fortified in a manner nearly similar. I may mention *Carn Madryn,* before described; the hill of *Boduan,* above *Nefyn,* covered with similar cells; *Moel ben Twrch,* between *Tre'r Caeri* and *Penmorfa;* and *Castell Gwgan,* remarkable for a small circular intrenchment; and to these I may add another fortified hill, called *Pen y Gaer,*

on the other side of the pass which leads from *Arfon*
to *Llyn;* all which makes it probable that this
country was the retreat of multitudes of *Britons,*
to escape the first fury of the *Saxon* invaders.

AFTER viewing the *Arffedoged-y-Gowres,* I descended to the village and church of *Llan-Ael-*
haiearn, the last dedicated to St. *Aelhaiearn,* or
the saint with an *iron eyebrow,* from a legend too
absurd to relate.   Near it is a fine well, once
much frequented for its reputed sanctity.   Continue descending: on the right are the high conic
hills of *Gern goch* and *Gern ddu,* the extremity of
the long chain which extends obliquely from *Snow-*
don, beginning at *Talmignèdd.*   Reach

LLAN AEL-
HAIEARN.

CLYNNOG, seated in a small grove near the
shore, on a plain near the foot of the hills.   The
church is the most magnificent structure of its kind
in *North Wales,* built in form of a cross; the
length from east to west is about a hundred and
thirty-eight feet, from north to south seventy.
Near the altar are three neat stalls, divided by
pillars supporting gothic arches, the seats of the
officiating priests.   The monuments are few: one
to *William Glynn de Lleiar,* with his figure, and
those of his wife and seven children: another to
his son-in-law *George Twisleton* esq; of *Aula*
Barrow in *Yorkshire,* and in right of his wife, of
Lleiar.   I imagine him to be the same with Colo-

CLYNNOG.

CHURCH.

nel *Twisleton*, an active officer under *Cromwell*, and the same who had the honor of defeating and making prisoner the gallant Sir *John Owen*[t].

ADJOINING the church is the chapel of St. *Beuno*. The passage to it is a narrow vault covered with great flat stones, and of far greater antiquity than either church or chapel; which seem nearly coeval. *Leland* speaks of the first as *new worke*, and the architecture verifies his account. He speaks also of the old church, where St. *Beuno* lieth, being near the new[u]. The passage is the only part left. The chapel was probably built after that traveller had visited the place, in the room of the old church, which might have fallen to ruin. In the midst is the tomb[x] of the saint, plain, and altar-shaped. Votaries were wont to have great faith in him, and did not doubt but that by means of a night's lodging on his tomb, a cure would be found for all diseases. It was customary to cover it with rushes, and leave on it till morning sick children, after making them first undergo ablution in the neighboring holy well; and I myself once saw on it a feather bed, on which a poor paralytic from *Meirioneddshire* had lain the whole night, after undergoing the same ceremony.

MR OF ST. BEUNO.

[t] *Whitelock's Memorials*, 311, and 454, 599.   [u] *Itin.* v. 13.

[x] The editor is informed that this tomb has been removed, in consequence of an inadequate and fruitless search to discover the body of the saint. The offerings mentioned in a following page, are said to he discontinued. ED.

I HAVE given some account of St. *Beuno* in the preceding volume[y].   After he had assumed the monastic habit, he here founded a convent in 616. *Cadvan*, king of *North Wales*, was his great patron, and promised him much land: his son *Cadwallan* performed the promise, and received from the Saint a golden sceptre worth sixty cows.   The land was clamed in behalf of a little infant, and his title proved good: the king refused either to give other land in lieu, or to resign the present. *Beuno* cursed him, and went away; but was appeased by *Gwrddeint*, first cousin to the king, who overtook him, and gave the town of *Celynnog* for ever to GOD and St. *Beuno*, for his own soul's sake, and that of the wicked *Cadwallan*.   Long after his time, the *Carmelites*, or white monks, had here an establishment.   They were suppressed, but I cannot learn the period.   At the time of the *Lincoln* taxation, or the year 1291 the church was collegiate, consisting of five portionists or prebendaries; and it continued so to the dissolution[z]. The rectory is a sinecure annexed to the headship of JESUS College, *Oxford*; the poor vicarage is the gift of the bishop.   Its revenues at the dissolution are not recorded; but they must at one time have been very great: many of the kings and first people of the country appear on the list of benefactors. *Cadwaladr* gave *Grayanoc*; *Tegwared* gave *Porth-*

y Vol. i. p. 44.   z *Tanner*, 705.

amel; Cadell bestowed *Cylcourt;* prince *Merfyn, Carnguin; Cadwgan ap Cynfelyn, Bodfeilion* in *Llyn; Idwal* endowed it with *Penrhos* and *Clynog Fechan* in *Anglesey:* and besides these are numbers of others, for which I refer the reader to my authority*.

AT present there is, I believe, no fund to keep this venerable pile from falling to ruin. The offerings of calves and lambs, which happen to be born with the *Nôd Beuno,* or mark of St. *Beuno,* a certain natural mark in the ear, have not entirely ceased. They are brought to the church on *Trinity Sunday,* the anniversary of the Saint, and delivered to the churchwardens; who sell, and put the money they receive for them into a great chest, called *Cyff St. Beuno,* made of one piece of oak, secured with three locks. From this the *Welsh* have a proverb for attempting any very difficult thing, "You may as well try to break up St. "*Beuno's* chest." The little money resulting from the sacred beasts, or casual offerings, is either applied to the relief of the poor, or in aid of repairs.

THOSE who are curious in druidical antiquities, may see a very uncommon *Cromlech* on the tenement of *Bachwen,* about half a mile from this place. The inclination of the upper stone is to

OFFERINGS TO.

A CROMLECH.

* *Dugdale Monast.* ii. 919.

the west; on its surface are numbers of small
shallow holes, with two or three larger than the
rest, possibly for some purpose of augury. At
thirty paces distance is an upright stone, placed,
as is supposed, to mark the limits of approach to
the people, while the rites were performing by the
Druid-priest.

THE distance from *Clynnog* to *Caernarvon* is
ten miles; a continued plain: the mountains recede
gradually from the sea, so as to leave a considerable extent of level ground as we approach the
capital of the county. The road is excellent, and
the greatest part has the merit of being made at
the expence of the parishes. The shore is low,
gravelly, or sandy: and forms one side of the bay
of *Caernarvon.*

CROSS the *Llyfni,* a rapid stream flowing out of
Llyn Nanlle. I heard here of a strong camp,
called *Carreg y Dinas;* of which I find this note
in the MS. travels of the late ingenious Dr. *Mason*
of *Cambridge.* He mentions it as being placed
upon the *Isthmus* of the *Llyfni,* opposite to the
house of *Lleiar.* The three sides to the river are
very steep; the fourth is defended by two fosses
and two banks, made chiefly of stone, especially
the inner one, which is six yards high. In the
middle is a mount, possibly the ruins of a tower.
The entrance is at the east, between the ends of
the banks.

ABOUT three miles, turn to the left, to visit *Dinas Dinlle,* a vast mount of gravel and sand, on the verge of a great marsh, upon the shore. On the top is a large area, surrounded by an amazing agger, seemingly formed by the earth scooped out of the summit. Within are remains of foundations of buildings, of an oblong form, constructed with earth and round stones; and in one part is a tumulus of the same materials. On the outside of the agger, on one part, is a very deep ditch, with another high rampart; and the ground towards the base seems every where to have been smoothed by art. There is a regular entrance at one end; on the other, the ground slopes to the sea, and is quite open, a defence being there needless. The waves have made great depredations, and worn one side into a cliff. I must attribute this fortress to the *Romans;* and am the more confirmed in my notion, as I am informed that coins have been found here, among which was one of *Alectus.* The *Romans* might possibly be induced to form this post, to secure a landing-place for any necessaries the country might want; for the entrance into the port of *Segontium* is often, even at present, very difficult; and must have been much more so in the earlier times of navigation.

THAT intelligent traveller and able botanist Mr. *Thomas Johnson*[b] speaks thus of *Dinas Dinlle,*

[b] An ingenious apothecary, the editor of *Gerard's Herbal.* He

" Stationem hîc in ipso littore *Romani* milites ha-
" buerunt, cujus adhuc satis clara vestigia manent."
Possibly there may be another of the same kind;
for I find in the old maps both of *Saxton* and
Speed, the name *Caer Ierienrode*(¹), a little lower
down at the mouth of the *Llyfni;* and by the
addition of the word *Caer*, it must have been a
fortified place.

WHEN I made my visit to *Dinas Dinlle*, I was
under the guidance of a worthy friend, and learned
antiquary, the Reverend *Richard Farrington* (now
deceased). He conducted me to his residence at
Dinas Dinorthwy(²), about four miles distant. In
the way he shewed to me *Dinas y Prif*, or, The
Post of the Chieftain; a small camp, about forty-
four yards square. Each corner is elevated above
the ramparts; and within are the foundations of
some stone buildings. By the name it might be
the summer station of the *Roman* commander in
chief, resident in winter at *Segontium*.

travelled through *North Wales* in 1639, to collect plants. He published his tour in 1641, a small volume, under the title of *Mercurius
Botanicus*. He was slain in the defence of *Basingstoke* House, in
1644.

(¹) This is the *Caer Arianrhod* of the Mabinogi of Math ap Math-
onwy, and no spot in Wales is more associated than the district
near it with the Celtic gods and goddesses, among whom Arianrhod was a sort of Venus. J.R.

(²) In Welsh spelling this would be *Dinorddwy*, and it puts one
again in mind of the Ordovices. J.R.

·From *Dinas* I visited *Glynllifon*, a house built GLYNLLIFON. by the late Sir *John Wynne*, seated near the little river *Llifon*, issuing from the *Cilgwyn* mountain. *Cilmen Troed-du*, or *Cilmin* with a *black foot*, one of the fifteen tribes of *North Wales*, and nephew to *Merfyn Frych*, prince of *Wales*, slain in 841, had his residence on this spot.   *F*rom him are descended the family of the *Glynnes*, who took their name from the place.   They bear, in allusion to the name of their ancestor, a man's leg, *coupè a la cuisse*, sable.   A ridiculous legend tells you, that *Cilmin*'s leg became so discoloured by escaping from a dæmon, whose books he had assisted a magician to steal.   In leaping over a brook, which was to be the limit of the pursuit, *Cilmin*'s left leg plunged into the water, and assumed its sable dye. Our stories are absurd; but not more so than an Eastern tale.   *Glynllifon* came into possession of the late Sir *John Wynne*, by the marriage of his father, *Tho. Wynne* esq;[c] of *Boduan*, with *Frances* second daughter to *John Glynne* esq; of *Glynllifon*.

CONTINUE my journey on a turnpike road. Cross, at *Pont Newydd*, the *Gwyrfai*, which flows from *Llyn Cwellyn;* and soon after cross the *Seiont*, and reach CAERNARVON.   CAERNAR VON.

THIS town is justly the boast of *North Wales,*

---

[c] Afterwards created a baronet.   He died in *April* 1749.

for the beauty of its situation, the goodness of its
buildings, the regularity of the plan, and, above all,
the grandeur of the castle, the most magnificent
badge of our subjection. The place sprung from
the ruin of the antient *Segontium;* but it does not
owe its name to *Edward* I. as is generally supposed. *Giraldus Cambrensis* mentions it in his
journey of the year 1188[d]; and *Llewelyn the Great*
dates from it a charter in the year 1221[e]. I greatly
suspect the *Caernarvon* of those times to have been
no other than the antient *Segontium,* whose name
the *Welsh* had changed to the apt one of *Caer ar
Fôn*([1]), or, The strong hold opposite to *Anglesey.*
But the present town was in all probability a creation of our conqueror. A judicious warrior such
as *Edward,* could not fail profiting of so fit a situation for curbing the newly-conquered country. It
had natural requisites for strength; being bounded
on one side by the arm of the sea called the *Menai;*
by the estuary of the *Seiont* on another, exactly
where it receives the tide from the former; on a
third side, and part of the fourth, by a creek of the

[d] *Iter. Cambr.* 865. Sir *Richard Hoare's* ed. vol. ii. p. 83.

[e] This charter is to the canons of *Penmon.* *Sebright MSS.*

([1]) As Pennant was perfectly aware that the part of the county
in which the town stood was called *Arfon,* it is curious that he
should have treated its name as he has: it can only be *Caer yn
Arfon,* or the Fort in Arvon, a name which sounds anything but old,
and confirms his view that it is not on the site of Segontium, though
near it. J.R.

Menai; and the remainder has the appearance of having the insulation completed by art. *Edward* undertook this great work immediately after his conquest of the country in 1282; and completed the fortifications and castle before 1284; for his queen, on *April* 25th in that year, brought forth within its walls *Edward,* first prince of *Wales* of the *English* line. It was built within the space of one year, by the labor of the peasants, and at the cost of the chieftains of the country, on whom the conqueror imposed the hateful task[f]. *Henry Ellerton,* or *de Elreton,* was appointed master mason of the castle[g], and perhaps was the architect; and under him must have been numbers of other skilful workmen: for I dare say that the *Welsh* peasants were no more than cutters of wood and hewers of stone. It is probable than many of the materials were brought from *Segontium,* or the old *Caernarvon;* and tradition says, that much of the limestone, with which it is built, was brought from *Twr-Celyn* in *Anglesey;* and of the grit-stone, from *Vaenol* in this county. The *Menai* greatly facilitated the carriage from both places.

THE walls and the castle, with regard to their exterior, are at present exactly as they were in the time of *Edward.* The former are defended by numbers of round towers, and have two principal

---

[f] *Sebright MSS.*   [g] *Sebright* and *Gloddaeth MSS.*

gates: the east, facing the mountains: the west, upon the *Menai*. The entrance into the castle is very august, beneath a great tower, on the front of which appears the statue of the founder, with an half drawn sword in his hand, as if menacing his newly-acquired unwilling subjects. The gate had four portcullises, and every requisite of strength. The court is oblong. The towers are very beautiful; none of them round, but pentagonal, hexagonal, or octagonal: two are more lofty than the rest. The Eagle tower is remarkably fine, and has the addition of three slender angular turrets issuing from the top. The Eagle upon the tower, (says my antiquary friend) is, with good reason, supposed to be *Roman*, and that *Edward* found it at old *Segontium*. *Edward* II. was born in a little dark room in this tower([1]), not twelve feet long, nor

---

([1]) The history of *Caernarvon* castle has been ably investigated by the late Mr. *Hartshorne;* who has proved conclusively that the erection of this grand fabric was commenced in the autumn of 1283, and carried on at different intervals until 1322, thus extending over a term of 38 years. The Royal effigy which adorns the entrance gate was placed there in *April* 1320, in the 13th year of *Edward* II; and in all probability it represents that monarch, and not his redoubted father. There seems to be no foundation for the conjecture, which is approved by *Pennant*, that the eagles on the top of the Eagle tower are *Roman*, or that they were brought from the old *Segontium*. This famous tower is shown by Mr. *Hartshorne* to have been roofed over in 1316, and the floors in it to have been laid down in 1317. The fact that *Edward* II. was born at *Caernarvon* on the 25th of *April* 1284 is unquestionable; but the precise situation of the place where he was born there is uncertain. "The little dark room" in the Eagle tower, described by *Pennant*, and so confidently reputed to

eight in breadth: so little did, in those days, a royal consort consult either pomp or conveniency. The gate through which the affectionate *Eleanor* entered, to give the *Welsh* a prince of their own, who could not speak a word of *English*, is at the farthest end, at a vast height above the outside ground; so could only be approached by a draw-bridge. In his sixteenth year, the prince received the homage of his duped subjects at *Chester*[h], invested, as marks of his dignity, with a chaplet of gold round his head, a golden ring on his finger, and a silver sceptre in his hand[i].

QUEEN'S GATE.

THE walls of this fortress are about seven feet nine inches thick; and have within their thickness a most convenient gallery, with narrow slips, for the discharge of arrows. The walls of the Eagle Tower are near two feet thicker. The view from its summit is very fine, of the *Menai*, *Anglesey*, and the nearer parts of the *British Alps*.

The first whom I find appointed by *Edward* to

be this prince's birthplace, appears to have been built subsequently. The tradition that *Edward* II. was born in the Eagle tower was universally accepted before Mr. *Hartshorne* published the result of his inquiries: but there are grounds for believing that an earlier tradition once existed, which assigned another portion of the castle as the birthplace of the son of *Eleanor*. Mr. *Hartshorne's* paper is printed in the *Archæological Journal*, Vol. vii. p. 237; and there is a short summary of his arguments in the *Archæologia Cambrensis* for 1848. A paper on the same subject by Professor *Babington* will be found in the *Archæologia Cambrensis* for 1879. T.P.

[h] *Powel*, 382.   [i] *Dodridge's Wales*, 6.

be governor of the castle, was *John de Havering*, with a salary of two hundred marks; for which he was obliged to maintain constantly, besides his own family, fourscore men, of which fifteen were to be cross-bowmen, one chaplain, one surgeon, and one smith; the rest were to do the duty of keepers of the gates, centinels, and other necessary offices[k].

IN 1289, I find that the king had appointed *Adam de Wetenhall* to the same important office[l].

THE establishment for town and castle was as follows:

THE constable of the castle had sometimes sixty pounds, at others only forty.

THE captain of the town had 12*l*. 3*s*. 4*d*. for his annual fee; but this office was sometimes annexed to the former, and then the fee was 60*l*. for both.

THE constable and the captain had twenty-four soldiers allowed them for the defence of the place, at the wages of 4*d*. per day each. Surely this slight garrison was only during peaceful times!

THE porter of the gates of the town had for his annual fee 3*l*. 10*s*[m].

I CANNOT discover more than two instances of this place having suffered by the calamities of war.

---

[k] *Sebright MSS.*
[l] *Ayloffe's Rotuli Walliæ*, 98.   [m] *Dodridge*, 56.

In the great insurrection of the *Welsh*, under *Madoc*, in 1294, they surprised the town during the time of a fair, and put many *English* to the sword[n]; and, according to Mr. *Carte*[o], took the castle, that of *Snowdon (Conwy)*, and made themselves masters of all *Anglesey*.

IN the seventeenth century, Captain *Swanly*, a parlementarian officer, took the town in 1644, made four hundred prisoners, and got a great quantity of arms, ammunition, and pillage. The royalists afterwards repossessed themselves of the place. Lord *Byron* was appointed Governor; was besieged by General *Mytton* in 1646, and yielded the place on the most honorable terms. In 1648, General *Mytton* and Colonel *Mason* were besieged in it by Sir *John Owen;* who hearing that Colonel *Carter* and Colonel *Twisselton* were on their march to relieve the place, drew a party from the siege, in order to attack them on the way. The parties met near *Llandegai:* Sir *John* was defeated, and made prisoner; and after that all *North Wales* submitted to the parlement[p].

THE quay forms a most beautiful walk along the side of the *Menai*, and commands a most agreeable view. QUAY.

CAERNARVON is destitute of manufactures, but has a brisk trade with *London*, *Bristol*, *Leverpool*, TRADE.

[n] *Powel*, 380   [o] *Carte*, ii. 237.   [p] *Whitelock*, 87. 208, 311.

and *Ireland*, for the several necessaries of life. It
is the residence of many genteel families; and contains several very good houses; a very antient
one, called *Plâs Pulesdon*, is remarkable for the
ROGER DE   fate of its first owner, Sir *Roger de Pulesdon*, a
PULESDON.
distinguished favorite of *Edward* I. He had been
appointed sheriff and keeper of the county of *Anglesey*[q] in 1284. What office he held here, I know
not; but in 1294, being directed to levy the sub-
sidy for the *French* war, a tax the *Welsh* had never
been accustomed to, they took up arms, and hanged
de Pulesdon and several of his people. This was
a signal for a general insurrection: *Madoc*, a relation of the late Prince *Llewelyn*, headed the people
of this country. *Edward* marched against them in
person, and with great difficulty reduced the insur-
gents to submit again to his yoke[r].

CHAPEL.   THE church is no more than a chapel to *Llan
Beblic;* and probably was originally only a chapel
to the garrison.

CHARTER.   EDWARD I. bestowed on *Caernarvon* its first
royal charter, and made it a free borough. Among
other privileges, none of the burgesses could be
convicted of any crime committed between the rivers *Conwy* and *Dyfy*, unless by a jury of their
own townsmen[s]. It is governed by a mayor, who,

 Ayloffe's Rotuli Walliæ, 89.
[r] *Matt. Westm.* 423.   [s] *Sebright MSS.*

by patent, is created governor of the castle. It has one alderman, two bailiffs, a town-clerk, and two serjeants at mace. The representative of the place is elected by its burgesses, and those of *Conwy, Pwllheli, Nefyn,* and *Crickaeth.* The right of voting is in every one, resident or non-resident, admitted to their freedom[t]. The first member was *John Puleston;* and the second time it sent representatives, which was in the 1st of *Edward* VI. it chose *Robert Puleston,* and the county elected *John*[u]; as if both town and county determined to to make reparation to the family for the cruelty practised on its ancestor.

CORPORA-TION.

FREE MEM-BERS.

THE mother church of *Caernarvon,* about half a a mile south-east of the town, is called *Llan Beblic,* being dedicated to St. *Peblic* or *Publicius,* (according to our historians) son of *Maxen Wledic* (*Maximus* the tyrant) and his wife *Helen,* daughter of *Euddaf.* It is said that he retired from the world and took a religious habit[x]. *Richard* II. bestowed this church, and the chapel of *Caernarvon,* on the nuns of St. *Mary*'s in *Chester,* in consideration of their poverty[y]. I find in the recital of another charter of the same prince, that his grandfather *Edward* II. had bestowed on those religious the advowson of *Llangathen* in *Caermarthenshire*[z]:

LLAN BEB-LIC.

---

[t] *Willis*'s *Notitia Parliam.* iii. Part i. 76.
[u] The same, Part ii. pp. 9, 10.   [x] *Rowlands' Mona Antiqua,* 165.
[y] *Sebright MSS.*   [z] The same.

both which, on the dissolution, were annexed to
the see of *Chester*, and remain to this day under
the patronage of the Bishop of *Chester*. In the
church is the tomb of a son[a] of Sir *William Gryffydd* of *Penrhyn*, who died in 1587, and *Margaret*,
daughter to *John Wynn ap Meredydd*. Their
figures are in white marble, lying on a mat, admirably carved: he is in armour; she has on a
short quilled ruff, and quilled ruffles at her wrists;
in a long gown, and a sash round her waist.

ROMAN
FORT.

NEAR the steep bank of the river *Seiont*, at a
small distance from the castle, is an antient *Roman*
fort. On two sides, the walls are pretty entire;
one is seventy-four yards long; the other, which
points to the river, is sixty-four. The height ten
feet eight inches. The thickness six feet. Much
of the facing is taken away, which discovers the
peculiarity of the *Roman* masonry. It consists of
regular courses; the others have the stones disposed
in zigzag fashion. Along the walls are three parallel lines of round holes, not three inches in
diameter, nicely plaistered within, which pass
through the whole thickness. There are other
similar holes, which are discovered in the end of
the wall, and seem to run through it lengthways.
I can neither discover the use of one or the other.

The name of this son appears from the inscription, some parts of
which are evidently transposed, to have been " *William.*"

Those that run through the walls are supposed to
be for the purpose of annoying an enemy with
arrows; but from the smallness of the diameter, a
compass of aim in directing the shot is wanting.
Near the corner of one of the walls is a heap of
stones, the ruins of a tower; for on digging, some
years ago, the foundation of a round one was discovered. It was paved, and in it were found the
horn of a deer and skeletons of some smaller animals; and seems intended to secure a landing-
place from the *Seiont,* at time of high-water.
I was informed, that in *Tre'r Beblic,* on the
opposite shore, had been other ruins, the work of
the same people. This very curious antiquity, is
at present most shamefully disfigured by walls, and
other buildings, insomuch that I fear my description will in a manner become unintelligible.

AT a small distance above this, and about a
quarter of a mile from the *Menai,* is the antient
Segontium, to the use of which the fort had been SEGONTIUM.
subservient. It forms an oblong of a very considerable extent, seemingly about six acres, placed
on the summit of rising ground, and sloping down
on every side. In several parts are vestiges of
walls; and in one place appears the remnant of a
building made with tiles, and plaistered with very
hard and smooth mortar: this seems to have been
part of a *hypocaust.* The mortar in all other parts

is very hard, and mixed with much gravel and
sand. At present a public road passes through the
midst of this antient station, beyond which the
Romans had only a small out-post or two in this
county. A gold coin, of about seventeen shillings
weight, was found here, inscribed T. DIVI AVG.
FIL AVGVSTVS.

CAMDEN suspects that this might have been the
Setantiorum Portus of *Ptolemy*, being willing to
read it *Segontiorum*[b]; but the situation of the
former is certainly at the mouth of the *Ribble*.
He may be right in supposing it to have been in
after times named *Caer Custenin*, or the Castle of
Constantine[c], and that *Hugh Lupus*, who certainly
invaded *Anglesey* in 1098, had here a temporary
post. How far the relation of *Matthew* of *Westminster*, that *Constantius*, father of *Constantine*,
was interred here, may be depended on, I will not
say; nor whether, as the historian farther asserts,
Edward caused the body to be taken up, and ho-
norably re-buried in the church, I suppose of St.
Publicius[d]. Mr. *Rowlands* says, that *Helen*, the
mother of *Publicius*, had a chapel here, which he
tells us was in being in his days[e]. A well, near the
fort, bears the name of that princess; and some

---

[b] ii. 798.

[c] *Nennius.*   [d] *Mat. Westm.* 411.

[e] *Mona Antiq.* 163. *Helen* was born at *Segontium.*

very slight remains of ruins are to be seen adjacent. Tradition says, the chapel stood on that spot.

THE traveller who wishes to visit *Snowdon*, from this town, may have a very agreeable ride. After crossing the *Fai* or *Gwyrfai*[1], at *Pont y Bettws*, about four miles and a half from *Caernarvon*, he will find about the village of *Bettws Garmon*, or *Is-Gwrfai*, a beautiful cascade fronting him, as he passes up a valley; which consists of verdant meadows, watered by the same river, and bounded by hills rising fast into alpine majesty. He will go under *Moel Elian*, a noble mountain of a stupendous bulk, cloathed with a smooth green turf, and most regularly rounded. He will pass on the right near *Castell Cedwm*, said by Mr. *Rowlands* to be one of the guards to the entrance into *Snowdon:* it is a great rock, which I did not ascend, so cannot certify whether it had any works like those of other *British* posts. The lake *Cwellyn* here almost fills the valley; a water famous for its Char, which are taken in nets in the first winter months, and after that season retire to inaccessible depths. In former times, this water was called, from the steepness of its banks, *Llyn y Torlennydd*. Above, on the right side of the lake, soars the magnificent *Mynydd Mawr*, smooth on the top, but the sides

[1] This river issues out of *Llyn Cwellyn*, and separates the two hundreds of *Uwch-Gwrfai* and *Is-Gwrfai*.

receding inwards in a semicircular form, exhibit a tremendous precipice.   Soon after this, the vale expands; *yr Wyddfa* appears full in view.   The traveller will pass by LLYN Y GADER, and join in my former tour at *Bedd Kelert.*

END OF THE SECOND VOLUME.

CARNARVON: PRINTED BY H. HUMPHREYS, CASTLE SQUARE.

Lightning Source UK Ltd.
Milton Keynes UK
UKOW05f2325050417
298453UK00018B/471/P